Suicide a

About the Authors

Erminia Colucci holds a PhD in Cultural Psychiatry (Australia) and is currently completing an MPhil in Ethnographic Documentary/Visual Anthropology (UK), and is a registered psychologist (Italy). Erminia's areas of specialization are suicidal behavior and prevention in different cultural contexts, spirituality, and religion, violence against women and mental health/suicide, women/human rights, and qualitative research methods including arts/visual-based methods. She is the National Representative for Italy of the World Suicidology Net, Chair (together with Heidi Hjelmeland) of the International Association for Suicide Prevention SIG on Culture and Suicidal Behaviour, and Co-Chair of the World Association of Cultural Psychiatry SIG on Arts, Media, and Psychiatry. In addition to academic writing, she has also produced photographic exhibitions and film-documentaries on her research and teaching interests.

Heidi Hjelmeland is Professor of Health Science at the Norwegian University of Science and Technology, Trondheim, as well as Senior Researcher at the Norwegian Institute of Public Health, Oslo, Norway. She has done research in suicidology since 1992 and has several ongoing research projects in Europe and Africa. She has published on various aspects of suicidal behavior such as epidemiology, attitudes, intentionality, meaning, communication, gender, and culture, as well as on theoretical and methodological issues. She is Co-Editor of the journal *Suicidology Online* and member of the Editorial Boards of *Crisis* and *Suicide and Life-Threatening Behavior*.

David Lester has doctorates from Cambridge University (UK) and Brandeis University (USA). He has written extensively on suicide, homicide, the fear of death, and other issues in thanatology. He was President of the International Association for Suicide Prevention and is Distinguished Professor of Psychology at the Richard Stockton College of New Jersey.

B. C. Ben Park has a doctoral degree in sociology (Maxwell School of Citizenship and Public Affairs at Syracuse University, NY) and a master's degree in sociology (College of William and Mary, VA). He is currently an Associate Professor in Human Development and Family Studies at Pennsylvania State University in DuBois, PA. The major strand of his research has focused on politically motivated suicide as well as other types of self-destructive behavior. His research program also involves intergenerational value socialization and cultural identity issues among the children of Korean immigrants in the US.

Suicide and Culture:
Understanding the Context

Erminia Colucci and David Lester (Editors)
with Heidi Hjelmeland and B. C. Ben Park

Library of Congress Cataloging-in-Publication Data

is available via the Library of Congress Marc Database under the
LC Control Number: 2012944819

Library and Archives Canada Cataloguing in Publication

Suicide and culture : understanding the context / Erminia Colucci and David Lester, editors ; with Heidi
Hjelmeland and B.C. Ben Park.

Includes bibliographical references.
ISBN 978-0-88937-436-2

1. Suicide. 2. Culture. 3. Suicide–Prevention. 4. Suicide–Research. 5. Culture–Research. I. Colucci,
Erminia, 1976- II. Lester, David, 1942- III. Hjelmeland, Heidi IV. Park, B. C. Ben (Byeong Chul Ben),
1956-

HV6545.S799 2012   362.28   C2012-905137-3

Cover images by Erminia Colucci © 2012

PUBLISHING OFFICES
USA: Hogrefe Publishing, 875 Massachusetts Avenue, 7th Floor, Cambridge, MA 02139
           Phone (866) 823-4726, Fax (617) 354-6875; E-mail customerservice@hogrefe-publishing.com
EUROPE: Hogrefe Publishing, Merkelstr. 3, 37085 Göttingen, Germany
           Phone +49 551 99950-0, Fax +49 551 99950-425, E-mail publishing@hogrefe.com

SALES & DISTRIBUTION
USA: Hogrefe Publishing, Customer Services Department,
           30 Amberwood Parkway, Ashland, OH 44805
           Phone (800) 228-3749, Fax (419) 281-6883, E-mail customerservice@hogrefe.com
EUROPE: Hogrefe Publishing, Merkelstr. 3, 37085 Göttingen, Germany
           Phone +49 551 99950-0, Fax +49 551 99950-425, E-mail publishing@hogrefe.com

OTHER OFFICES
CANADA: Hogrefe Publishing, 660 Eglinton Ave. East, Suite 119-514, Toronto, Ontario M4G 2K2
SWITZERLAND: Hogrefe Publishing, Länggass-Strasse 76, CH-3000 Bern 9

Hogrefe Publishing
Incorporated and registered in the Commonwealth of Massachusetts, USA, and in Göttingen, Lower Saxony,
Germany

Printed and bound in the USA
ISBN 978-0-88937-436-2

Dedication

In memory of Prof. Guido Petter, an inspiring scholar, a talented writer, and a great man.

Endorsements of the Book

Suicide is fundamentally a social act, suffused with personal and collective meaning. In this volume by Colucci and Lester, a group of international scholars explore the cultural contexts, causes and consequences of suicide. This engagement with culture provides insights into the social determinants of suicide and promises renewed attention to lived experience. By taking culture seriously, the contributors have produced a path-breaking book that can inform the next generation of suicide research, clinical practice and prevention.

Laurence J. Kirmayer, MD, James McGill Professor & Director, Division of Social & Transcultural Psychiatry, McGill University, Montreal, Quebec, Canada; Head of Social Axis, FRSQ Suicide Research Network; Director of Culture & Mental Health Research Unit, Montreal, Quebec, Canada; Editor-in-Chief of Transcultural Psychiatry

Are conventional biological and medical models used by psychiatry sufficient to understand (and to prevent) suicide? This unconventional and innovative book provides theoretical analyses and field studies that consider suicide not just as an event determined by some psychiatric disease but rather as a complex phenomenon determined by cultural and social determinants. The book offers convincing arguments and a broad spectrum of concrete multinational and multicultural examples showing the role of culture in determining suicidal behaviour. This perspective has significant implications for public health: A deeper cultural understanding should be seen as the way towards more effective prevention strategies. This book tells us that it is time for psychiatry to pay more attention to different epistemological models and to different disciplines in order to really understand and effectively prevent suicide. It is an eye-opening book which also will hopefully open the minds of all professionals concerned with suicide and suicide prevention encouraging them to use more culture-oriented and multidisciplinary approaches and attitudes.

Prof. Benedetto Saraceno, MSc, MD, FRCPsych, Calouste Gulbenkian Professor of Global Health, University Nova of Lisbon, Portugal; Director of WHO Collaborating Center on Mental Health, University of Geneva, Switzerland

Suicide and Culture: Understanding the Context is a wise, excellent, and original book, full of details about the relevance and importance of culture in the suicidology field. Uptodate and modern, it is an important book for all persons involved in suicide prevention and provides clear insight into the role of culture in suicidal behavior. This book shows that it is impossible to understand human beings if they are divorced from their culture.

Prof. Sergio Perez, MD, Founder of World Psychiatric Association's Suicidology Section and Founder of World Suicidology Net

This volume brings together fundamental questions about the meaning and construction of suicide as a social phenomenon expressing wider social ills and structures as well as individual dispositions. By necessity the authors have to tackle the meaning of culture and unpack research traditions, including epidemiological and more hermeneutic research methods. They take up prejudices found within and across these traditions and push for interdisciplinary maturity to better understand the complexities involved in suicidal acts. The chapters incisively take up the relevance of religion, present national and international comparisons of rates and meanings, and the impact on indigenous peoples and migrants. Including original new data as well as summaries of previous literature, the book provides a valuable and provocative set of issues that surely will motivate researchers, policy makers, and clinicians to progressively understand and prevent suicide among people from diverse cultural backgrounds. This valuable book, if well used, will not only help to save human life and human capital, but also help society to understand a fundamental philosophical issue facing us all: the meaning of life and the value we place upon it.

Prof. Kamaldeep Bhui, BSc, MBBS, MSc, MSc, MD, FRCPsych, Professor of Cultural Psychiatry & Epidemiology, Wolfson Institute of Preventive Medicine, Queen Mary University of London, UK

While we often hear that most suicides are associated with mental disorders, a majority are also associated with "social disorders," including those in the cultural, economic, religious, and familial structures of society. The present book shows how culture exists independent of the individual psyche and biology. It provides new analyses including the relationship between cultural approval of suicide and suicide attempts in India, Australia, and Italy, and the role of cultural change in producing a fourfold increase in suicide rates over just 20 years in Korea. By calling attention to the role of culture in shaping suicide risk, it should stimulate work which will integrate the hegemonic individual perspective with the fertile but neglected social perspective on suicide.

Prof. Steven Stack, Departments of Psychiatry & Criminology, Wayne State University, Detroit, MI USA

I was completely captivated by the book, which is a landmark in the study of culture and suicide. A perfect mix of precision and compassion.

Prof. Lakshmi Vijayakumar, MBBS, DPM, PhD, FRCPsyc, Founder of SNEHA; Honorary Associate Professor, Melbourne University, Australia; Adjunct Professor, Australian Institute for Suicide and Research Prevention, Griffith University, Australia

Culture has indeed been sorely neglected in suicidology. This book addresses the bias in suicidology of looking at pathology, including depression, and neurobiology, and in particular seeing suicide as an individual phenomenon. The authors show that suicide enters the mind through culture, that it is a cultural phenomenon, a cultural syndrome or idiom, and at its core a social problem. This book is a wake-up call to suicidologists.

Prof. Michael Kral, PhD, Associate Professor of Psychology and Anthropology, University of Illinois at Urbana-Champaign, IL

Foreword

Cultures inevitably affect the way individuals express emotional distress. For a considerable period of time, suicide in all its manifestations has been of great interest in not only epidemiological and psychiatric contexts but also in social and cultural dimensions as well. There has been sufficiently rigorous epidemiological evidence to indicate that rates of suicide do vary across nations and cultures as well across time periods. These variations are related to a number of factors – some clearly understood and others not so. Cultures influence the method of suicide and underlying attitudes to self-harm and suicide. The challenge and ethical dilemma for mental health professionals is to determine whether all cases of suicide have an underlying psychiatric disorder. The role of the psychiatrist in both assessing suicidal intent as well as their role in public mental health and suicide prevention therefore is significant. In addition, embedded within the culture, religion plays a key role in social attitudes to suicide and suicidal attempts. Furthermore, across cultures, sometimes suicidal behaviour is legally proscribed making it impossible to understand the factors leading to suicide and also putting preventive strategies in place.

It is important that not only clinicians but also other stake holders including policy makers take this matter seriously and this volume provides up-to-date research materials and cultural meanings of suicide with additional background. In addition, this volume not only continues the debate on whether cultural variations can explain the rates and types of suicide, but it also discusses how biological factors are in themselves culturally influenced. It provides plenty of thought-provoking material and data and will be of great interest to those who deal with the sequelae and consequences of suicide, but also to those who are interested in culture and its impact on suicide.

Dinesh Bhugra, CBE, FRCP, FRCPsych, PhD
Professor of Mental Health and Cultural Diversity
Institute of Psychiatry, King's College London
Immediate Past President, Royal College of Psychiatrists

Preface

This book is about suicide and culture, a topic that has been neglected in suicid-ology. It differs greatly from the organization of other books that have appeared on this issue, which typically contain chapters on "Suicide in Asia" and "Suicide in Sub-Saharan Africa" or suicide in particular countries.

The present book first examines some of the issues in the study of culture and suicide, beginning with a plea for the role of culture in an era when biological models of suicide have become popular. This is followed by a debate in Chapters 2 and 3 between the two editors on what "the cultural meaning of suicide" means. This section ends with a review of research and theorizing on the role of culture in suicidal behavior in Chapter 4.

The research section begins by presenting the results of a quantitative and qual-itative study by Erminia Colucci on the meaning of suicide in three cultures – Australian, Indian, and Italian. Chapter 6 reviews a body of research conducted by Ahmed Abdel-Khalek and David Lester comparing correlates of suicidal behavior in Kuwait and the US, with a critique of this research – what it has accomplished and where it has failed. Chapter 7 reviews what is known about a culturally-bound form of suicide – sati in India.

In Chapter 8, Ben Park explores the role of cultural conflict for understanding suicide in South Korea, and Chapter 9 presents our conclusions.

Table of Contents

The Issues

Suicide Research and Prevention: The Importance of Culture in "Biological Times"

Heidi Hjelmeland

Suicide is recognized as a multifactorial phenomenon that can be approached from a range of different perspectives. In his monumental book *Definition of Suicide*, Shneidman (1985) listed the following perspectives: theological, philosophical, demographic, sociological, psychodynamic, psychological, cognitive, biological, evolutionary, constitutional, biochemical, legal, prevention, global, political, and supranational. The importance of the sociocultural context in the development, treatment, and prevention of suicidal behavior should be self-evident from this, and this is widely acknowledged.

Although Shneidman did not mention psychiatry explicitly, there is no doubt that psychiatry is currently one of the most powerful bases for suicidology. In fact, it has been proposed recently to include suicidal behavior as a mental disorder in the upcoming DSM-5 (Berman, 2011; Classen, 2011). This may be perceived as an attempt from (parts of) the psychiatric profession to monopolize suicide prevention. Moreover, it is evident that psychiatry, as well as the behavioral sciences, have developed in a very biological direction (Brinkmann, 2009) and, with the focus on biological and genetic explanations of human behavior on the increase, the focus on cultural explanations is decreasing (Brinkmann, 2009; Lipton, 2010). This will inevitably have implications for suicidology. Indeed, as outlined further below, we may be witnessing a current "biologification" of suicidology. Hence, this biological turn may become, or perhaps already is, an important (political) challenge for the promotion of the importance of cultural issues in suicide research and prevention (Hjelmeland, 2010, 2011).

Alarcón (2009), a leading cultural psychiatrist, claimed that maintaining the focus on cultural issues is an uphill battle in psychiatry, which may make it an uphill battle in suicidology as well. However, there is no doubt that culture is crucial in suicide research and prevention (e.g., Boldt, 1988; Colucci, 2006; Hjelmeland, 2011), and this is the focus of the present chapter. It should, however, be mentioned at the outset that psychology is, of course, also extremely important in understanding suicidality. According to Shneidman (1985), psychology is *the* most important perspective in suicidology. According to systems theory (Engel, 1977), it is psychology that binds together the biological and sociocultural perspectives. However, the psychological perspective is not discussed in depth in this chapter. The main focus here is on the relationship between biology and culture.

Below, I present evidence that suicidology is currently increasingly biologized, and I discuss some (potential) consequences of this trend, followed by an outline of the importance of including a cultural perspective in *all* suicide research and prevention, even (and particularly) in "biological times." First, however, I discuss why a focus on biology is important in a chapter and book on culture and suicide.

Why all the Focus on Biology in this Chapter on Culture?

The main reason to focus on biology is that the natural sciences traditionally have a much higher status and legitimacy and, hence, power compared to the humanistic and social sciences (Brinkmann, 2009). In fact, we sometimes get the impression that natural science (including biology) is considered to be the only *real* kind of science. Moreover, there are strong monetary interests here. If it were possible to find some biological, neurological, or biochemical markers of suicidality, the next step would be to develop medications to treat what is often, although erroneously, referred to as a "chemical imbalance" in the brain. According to Rose (2007), "Whether it is brain scans or genetic tests, all pathways through the brain seem to end in the use of psychopharmaceuticals" (p. 208). Therefore, pharmaceutical companies are eager to fund biological research on suicidal behavior and, indeed, many of the biological projects in the field are funded by the pharmaceutical industry as evidenced by authors' declarations of interest in published articles. This may contribute to an increased focus on biological research at the expense of equally or more important kinds of research, such as cultural research.

This, in turn, makes it important to be vigilant and aware of the potential consequences (and dangers) of such a development. It is important that the biological perspective develops in *interplay* with the humanistic and social sciences rather than at the cost of them. We must never lose sight of the fact that suicidality is a complex, multifactorial phenomenon (Shneidman, 1985), and that the "road to suicide" differs across cultural groups as well as across individuals within the different cultural groups. Thus, the sociocultural context and, hence, a cultural perspective, is *crucial* in suicide research and prevention. Suicide should never be reduced to a simplistic biological condition that can the treated with medicines for, by doing that, we would go back to a very mechanistic view of human beings. People are not mechanical machines, responding automatically to biological stimuli, but complex, reflecting, meaning-seeking, relational and goal-oriented beings, and suicide is by definition a conscious, *intentional* act that cannot be reduced to a cause-and-effect relationship with a biological factor. In the words of Lipton (2010), "because we are not powerless biochemical machines, popping a pill every time we are mentally or physically out of tune is not the answer" (p. xxvi). If we get to a point where we try to medicate away the effect of negative life experiences leading to suicidality, which seems to be the aim of some of the biological research in the field, this may have serious effects for our development as human beings.

Manifestations of a Current "Biologification" of Suicidology

An increased focus on biology in suicide research is apparent in a number of ways. First, a biological turn of the suicidological "language" seems to be developing. For instance, common risk factors are referred to as "endophenotypes" (i.e., genetically induced biological markers; Gottesman & Gould, 2003), whether they are biological or not. Some examples of these markers are partner violence, criminal behavior, firearm ownership (Larkin & Beautrais, 2010), and hopelessness (Lazary et al., 2012). Also, suicidal behavior is itself now referred to as a "phenotype" (e.g., Mann & Currier, 2011). Moreover, since 2003, the concept "suicidal brain" has appeared in the titles of several articles and book chapters (e.g., Audenaert, Peremans, Goethals, & van Heeringen, 2006; Desmyter et al., 2011; van Heeringen, Godfrin, & Bijttebier, 2011; van Heeringen & Marusic, 2003). To refer to suicidal brains rather than to suicidal minds or suicidal persons can be described as a prototypical biological reductionist use of language common within the framework of the biomedical illness model.

Of course, not everyone is using biological concepts such as those referred to above. The biological literature still is only a relatively small part of the suicidological field. However, when texts like these are read together by means of "symptomal reading" (Althusser, 1968/1970), the development of a more biological turn in the language is discernible. Language is power and influences thoughts and actions. The way we use language has implications for how we think and how we act with regard to suicidal behavior and suicidal people. This, in turn, has implications for how we approach suicide prevention.

A second manifestation of a biological turn in suicidology is an increased interest and enthusiasm for (neuro)biological research on suicide. With the new developments in technology, various kinds of brain-imaging studies have received

increasing attention and their potential to contribute to suicide prevention is
emphasized (e.g., Audenaert et al., 2005, 2006; Desmyter, van Heeringen, &
Audenaert, 2011; Jollant, Lawrence, Olié, Guillaume, & Courtet, 2011;
Mann, 2005). With the high status of (neuro)biological research, the monetary
interests involved in such research, and the constant emphasis of how promising
the results from such studies are, there is every reason to assume that this type of
research will increase in the years to come (Restak, 2006).

Researchers have searched for a long time for the genetic underpinnings of suicide, and the mapping of the complete human genome created high expectations
with regard to the potential of such research – a third example of the biologification of suicidology. In their review of genetic studies to date, Wasserman,
Sokolowski, Wasserman, and Rujescu (2009) listed a number of genes that are
of interest in relation to suicidal behavior and, for each of the (candidate) genes
presented, they concluded that more studies are needed to clarify the relationship.
Marusic and Farmer (2001) called for more molecular genetic research "because
this may allow targeting of psychosocial or pharmacotherapeutic interventions at
persons of high suicide risk" (p. 196). Thus, there is reason to believe that genetic
research will increase significantly in the years to come, perhaps focusing more on
biological and clinical endophenotypes relevant to suicide than on suicide *per se*
(Mann et al., 2009).

Fourth, depression is claimed to be the most important risk factor for suicide,
and even granted causal status by some (e.g., Isacsson & Rich, 2003). About a
decade ago, Isacsson (2000) stated that treatment with antidepressants (a biological treatment) might be a medical breakthrough in suicide prevention. Indeed,
three years later he claimed that the increased use of antidepressants had saved
2,500 Swedish lives in the last ten years (Isacsson, 2003). Much research on this
has been conducted, and the topic has been debated since then.

A curiosity (or maybe not?) can be mentioned as a fifth example of a current
biologification of suicidology. The Action Alliance for Suicide Prevention (2011)
Research Task Force in the USA included a survey, conducted in the autumn of
2011, asking suicide researchers and others involved in suicide prevention to suggest the aspirational research goals that they thought would most likely contribute
to the reduction of the suicide rate in the next five to ten years. To clarify to the
participants what was meant by aspirational research goals one of the first examples was "To develop medications that can quickly reduce suicidal thoughts and
plans in distressed people." This can either be a coincidence or be symptomatic of
a biological *Zeitgeist* in the field. In the next round of this survey, all the suggestions from participants were summarized and condensed into 12 strategic aspirational goals to be further discussed. "Find better ways to use existing and new
biological treatments (e.g., medications) to prevent suicidal behavior" was listed

among the 12, indicating that many of the participants had made suggestions along this line. All of these examples of a "biologification" of suicidology presented above are discussed critically below.

Culture is Crucial

According to Bhugra and Bhui (2007), "People eat, drink and breathe culture" (p. xvii), and Geertz (1973) maintained that: "there is no such thing as a human nature independent of culture ... We are ... incomplete or unfinished animals who complete or finish ourselves through culture" (p. 49). In the words of Markus and Hamedani (2007), "biological beings become human beings through their engagement with the meanings and practices of their social world" (p. 32). In other words, culture is fundamental to people's lives and, hence, will be of crucial importance to their suicidality as well since suicidality is about what kinds of lives people have. Boldt (1988) emphasized that the meaning of suicide is culture-specific and that "no one who commits suicide does so without reference to the prevailing normative standards and attitudes of the cultural community" (p. 106). Thus, to prevent suicide we need to understand what suicidal behavior *means* to people in their particular sociocultural context(s) (Boldt, 1988; Colucci, 2006; Hjelmeland & Knizek, 2011).

Tseng (2007) has emphasized that "... culture has a significant pathofacilitating effect on suicidal behavior" (p. 106), that is, cultural factors contribute significantly to the occurrence of suicidal behavior in a society. Prevalence and risk factors for suicidal behavior do indeed vary across regions, countries, and parts of the world (Vijayakumar, John, Pirkis, & Whiteford 2005a; Vijayakumar, Nagaray, Pirkis, & Whiteford, 2005b;) implying that culture may play an important role in suicidal behavior. Thus, studies in or from different cultural contexts can teach us something about suicidal phenomena (suicidal ideation and nonfatal and fatal suicidal behavior). Such studies will enhance our understanding of what suicidal behavior *means* in different cultural contexts (Hjelmeland & Knizek, 2011). This is important in order to develop the field of suicidology itself, as well as to enable us to develop culture-sensitive knowledge bases for suicide prevention. Also, by looking at suicidal behavior in or from a different cultural context than our own, we can see this behavior in our own culture in a new light and, therefore, get a better understanding of what this behavior means and thus how it best can be prevented (Hjelmeland & Knizek, 2011).

For instance, the strong relationship between mental disorders and suicide, namely that more than 90% of those who kill themselves suffered from one or more mental disorders, established as a "truth" in the West (e.g., Cavanagh, Carson, Sharpe, & Lawrie, 2003) is not found in other parts of the world (e.g., Chan, Hung, & Yip, 2001; Kizza, Knizek, Kinyanda, & Hjelmeland, in press; Phillips et al., 2002; Vijayakumar et al., 2005a; Yang et al., 2005; Zhang, Conwell, Zhou, & Jiang, 2004). Perhaps the weaker relationship between depression (and other mental disorders) and suicide found outside the West is *not* the anomaly? No one has ever been able to show *how* depression and other mental disorders are related to suicide. In fact, the evidence base for this Western truism is rather weak (Hjelmeland, Dieserud, Dyregrov, Knizek, & Leenaars, 2012). The vast majority, around 95% or more, of people with a diagnosis of depression do *not* kill themselves (e.g., Blair-West, Mellsop, & Eyeson-Annan, 1997). What separates those relatively few depressed people who do kill themselves from those who do not? It is certainly not the depression. Perhaps this relationship, then, is overemphasized in the West because psychiatry there has such a strong position in suicidology? Psychiatrists are medical doctors and hence natural scientists and, as such, they have a higher status than other professional groups. This is then an example of how studies from different cultural contexts can teach us something about the phenomenon of suicide. Perhaps we in the West are looking in the wrong places for the solution to the "enigma" of suicide?

Moreover, taking the numerous definitions of culture into consideration (for references, see Colucci, 2006; Hjelmeland, 2010), it is safe to say that *all* countries are multicultural one way or the other and that currently, "within any specific regions, the populations are rapidly becoming diversified" (Yu, Lui, & Lin, 2007, p. 403). Thus, even if we are not particularly interested in what goes on elsewhere in the world, we need to take cultural aspects of suicidal behavior into consideration in our own multicultural societies, everywhere. In Medin, Unsworth, and Hirschfeld's (2007) statement that "psychology needs cultural research to be legitimate" (p. 615), "psychology" can indeed be replaced by "suicidology." If we want to *understand* suicidal behavior and suicidal people, it is absolutely essential to take the cultural context into consideration in *all* kinds of suicidological research, including biological research (e.g., Hjelmeland, 2010). Some reasons for this are outlined in the following section.

Why Culture is Important Even in Biological Research

First it should be emphasized that (neuro)biological research in suicidology is important. However, there are some important limitations, as well as potentially problematic consequences of such research, that we need not only to be aware of, but to deal with properly. Brinkmann (2009) pointed to one of the perhaps most problematic consequences, namely that biological research takes the focus away from other equally or more important types of research. If future suicidological research is dominated by the biological aspects of suicidal behavior, we run the risk of going back to a very mechanistic view of human beings, reducing suicide, a conscious and intentional act as well as a highly existential issue, to a mere biological "fault" or "chemical imbalance" that can be treated with medications. This would be a dangerous development, and reasons for why it is absolutely crucial to take the sociocultural context into consideration in biological research are outlined below.

Genetic Studies

According to Chen et al. (2007), "Biology is not 'culture free,' and findings derived from the field of biological psychiatry need to be understood in the context of culture and ethnicity to avoid misleading and mis-interpretation" (p. 78). For example, most of the phenotypes are not genetically conditioned but culturally induced (Stuppia, 2009), and the same genotype can result in very different phenotypes depending on the cultural context (Kim, Sherman, & Sasaki 2009). This also applies to the phenotype of suicide. However, this information seems to be lost in the focus on biology. It is well recognized in genetics that intentional behavior (e.g., suicide) cannot be reduced to the deterministic cause-and-effect level of a gene (Colbert, 2001). It is also unlikely that several genes in interplay will be able to "cause" such a complex behavior without input from the environment (i.e., certain kinds of experiences). The genetic influence on a complex phenomenon such as (suicidal) behavior would have to be infinitely complex, involving all the developmental, environmental, social, and cultural influences that a human being is exposed to. Rutter (2006) observed that:

> First, the genes may code for some polypeptide that is indirectly relevant but yet not involved in the main causal chain. Second, not only are multiple genes affecting proteins involved, but also there are multiple genetic elements that influence the operation of any single gene affecting protein. Third, there are environmental influences on gene expression – the key process that determines the functional operation of genes. Fourth, some genetic effects are contingent on an interaction with specific environmental influences so that any understanding of the causal pathway must incorporate identification of the mechanisms underlying that interplay. Fifth, there will be influences operating on the pathway to the behavior that involve thought processes. (pp. 174–175)

As emphasized above, people are reflective beings and suicide is, by definition, a conscious, intentional act resulting from people's life experiences, experiences that, in turn, will influence the expressions of their genes. In the words of
Church (2009), "Not just from day to day, but from second to second, genetic cas-
cades are turned on or off by our experience" (p. 81).

In addition, we have cultural complexities. "Not only may several different
genes, or multiple alleles of the same gene, lead to the same trait, but which ones
do so may vary geographically" (Rutter, 2006, p. 163). The findings from quantitative genetics must be interpreted with great caution since there is little evidence
as to whether genetic influences operate the same way in different ethnic groups,
or even across different segments in the same ethnic or cultural group. Research
findings may be highly population dependent. Furthermore, it is widely acknowledged that suicidal individuals constitute a highly heterogeneous group both
across and within different ethnic, cultural and population groups. Rutter (2006)
noted that, even within a relative homogeneous population, there will be individual differences with regard to which genes have contributed to a behavior and that,
"when dealing with populations that differ in either their genetic makeup or their
life circumstances, or both, the findings may not be the same" (p. 159). Therefore,
there is reason to ask whether we can expect much useful knowledge from genetic
studies on suicidal behavior. Suicidological studies on genes rarely mention such
sociocultural complexities.

Researchers of genetics in suicidology do, however, recognize the importance of
environmental factors to some extent. For instance, they often refer to the stress-
diathesis model (Mann & Arango, 1992) in which a genetic predisposition is the
diathesis (vulnerability) that, in interplay with later life stressors (risk factors),
"causes" suicidal behavior. However, here the sociocultural context is also crucial
since what constitutes a risk factor varies across cultures (Vijayakumar et al.,
2005b). Furthermore, "Even though this model considers environmental events,
there is no room for intentionality or purpose in it. If a person is subjected to a
stressful event, the event triggers a genetic tendency; then the genetic pre-
programming takes over the person's control of his/her behavior" (Colbert,
2001, p. 88). In other words, in the stress-diathesis model, contextual factors are
reduced to mere triggers and their meaning and significance for the individuals
are thus completely disregarded. Such models cannot explain why the different risk
factors contribute to suicide in some but not in most people experiencing them, or
why some risk factors are more important in some cultural contexts than in others.

It is also a question of the *relative* importance of a genetic predisposition
compared to environmental and contextual factors. For example, Markus and
Hamedani (2007) argued that, "before looking for ... the genetic underpinnings
of a given behavior, it would seem wise, and also scientifically sound, to

determine whether a given observed behavior can still be observed once the context shifts" (p. 29). This statement actually may be perceived as an argument for doing cultural research *before* conducting biological research. Perhaps even *instead* of, especially if Francis (2011) is correct in that the payoff of studies on genetic contributions to complex phenomena is uncertain, at best. Colbert (2001) actually claims that genetic psychiatric research is more about statistical manipulations than actual science, and Rogers and Lester (2010) maintained that the biological suicide research "sheds little, if any, light on the etiology of suicide" (p. 56).

The environment or sociocultural context[1] is crucial regardless of the genetic make-up of the individual. Hence, it is important to understand the context making the person suicidal rather than merely treating their symptoms of anguish, despair, or mental pain with medications. This might even make some of the biological research on suicide superfluous but, at the very least, the sociocultural context needs to be taken into consideration in interpreting the results of biological research.

Antidepressants

The effects of medication have been shown to be culture dependent (Yu et al., 2007), which means, for example, that the cultural context must be considered when using antidepressants. This is often disregarded in the research on the suicide preventive effects of antidepressants, even though research results are mixed with regard to such an effect and the topic, therefore, has been debated during the last decade. In 2010, this debate was summarized in a discussion paper in the *British Journal of Psychiatry* in which Isacsson and Rich argued that "treatment with antidepressants prevents suicide" (p. 429), whereas Juredini and Raven maintained that the evidence base for such a relationship is weak (Isacsson & Rich vs. Jureidini & Raven, 2010). In this debate article, Isacsson and Rich argued *for* a *worldwide* decrease in suicide rates due to the increased use of antidepressants. Governments, for example, will perhaps welcome such simple solutions to complex problems. Researchers have, however, a duty to not contribute to untenable simplification (Hjelmeland, 2011), particularly since we *know* that the relationship between the use of antidepressants and suicidality is rather complex. This was demonstrated in a meta-analysis of 372 double-blind randomized placebo-controlled trials showing that the effect was strongly dependent on age. Only

---

[1]   Whatever we want to call it – researchers on biological factors seem to prefer environment, perhaps because of its biological connotation?

among older adults (age > 64) was the risk of suicidality found to be reduced with use of antidepressants, whereas there was no effect for the age group 25–64 and even an increased risk for those under 25 years (Stone et al., 2009). Although this meta-analysis focused on age differences, there are reasons to believe that the effect is also culture-dependent (Yu et al., 2007). It is, therefore, crucial to take the cultural context into consideration in studies of antidepressants as well as in their use for suicide prevention.

The basis for the strong faith in the suicide preventive effect of antidepressants is the belief that depression is a causal factor in suicidality (e.g., Isacsson & Rich, 2003). However, as mentioned above, the strong relationship between depression and suicide, often referred to in the West, is not found in other parts of the world (e.g., Chan et al., 2001; Kizza et al., in press; Phillips et al., 2002; Vijayakumar et al., 2005a; Yang et al., 2005; Zhang et al., 2004). Moreover, of all the psychiatric diagnoses, depression is the one that raises most questions concerning cross-cultural validity (Fernando, 2003; Jadhav & Littlewood, 1994; Kleinman & Good, 1985). In fact, the transcultural meaning of *all* the traditional psychiatric diagnoses (related to suicide) is very uncertain since they are based on a unicultural, ethnocentric Western psychiatry (Fernando, 2003). This is also important to consider with regard to the current attempt to get suicidal behaviors included as mental disorders in the DSM-5, particularly since psychiatry has a relatively bad track record in terms of recognizing cultural issues in assessment and treatment of mental disorders (Hughes, 1998; Jenkins, 1998; Kirmayer, 1998; Lewis-Fernandez, 1998; Mezzich et al., 1999). It remains to be seen which place culture will have in the DSM-5.

Based on all the above considerations, it would under any circumstances be a bad idea if psychiatry monopolized suicide prevention by including suicidal behavior as a diagnosis in the DSM-5, particularly since psychiatry is moving in a biological direction and since the connection between psychiatry and the pharmaceutical industry is so close – too close, according to some. For instance, in a letter in connection with Lauren Mosher's withdrawal from the American Psychiatric Association circulated on the internet and referred to by Rose (2007), Mosher states that "At this point in history, in my view, psychiatry has been almost completely bought out by the drug companies .... No longer do we seek to understand whole persons in their social contexts – rather we are there to realign our patients' neurotransmitters" (p. 218).

Neuro-Imaging Studies

It is also important for (neuro)biological researchers to recognize that the "suicidal brain" is placed inside the skull of a whole person, and this person is embedded within his or her specific sociocultural context, a cultural context that consists of several different cultural contexts simultaneously, and many factors in these contexts are *crucial* in the suicidal process, regardless of the individual's biological and genetic makeup. Such an awareness seems, to a large degree, to be absent in (neuro)biological research on suicidal behavior. Although it is recognized that suicide is a multidimensional phenomenon and thus a multidimensional approach is important in research, the focus seems to be on intrapersonal factors only. For instance, Desmyter et al. (2011), in their review of structural and functional neuroimaging studies of the suicidal brain, emphasize "that it is of great importance to realize that one behavior can consist of multiple underlying cognitions, emotions, and thus neurobiological mechanisms." Mann et al. (2006), in their conclusion of their meta-analysis of whether biological tests can predict suicide, stated that, "Predicting risk for completed suicide requires a multidimensional approach that includes biological, clinical, and neuropsychological indices" (p. 472). No mention of contextual or cultural factors was made. Suicidality clearly is defined as something *in* the individual, and the solutions to the problem of suicidality is thus also sought *within* the suicidal individual. It is the individual, rather than the context, making the individual suicidal that is the target for intervention. However, "we now know that culture exerts a more powerful effect than strictly biological factors in shaping our brains" (Restak, 2006, p. 215).

Transcultural neuroimaging has shown that cultural background influences neural activity (Stompe, 2009). Thus, the sociocultural context needs to be considered when interpreting brain images (Restak, 2006). In the words of Restak, "Change the context and you change the brain's response" (p. 86). We know that biological patterns in the brain can be created and changed by experience (e.g., Schwartz & Begley, 2002). Since experiences occur in particular cultural contexts, it should be self-evident why cultural issues must be taken into consideration in the analysis of biological data (e.g., Hjelmeland & Knizek, 2011).

The development of new brain-imaging techniques have contributed to a return toward a mechanistic view of human beings in psychiatry and, hence, in suicidology. As mentioned above, a potential consequence of finding biological markers for suicidal behavior is that this makes it easy to propose biological treatments, such as medication, as the best, cheapest, and easiest possible intervention. As a result of the high cost of brain-imaging equipment, it is not likely that culture-specific MRI studies will be conducted on a large scale, especially in low income countries, but it is not unlikely that, for instance, some pharmaceutical companies will generalize the effect of medicines from one cultural context to another (it has been known to happen) although, as mentioned above, there is evidence of culture, both the clinician's culture as well as the patient's culture, influencing the effect of drugs (Yu et al., 2007). This research also raises numerous ethical issues, which are, however, beyond the scope of this chapter to discuss.

It is also important to highlight some limitations of brain-imaging research. Restak (2006) has referred to brain-imaging studies as neo-phrenology. Where the old phrenologists measured peoples' skulls, the brain-imaging people measure inside peoples' skulls. Restak further maintains that the brain patterns involved in complex behavior (in our case suicidal behavior) involve multiple circuits that are spread throughout wide parts of the brain and that vary from one person to another. "That's why it's so risky and often just plain wrongheaded to attempt too rigid a localization of complex and multidetermined behaviors to specific locations within the brain" (Restak, 2006, p. 203). He further observed that "a lot of correlations can be established between brain and behavior (. . ..) [and that] the brain is too highly interconnected for any simplistic one-to-one correlation between a single brain area and our complex and nuanced human faculties" (p. 214).

I discussed the biologification of suicidological language earlier. We need to be conscious of what words we use. To reduce a suicidal person to a "suicidal brain" may contribute to a view that suicidal people are mechanical machines who, with proper medication, can function normally again, that is, become nonsuicidal. It is perhaps not what the authors had in mind when they used this concept. Perhaps it was just an attempt to describe what goes on in the brain when someone is suicidal. However, as mentioned above, language is power, and we need to be conscious of how we use it. Also, to refer to clearly nonbiological risk factors as endophenotypes contributes to biologize complex intentional behavior and should be avoided.

Can Epigenetics Aid the Argument for the Importance of Culture?

Epigenetics is defined as "the study of heritable changes in gene expression that are not due to changes in DNA sequence" (Eccleston, DeWitt, Gunter, Marte, & Nath, 2007, p. 395). Epigenetics studies the sources of expression or suppression of genes. In other words, "Epigenetics studies the environment" (Church, 2009, p. 48). Epigenetics studies how experiences effect genetic expression (Getz, Kirkengen, & Ulvestad, 2011) and, according to Francis (2011), "Social interactions are a particularly important source of gene regulation" (p. 29). Thus, much of what was presented above in terms of the importance of sociocultural context is epigenetics.

Although the concept of epigenetics was coined already in 1957 (Autry & Monteggia, 2009), it has only recently begun to appear in the medical and suicidological literature. It was recently claimed that the traditional biomedical production of knowledge has hindered insight in the medical significance of peoples' experiences and that epigenetics will contribute to a holistic understanding of the relationship between body, mind, and spirituality (Getz et al., 2011). In the words of Church (2009):

> Yet our experiences themselves are just part of the picture. We take facts and experiences and then assign meaning to them. What meaning we assign, mentally, emotionally, and spiritually, is often as important to genetic activation as the facts themselves. We are discovering that our genes dance with our awareness. Thoughts and feelings turn sets of genes on and off in complex relationships. Science is discovering that while we may have a fixed set of genes in our chromosomes, which of those genes is active has a great deal to do with our subjective experiences, and how we process them. (p. 36)

People's experiences are thus biologically relevant in that they actually affect the expression of genes without altering the DNA. Experiences always occur in a unique sociocultural context. Perhaps then, the "new" ideas from epigenetic research will contribute to a greater awareness of the crucial importance of culture in all suicidology research, including biological research? According to Tsai, Hong, and Liou (2011), "Epigenetic analyses in the brain of suicide subjects offer a possible explanation for the difficulty of geneticists in trying to link genetic polymorphisms to SB [suicidal behavior]" (p. 813).

However, it is important to be aware of how this is used. For instance, Labonte and Turecki (2010) argued that early life adversity, such as child sexual abuse, is a well-recognized risk factor for suicidal behavior. Recent research now indicates that such experiences can induce suicidal behavior "by affecting gene function via epigenetic reprogramming" (p. 292) and that epigenetics "may allow us to better understand through which biological processes environmental stressors and life adversity increase suicide risk" (p. 292). Although they do recognize the importance of environmental stressors, their focus is on the biological processes and, thereby, they seem to reduce suicidal people to biological and mechanic machines that react to a change of the genes by killing themselves. But individuals are intentional, reflective, meaning-seeking, and relational. After all, "a choice can invalidate a genetic influence" (Colbert, 2001, p. 88).

Multidisciplinary Collaboration is Crucial

It should be clear from the above that culture is crucial, and some might wonder whether we need biological research in suicidology. We do. In particular, research in neuroplasticity may have great potential to contribute to suicide prevention. Interpersonal neurobiology has, for instance, shown great potential in psychotherapy (e.g., Badenoch, 2008). However, based on the abundant evidence, of which only some has been presented above, that sociocultural issues are crucial (even in biological suicide research), perhaps funding sources should require that researchers outline how they plan to integrate a cultural perspective in, for instance, their genetic and neuroimaging research? Biological research in isolation can contribute relatively little to suicide prevention unless the sociocultural issues are properly dealt with. One way to move the suicidological field forward is, therefore, multidisciplinary collaboration (e.g., Bertolote, 2004; De Leo, 2002a, 2002b, 2004; Hjelmeland, 2011). Research projects should be constructed so that neurologists, psychiatrists, psychologists, sociologists, and anthropologists can collaborate to *integrate* the effect of potential biological markers with psychological, social, and cultural issues. In the words of Rutter (2006):

> It continues to prove quite difficult to identify genes for multifactorial traits (somatic or psychological) because most genes have such small effects and because their effects are often contingent on environmental circumstances ... there is every reason to suppose that "The new genetics" will deliver the goods but it will do so only if it combines effectively with other branches of science. (p. 5).

However, to achieve true multidisciplinary collaboration, there may be a need for a change of attitude in some circles. Tendencies of a "trench mentality," where professionals look down at or even dismiss the contributions from other disciplines, are frequently met (Hjelmeland, 2011). This is particularly strange and unfortunate in suicidology since suicide is a multifactorial phenomenon which can be studied from numerous theoretical perspectives (Shneidman, 1985).

Another issue to be considered in multidisciplinary collaboration is that culture influences the different disciplines. Both biomedicine and psychiatry are culturally constructed bodies of knowledge (Kirmayer, 2007), and here anthropologists may make important contributions. However, in multidisciplinary collaboration we face another cultural challenge, namely, that professionals from different disciplines need to communicate *in depth* with one another. With the increasing specializations in each of the collaborating disciplines, each with its own specialized language, this is not easy. With multidisciplinary collaboration we thus run the risk of ending up in a paradoxical situation. In order to broaden our horizon by having people from several disciplines working together, terminological difficulties result in the development of a reductionist pidgin-language that everyone can understand. But, at the same time, we lose the potential of the specialties of each of the individual disciplines. Together with the loss of the discipline-specific precision in terminology, we lose the specific understandings of each of the disciplines. Multidisciplinary approaches must focus especially on keeping up the specific terminology and methodology of the discrete disciplines, but also overcome the difficulties this creates for cross-disciplinary communication (Knizek, 1997).

The Need for a Paradigm shift

There is another, equally (or even more) important way to move the suicidological field forward, but for that we need a paradigm shift. Even if we manage to create truly multidisciplinary collaborative projects, with the current high emphasis on research of risk factors, whether these are biological, psychological, or social, it is not likely to bring us far in terms of *understanding* suicidal behavior and suicidal individuals in a cultural context (Hjelmeland & Knizek, 2011). First, it would be impossible to include all possible contributory (risk) factors in the same statistical analysis. Even if we could, we are left with the problem that culture is not a measurable variable (Jenkins, 1994). It cannot be measured on a scale from 1–10 where we can say that some have a lot of culture while others have little, or, in terms of presence or absence, where we can say that some have culture while others do not (Hjelmeland, 2010). Hence, culture cannot be included in a quantitative analysis to study its contribution to suicidal behavior.

Cohen (2007) has stated that "very few (or perhaps no) methodological problems become easier when culture is added to the picture" (p. 196). Medin and colleagues (2007) have described studying culture as "describing a moving target" (p. 637). It adds to the problems that, "The methods themselves have assumptions built into them about what culture is" (Cohen, 2007, p. 230). So what do we do? To increase our understanding of how culture contributes to suicidal behavior, we need a paradigm focusing on meaning and interpretation where the methodology employed is qualitative (Colucci, 2006; Hjelmeland & Knizek, 2010, 2011). Qualitative studies that focus on the *meanings* of suicidal behavior in different cultural contexts are more relevant for suicide prevention than much of the quantitative risk factor research that is currently being conducted in abundance (Hjelmeland & Knizek, 2010, 2011). It is high time to recognize the limitations of prediction, whether it is biological or otherwise, and instead focus on *understanding* suicide

at the individual level in different sociocultural contexts (Colucci, 2006; Hjelmeland, 2010; Hjelmeland & Knizek, 2010, 2011; Rogers & Lester, 2010). We need
in-depth interviews with the real experts, namely, the suicidal individuals themselves, in different cultural contexts. With reference to the topic of this chapter,
we can borrow the words from Restak (2006): " the answers provided by neuroscience aren't necessarily definitive. *Indeed, they often aren't as valid as information gathered from individual sources (asking questions, making behavioral
observations, etc.)*" (p. 202; italics not in the original). He goes on to say that,
"Keeping that fact in mind won't be easy, however, especially when some are
claiming that neuroscience will reveal definitive and reliable information about
people" (p. 202). Nevertheless, this is the way to go if we are interested in bringing the suicidological field forward (Hjelmeland & Knizek, 2010, 2011). Such
research, too, will benefit from multidisciplinary collaboration.

Concluding Remarks

This chapter hopefully makes clear that culture is indeed crucial in all suicide
research and prevention, including research from a biological perspective. Reducing thinking, feeling, and acting people to their brains and disregarding the sociocultural contexts that their brains develop in will impoverish our lives and impede
us from understanding central dimensions of ourselves (Brinkmann, 2009). "The
future should belong to a pluralistic and cross-disciplinary approach to the psyche
that, on the one hand, implies a corrective to the current brain fetishism and on the
other hand recognizes that the psyche is biological as well as cultural. Human
beings' mental lives are molecular, biological, *and* meaningful to persons"
(Brinkmann, 2009, p. 160, author's translation).

The chapter started with underlining the strong position psychiatry has in
suicidology and arguing that the current emphasis on biological approaches in
psychiatry has implications for suicidology. It will end with the words of
Lewis-Fernandez and Kleinman (1995): "Psychiatry can no more afford to be
contextless than it can afford to be mindless or brainless" (p. 444). The same
indeed applies to suicidology.

References

Action Alliance for Suicide Prevention. (2011). *Research Task Force.* Available online at http://
    actionallianceforsuicideprevention.org/?page_id=359

Alarcón, R. (2009, September). *Diagnosis in cultural psychiatry.* Roundtable presentation at the Second World Congress of Cultural Psychiatry: Cultural Brain and Living Societies, Norcia, Italy.

Althusser, L. (1968/1970). *Att läsa kapitalet 1* [To read the Capital]. Lund, Sweden: Bo Cavefors Bokförlag.

Audenaert, K., Peremans, K., Goethals, I., Otte, A., Dierckx, R., & van Heeringen, C. (2005). Functional brain imaging of the suicidal brain. *Nuclear Medicine Communications, 26,* 391–393.

Audenaert, K., Peremans, K., Goethals, I., & van Heeringen, C. (2006). Functional imaging, serotonin and the suicidal brain. *Acta Neurologica Belgica, 106,* 125–131.

Autry, A. E., & Monteggia, L. M. (2009). Epigentics in suicide and depression. *Biological Psychiatry, 66,* 812–813.

Badenoch, B. (2008). *Being a brain-wise therapist: A practical guide to interpersonal neurobiology.* New York: W. W. Norton & Company.

Berman, L. (2011). From the President. *IASP News Bulletin,* May/June, 2.

Bertolote, J. (2004). Suicide prevention: At what level does it work? *World Psychiatry, 3,* 3.

Bhugra, D., & Bhui, K. (2007). Preface. In D. Bhugra & K. Bhui (Eds.), *Textbook of cultural psychiatry,* pp. xvii–xviii. Cambridge, UK: Cambridge University Press.

Blair-West, G. W., Mellsop, G. W., & Eyeson-Annan, M. L. (1997). Down-rating lifetime suicide risk in major depression. *Acta Psychiatrica Scandinavica, 95,* 259–263.

Boldt, M. (1988). The meaning of suicide: Implications for research. *Crisis, 9,* 93–108.

Brinkmann, S. (2009). *Mellem synapser og samfund.* [Between synapses and societies]. Århus, Denmark: Aarhus universitetsforlag.

Cavanagh, J. T. O., Carson, A. J., Sharpe, M., & Lawrie, S. M. (2003). Psychological autopsy studies of suicide: A systematic review. *Psychological Medicine, 33,* 395–405.

Chan, K. P. M., Hung, S. F., & Yip, P. S. F. (2001). Suicide in response to changing societies. *Child & Adolescent Psychiatric Clinics of North America, 10,* 777–795.

Chen, C.-H., Liu, S.-K., & Lin, K.-M. (2007). Culture, ethnicity and biological psychiatry. In D. Bhugra & K. Bhui (Eds.), *Textbook of cultural psychiatry,* pp. 72–80. Cambridge, UK: Cambridge University Press.

Church, D. (2009). *The genie in your genes. Epigenetic medicine and the new biology of intention.* Santa Rosa, CA: Energy Psychology Press.

Classen, C. (2011, September). The global burden of suicide in DSM-V and ICD 11. Plenary presentation at the 26th World Congress of the International Association for Suicide Research and Prevention, Beijing, China.

Cohen, D. (2007). Methods in cultural psychology. In S. Kitayama & D. Cohen (Eds.), *Handbook of cultural psychology,* pp. 196–236. New York: Guilford Press.

Colbert, T. C. (2001). *Blaming our genes: Why mental illness can't be inherited.* Tustin, CA: Kevco Publishing.

Colucci, E. (2006). The cultural facet of suicidal behavior: Its importance and neglect. *Australian e-Journal for the Advancement of Mental Health, 5*(3). Retrieved from www.auseinet.com/journal/vol5iss3/colucci.pdf

De Leo, D. (2002a). Struggling against suicide: The need for an integrative approach. *Crisis, 23,* 23–31.

De Leo, D. (2002b). Why are we not getting any closer to preventing suicide? *British Journal of Psychiatry, 181,* 372–374.

De Leo, D. (2004). Suicide prevention is far more than a psychiatric business. *World Psychiatry, 3*, 3.

Desmyter, S. van Heeringen, C., & Audenaert, K. (2011). Structural and functional neuroimaging studies of the suicidal brain. *Progress in Neuro-Psychopharmacology & Biological Psychiatry, 35*(4), 796–808.

Eccleston, A., DeWitt, N., Gunter, C., Marte, B., & Nath, D. (2007). Nature Insight: Epigenetics. *Nature, 447*, 396–440.

Engel, G. L. (1977). The need of a new medical model: A challenge for biomedicine. *Science, 196*, 129–136.

Fernando, S. (2003). *Cultural diversity, mental health and psychiatry: The struggle against racism*. New York: Brunner-Routledge.

Francis, R. F. (2011). *Epigenetics: The ultimate mystery of inheritance*. New York: W. W. Norton & Company.

Geertz, C. (1973). *The interpretation of cultures*. New York: Basic Books

Getz, L., Kirkengen, A. L., & Ulvestad, E. (2011). Menneskets biologi – mettet med erfaring. [Human biology – Saturated with experience]. *Tidsskrift for den norske legeforening, 131*, 683–687.

Gottesman, I. I., & Gould, T. D. (2003). The endophenotype concept in psychiatry: Etymology and strategic intentions. *American Journal of Psychiatry, 160*, 636–645.

Hjelmeland, H. (2010). Cultural research in suicidology: Challenges and opportunities. *Suicidology Online, 1*, 34–52.

Hjelmeland, H. (2011). Cultural context is crucial in suicide research and prevention. *Crisis, 32*, 61–64.

Hjelmeland, H., Dieserud, G., Dyregrov, K., Knizek, B. L., & Leenaars, A. A. (2012). Psychological autopsy studies as diagnostic tools: Are they methodologically flawed? *Death Studies, 36*, 605–626.

Hjelmeland, H., & Knizek, B. (2010). Why we need qualitative research in suicidology. *Suicide and Life-Threatening Behavior, 40*, 74–80.

Hjelmeland, H., & Knizek, B. L. (2011). What kind of research do we need in suicidology today? In R. O'Connor, S. Platt, & J. Gordon (Eds.), *International handbook of suicide prevention: Research, policy and practice*, pp. 591–608. Chichester, UK: WileyBlackwell.

Hughes, C. C. (1998). The glossary of 'culture-bound syndromes' in DSM-IV: A critique. *Transcultural Psychiatry, 35*, 413–421.

Isacsson, G. (2000). Suicide prevention: A medical breakthrough? *Acta Psychiatrica Scandinavica, 102*, 113–117.

Isacsson. G. (2003). Prevention av självmord har räddat 2 500 liv på tio år. [Prevention of suicide has saved 2,500 lives in ten years.] *Läkartidningen, 100*, 1160–1161.

Isacsson, G., & Rich, C. L. (2003). Getting closer to suicide prevention. *British Journal of Psychiatry, 182*, 457.

Isacsson, G., & Rich, C. L., versus Jureidini, J. & Raven, M. (2010). The increased use of antidepressants has contributed to the worldwide reduction in suicide rates. *British Journal of Psychiatry, 196*, 429–433.

Jadhav, S., & Littlewood, R. (1994). Defeat depression campaign: Some medical anthropological queries. *Psychiatric Bulletin, 18*, 572–573.

Jenkins, J. H. (1994). Culture, emotion, and psychopathology. In S. Kitayama & H.R. Markus (Eds.), *Emotion and culture*, pp. 307–335. Washington, DC: American Psychological Association.

Jenkins, J. H. (1998). Diagnostic criteria for schizophrenia and related psychotic disorders: Integration and suppression of cultural evidence in DSM-IV. *Transcultural Psychiatry, 35,* 357–376.

Jollant, F., Lawrence, N. L., Olié, E., Guillaume, S., & Courtet, P. (2011). The suicidal mind and brain: A review of neuropsychological and neuroimaging studies. *World Journal of Biological Psychiatry, 12,* 319–339.

Kim, H., Sherman, D., & Sasaki, J. (2009, September). *Gene x culture interaction: The effect of culture and the serotonin receptor polymorphism (5-HTR1A) on social support use.* Paper presented at the Second World Congress of Cultural Psychiatry: Cultural Brains and Living Societies, Norcia, Italy.

Kirmayer, L. J. (1998). The fate of culture in DSM-IV. *Transcultural Psychiatry, 35,* 339–342.

Kirmayer, L. J. (2007). Cultural psychiatry in historical perspective. In D. Bhugra & K. Bhui (Eds.), *Textbook of cultural psychiatry,* pp. 3–19. New York: Cambridge University Press.

Kizza, D., Knizek, B. L., Kinyanda, E., & Hjelmeland, H. (in press). Men in despair: A qualitative psychological autopsy study of suicide in Northern Uganda. *Transcultural Psychiatry.*

Kleinman, A., & Good, B. (Eds.) (1985). *Culture and depression: Studies in the anthropology and cross-cultural psychiatry of affect and disorder.* Berkeley, CA: University of California Press.

Knizek, B. L. (1997). Semiotics as the psychosomatic hope. In I. Rauch & G. F. Carr (Eds.), *Semiotics around the world: Synthesis in diversity,* pp. 949–952. New York: Mouton de Gruyter.

Labonte, B., & Turecki, G. (2010). The epigenetics of suicide: Explaining the biological effects of early life environmental adversity. *Archives of Suicide Research, 14,* 291–310.

Larkin, G. L., & Beautrais, A. (2010). Emergency departments are underutilized sites for suicide prevention. *Crisis, 31,* 1–6.

Lazary, J., Viczena, V., Dome, P., Chase, D., Juhasz, G., & Bagdy, G. (2012). Hopelessness, a potential endophenotype for suicidal behavior, is influenced by TPH2 gene variants. *Progress in Neuro-Psychopharmachology & Biological Psychiatry, 36*(1), 155–160.

Lewis-Fernandez, R. (1998). A cultural critique of the DSM-IV dissociative disorders section. *Transcultural Psychiatry, 35,* 387–400.

Lewis-Fernandez, R., & Kleinman, A. (1995). Cultural psychiatry: Theoretical, clinical, and research issues. *Psychiatric Clinics of North America, 18,* 433–448.

Lipton, B. (2010). *The biology of belief: Unleashing the power of consciousness, matter and miracles.* Carlsbad, CA: Hay House.

Mann, J. (2005). What does brain imaging tell us about the predisposition to suicidal behavior. *Crisis, 26,* 101–103.

Mann, J. J., & Currier, D. (2011). Relationships of genes and early-life experience to the neurobiology of suicidal behaviour. In R. O'Connor, S. Platt, & J. Gordon (Eds.), *International handbook of suicide prevention: Research, policy and practice,* pp. 133–150. Chichester, UK: Wiley Blackwell.

Mann, J. J., & Arango, V. (1992). Integration of neurobiology and psychopathology in a unified model of suicidal behavior. *Journal of Clinical Psychopharmacology, 12*(2 Suppl.), 2S–7S.

Mann, J. J., Currier, D., Stanley, B., Oquendo, M. A., Amsel, L. V., & Ellis, S. P. (2006). Can biological tests assist prediction of suicide in mood disorders? *International Journal of Neuropsychopharmacology, 9,* 465–474.

Mann, J. J., Arango, V. A., Avenevoli, S., Brent, D. A., Champagne, F. A., Clayton, P., . . .
    Wenzel, A. (2009). Candidate endophenotypes for genetic studies of suicidal behavior.
    Biological Psychiatry, 65, 556–563.

Markus, H. R., & Hamedani, M. Y. G. (2007). Sociocultural psychology: The dynamic
    interdependence among self systems and social systems. In S. Kitayama & D. Cohen (Eds.),
    Handbook of cultural psychology, pp. 3–39. New York: Guilford.

Marusic, A., & Farmer, A. (2001). Genetic risk factors as possible causes of the variation in
    European suicide rates. *British Journal of Psychiatry, 179,* 194–196.

Medin, D. L., Unsworth, S. J., & Hirschfeld, L. (2007). Culture, categorization, and reasoning. In
    S. Kitayama & D. Cohen (Eds.), *Handbook of cultural psychology,* pp. 615-644. New York:
    Guilford.

Mezzich, J. E., Kirmayer, L. J., Kleinman, A., Fabrega, H., Parron, D. L., Good, B. J., Lin, K.-M.,
    & Manson, S. M. (1999). The place of culture in DSM-IV. *Journal of Nervous & Mental
    Disease, 187,* 457–464.

Phillips, M. R., Yang, G., Zhang, Y., Wang, L., Ji, H., & Zhou, M. (2002). Risk factors for suicide
    in China: A national case-control psychological autopsy study. *Lancet, 360,* 1728–1736.

Restak, R. (2006). *The naked brain: How the emerging neurosociety is changing how we live,
    work, and love.* New York: Three Rivers Press.

Rogers, J. R., & Lester, D. (2010). *Understanding suicide: Why we don't and how we might.*
    Cambridge, MA: Hogrefe Publishing.

Rose, N. (2007). *The politics of life itself: Biomedicine, power, and subjectivity in the Twenty-
    First Century.* Princeton, NJ: Princeton University Press.

Rutter, M. (2006). *Genes and behavior: Nature-nurture interplay explained.* Oxford, UK:
    Blackwell.

Schwartz, J. M., & Begley, S. (2002). *The Mind and the brain: Neuroplasticity and the power of
    mental force.* New York: Harper Perennial.

Shneidman, E. (1985). *Definition of suicide.* Northvale, NJ: Jason Aronson.

Stompe, T. (2009, September). *Transcultural neuroimaging.* Paper presented at the Second World
    Congress of Cultural Psychiatry: Cultural Brains and Living Societies, Norcia, Italy.

Stone, M., Laughren, T., Jones, L., Levenson, M., Holland, P. C., Hughes, A., Hammad, T. A.,
    Temple, R., & Rochester, G. (2009). Risk of suicidality in clinical trials of antidepressants in
    adults: Analysis of proprietary data submitted to US Food and Drug Administration. *British
    Medical Journal, 339,* b2880.

Stuppia, L. (2009, September). *Neuroscience and culture: Introduction.* Paper presented at the
    Second World Congress of Cultural Psychiatry: Cultural Brains and Living Societies, Norcia,
    Italy.

Tsai, S.-J., Hong, C.-J., & Liou, Y.-J. (2011). Recent molecular genetic studies and
    methodological issues in suicide research. *Progress in Neuro-Psychopharmacology &
    Biological Psychiatry, 35*(4) 809–817.

Tseng, W.-S. (2007). Culture and psychopathology: General view. In D. Bhugra & K. Bhui
    (Eds.), *Textbook of cultural psychiatry,* pp. 95–112. Cambridge, UK: Cambridge University
    Press.

van Heeringen, C., & Marusic, A. (2003). Understanding the suicidal brain. *British Journal of
    Psychiatry, 183,* 282–284.

van Heeringen, C., Godfrin, K., & Bijttebier, S. (2011). Understanding the suicidal brain:
    A review of neuropsychological studies of suicidal ideation and behaviour. In R. O'Connor,

S. Platt, & J. Gordon (Eds.), *International handbook of suicide prevention: Research, policy and practice*, pp. 151–167. Chichester, UK: Wiley-Blackwell.

Vijayakumar, L., John, S., Pirkis, P., & Whiteford, H. (2005a). Suicide in developing countries (2): Risk factors. *Crisis, 26,* 112–119.

Vijayakumar, L., Nagaray, K., Pirkis, J., & Whiteford, H. (2005b). Suicide in developing countries (1): Frequency, distribution, and association with socioeconomic indicators. *Crisis, 26,* 104–111.

Wasserman, D., Sokolowski, M., Wasserman, J., & Rujescu, D. (2009). Neurobiology and the genetics of suicide. In D. Wasserman & C. Wasserman (Eds.), *Oxford textbook of suicidology and suicide prevention*. Oxford, UK: Oxford University Press.

Yang, G.-H., Phillips, M. R., Zhou, M. G., Wang, L.-J., Zhang, Y.-P., & Xu, D. (2005). Understanding the unique characteristics of suicide in China: National psychological autopsy study. *Biomedical & Environmental Sciences, 18,* 379–389.

Yu, S.-H., Liu, S.-K., & Lin, K.-M. (2007). Psychopharmacology across cultures. In D. Bhugra & K. Bhui (Eds.), *Textbook of cultural psychiatry*, pp. 402–413. Cambridge, UK: Cambridge University Press.

Zhang, J., Conwell, Y., Zhou, L., & Jiang, C. (2004). Culture, risk factors and suicide in rural China: A psychological autopsy case control study. *Acta Psychiatrica Scandinavica, 110,* 430–437.

Culture, Cultural Meaning(s), and Suicide[1]

Erminia Colucci

"No one who kills himself does so without reference to the prevailing
normative standards, values and attitudes of the culture to which
he belongs"
Boldt (1988)

The epidemiological differences between countries in the rates of suicide have led
to research on the factors that predispose people in these countries to an increased
risk of suicide. Few of these studies have addressed culture or ethnicity as an
important dimension that might impact an individual's decision to take his or
her own life. This missing area in suicidology has been noted by many scholars,
including Hjelmeland and Knizek (2011), De Leo (2002), Eskin (1999), Kral
(1998), Leenaars, Haines, Wenckstern, Williams, and Lester (2003), Shiang
(2000), Tortolero and Roberts (2001), and Trovato (1986). In particular, we have
little understanding of the variation of a key aspect of suicide, hypothesized by
various authors as differing across cultures, namely, the meaning(s) of suicide
(Boldt, 1988; Douglas, 1967; Farberow, 1975; Leenaars, Maris, & Takahashi,
1997; Lester, 1997).

The chapter opens with a discussion of how culture is a central but highly
debated concept in suicidology. In spite of the difficulty in studying this construct,
scholars have recognized the relevance of culture and ethnicity for understanding
suicidal behavior. Particular attention is given to the importance and necessity of
understanding the cultural meanings of suicide rather than taking for granted that
the meanings, interpretations, and mental representations of suicidal behavior

---

[1] An earlier and shorter version of this paper appeared as Colucci (2006). Permission for
reproduction has been granted.

remain the same in different cultures and subcultures. After this, I will underline the need to establish culturally sensitive prevention strategies. The chapter concludes by providing suggestions for future research on the cultural context of suicidal behavior.

The Concept of Culture

The concept of culture is probably one of the most debated in any discipline that has dealt with it, and there is very little agreement on its definition. Already in the 50s Kroeber and Kluckholm (1952) reviewed more than one hundred definitions of *culture*, and there was little agreement between scholars; at best, the various definitions could be grouped into categorical types. Sixty years later, the term *culture* still does not have an unequivocal interpretation.

Marsella, Dubanoski, Hamada, and Morse (2000) proposed a definition of culture as:

> shared acquired patterns of behavior and meanings that are constructed and transmitted within social-life contexts for the purposes of promoting individual and group survival, adaptation, and adjustment. These shared patterns are dynamic in nature (i.e., continuously subject to change and revision) and can become dysfunctional. (p. 50)

The authors noted that culture is represented both externally and internally: externally in artifacts, roles, activity context and institutions, and internally in world-views, identities, meanings, values, attitudes, epistemologies, consciousness patterns, cognitive, somatic and affective processes, and the concept of self and personhood.

Other scholars have included in the definition of culture aspects of the man-made environment. For example, Al-Issa (1982) observed:

> Culture ... consists of the beliefs, values, norms, and myths that are shared by the group and symbolically transmitted to its members, as well as the physical environment, which is comprised of artifacts like roads, bridges, and buildings that are handed down from one generation to another. (p. 3)

Barrett (2001), after emphasizing that culture is very often taken to mean a set of qualities "who are not us," noted that culture, like biology, is a fundamental precondition of human existence, and culture mediates all human interactions. An important concept present in Barrett's definition of culture is the centrality of the individual:

> Culture, although it refers to ideas and beliefs held in common by a group of people, is mediated by and manifested within *individuals*. One's culture becomes incorporated into one's personality, into one's fundamental way of "being-in-the-world." (p. 7)

What authors such as Barrett point out is that the individual, endowed with self-reflection, critical abilities, and creative imagination, is capable of evaluating predominant norms, values, and social expectations and, therefore, can contemplate alternative meanings. Thus, "culture" is not an ontological reality that we simply *acquire* or inherit by being born into a certain setting but a system of beliefs, norms, values, and attitudes that are constantly construed, interpreted, and (re)negotiated. As such, culture cannot be reified, operationalized nor measured as a static dimension (which partially explains the difficulty in studying "culture" and, therefore, scarce attention paid to this construct in suicidology and other mental health disciplines). This was recognized by Tseng (2001) who noted that, "rather than a static set of ideas, beliefs, values and perspectives on the world, culture can be negotiated or contested." (p. 24)

There is often the presence of several value systems operating at one time within any cultural community, as underlined also by Boldt (1988) and Eckersley and Dear (2002). These latter authors stated:

> This is not to argue that cultures are monolithic, exerting a uniform effect on everyone, regardless of gender, class and ethnicity; nor that individuals are cultural sponges, passively absorbing cultural influences rather than interacting actively with them; nor that there is not a variety of subcultures marked by sometimes very different values, meanings, and beliefs. (p. 1892)

As is clear, even if culture has been recognized by many scholars and various disciplines as a central aspect of human life, the problem in the study of culture is mainly a problem of interpretation from two perspectives: from one side, the interpretation of what culture "is" and, from the other side, people's individual interpretation of their own cultures.

This is especially apparent in the study of the cultural aspects of suicide where our understanding is made particularly difficult by the complexity of the phenomenon and the difficulty in gaining direct access to the subjects under study.[2] The former problem was addressed by Kral (1998) who noted that, "Suicide, like everything else that is complexly human, takes place in a powerful social context" (p. 221).

The Relevance of Culture for Suicidal Behavior

Overall, the suicide rates of different countries tend to be relatively stable over time and very different from one another. For example, Lester (1987) found that suicide rates of European countries in 1975 were strongly associated with the suicide rates of those countries 100 years earlier. The difference in suicide rates persists when immigrants from these countries are examined in the US, Canada, and Australia (De Leo, 2002; Dusevic, Baume, & Malak, 2002; Lester, 1994).

Similar considerations lead Zonda and Lester (1990), in their study of suicide among gypsies in Hungary, to conclude that, "these national and regional variations in suicide rates point to the possible role of cultural factors" (p. 381). In addition, De Leo (2002), interpreting the World Health Organization (WHO) rates of suicide in different countries, noted that epidemiological studies provide evidence that social and cultural dimensions amplify any biological and psychological aspect. In particular, the male/female ratio appears to be particularly influenced by the cultural context (idem).

Other researchers have also noticed cultural differences in the epidemiology of suicidal behavior among a range of countries (see Colucci & Martin, 2007a, 2007b, for a review on youth suicide). In particular, Mayer and Ziaian (2002) and Vijayakumar (2005) pointed out different suicide patterns in Asia as compared to Western countries. For instance, the age distribution and male to female ratio are different: rates are highest in the elderly in Western countries, but in young people in Asia. In the former, the male to female ratio is greater at 3:1 (or more), whereas in the latter the ratio is smaller at 2:1, with some countries like India showing a very similar ratio (1.4:1) and China showing higher suicide among women (Vijayakumar, 2005). Emphasizing further the presence of important sociocultural differences among countries, the selective review of Vijayakumar, John, Pirkis, and Whiteford (2005) pointed out that, in some developing countries (e.g., India), being female, living in a rural area, and holding religious beliefs that sanction suicide, may have more relevance to suicide risk than the same factors

---

[2]   The "subjects" are, of course, deceased.

have in developed countries. On the other hand, being single or having a history of mental illness may be of less significance. Similar observations and reflections indicate how important it is for researchers to identify which findings have cross-cultural generality and which are culturally specific (Colucci & Martin, 2007b; Lester, 1992–93; Mishara, 2006).

Considerations of this kind led various scholars to recognize that suicide is a phenomenon that needs to be studied and understood in its social and cultural milieu. For instance, Tseng (2001) stated that "suicide, even though a personal act, is very much socioculturally shaped and susceptible to sociocultural factors" (p. 392), and Kazarian and Persad (2001) affirmed that the embrace of culture and a life-enhancing perspective to research and practice are likely to contribute to a better understanding of suicidal behavior and to improve individual, family, and community well-being. Range and collaborators (1999), after examining suicide among African Americans, Hispanic Americans, Native Americans, and Asian Americans, declared that suicide must be studied from all angles, and ethnic origin is one of the characteristics that must be recognized and considered in assessing risk and designing interventions.

In spite of the well-established and long-term interest in sociocultural aspects of suicidal behavior, research in this area is still in an embryonic stage. As Kral (1998) noted, "we are only beginning to look seriously at the power of cultural ideas like suicide" (p. 225). Roberts, Chen, and Roberts (1997) pointed out that: "In general, ethnicity has been little studied in relation to suicidal behaviors; results from the few studies that have examined ethnic differences have been equivocal" (p. 209). This observation was confirmed through a systematic literature review of youth suicide (Colucci & Martin, 2007a, 2007b).

Furthermore, as pointed out by Lester (1992–1993), although culture may influence the incidence of suicide, the circumstances of the act, the methods used, and the reasons for and the meanings of suicide, most researchers have focused on the association between culture and only the incidence of suicide. This was under-lined also by Marsella (2000) when he wrote:

> While it is true that much has been written about international variations in rates and patterns of suicidal behaviour, little systematic research has been conducted on the specific contributions of sociocultural factors to the rates, co-morbidity, meanings, motivations, and methods of suicidal behaviour. (p. 4)

The reason for this omission results from the fact that, even though some researchers have attempted to study the way in which culture influences suicidal behavior, the conceptual consideration (i.e., theory) of the interface between culture and suicide has been, with few exceptions (e.g., Durkheim, 1897/1997), an overall recent phenomenon (Kazarian & Persad, 2001).

As an example of a theoretical explanation, Cohen, Spirito, Apter, and Saini (1997) hypothesized that culture affects the development of psychopathology, which in turn affects suicide rates. Similarly, Tseng (2001) applied his theory of the effects of culture on psychopathology to suicidal behavior, indicating various effects of culture on suicide, although suggesting an arguable application of the pathological frame to suicidal behavior and a simplistic cause-effect link between the two:

(1) Culture contributes to the nature and severity of the distress that people may suffer. For example, Chinese and Korean cultures prohibit the union of certain couples. This distress may then contribute to the occurrence of suicidal behavior (the *pathogenetic effects* of culture);

(2) Culture can have *pathoselective effects* in a person's choice of suicide over other possible solutions to his problems (e.g., when facing bankruptcy). An example of this is the Ghanaian concept of *feree fanyinam owuo*, which makes death (including suicide) a preferable option than humiliation (Adinkrah, 2012);

(3) The *pathoplastic effects* of culture on suicide are illustrated by the manifestation of special forms of suicidal behavior in addition to individual personal suicide. These include behaviours such as family suicide, group suicide, and mass suicide or seppuku (traditionally observed in Japan) and sati (practiced in India);

(4) A *pathoelaborating effect* is illustrated by the complex terminologies used to recognize and distinguish different forms of suicide, as in Japan where laymen use different terms to refer to different kinds of suicide;

(5) The *pathofacilitative effects* are illustrated by the variation in the rates of and methods used for suicide in different societies;

(6) Many societies have a negative attitude toward suicidal behavior. For example, Muslims see suicide as an unforgivable sin, the Indian legal system views it as crime, and the Baganda in Uganda view suicide as an abominable act (Mugisha, Hjelemland, Kinyanda, & Knizek, 2011), whereas the Japanese see suicide as an honorable act of self-sacrifice in some circumstances (Young, 2002). Attitudes and stigma show the *pathoreactive effects* of culture on suicidal behavior.

The pathoreactive effect, I believe, is also expressed in the way society as a whole respond to suicide or lack of suicide when this is a socially accepted, expected, or forced response to certain life events and circumstances (see the chapter "Cultural Meanings of Suicide" in this book), and by society I also include health professionals and the set of assumptions, predispositions, and preconceptions we bring with us in our encounters with suicidal clients.

In this regard, the "cultural meanings" of suicide (as will be further discussed below) are particularly relevant in shaping society's response to the suicidal act and the kind of help and support provided to a suicidal person, if any. Thus, understanding the cultural meanings of suicide is essential for the development of culturally sensitive and appropriate suicide prevention strategies. This has also recently been observed by Osafo (2012) who found that the construed meaning of suicide (as an act) consistently mediated the attributions made about the suicidal person, and also influenced measures taken to prevent suicide. More specifically, the conception that suicide was a breach of divine and communal moralities (what the author labeled the "moral framework") facilitated views about the suicidal person as a sinner, a transgressor, and a criminal, which resulted in a preference for proscriptive measures to prevent suicide, such as endorsement of the penal code against suicide and the religious threat of punishment in the afterlife. When conceived as a health crisis or pathology (the "mental health" framework), the suicidal person was seen as needful and unwell, and prevention was viewed from a care-oriented and treatment approach.

The Cultural Meanings of Suicide

Some scholars have reflected on the way culture affects the particular meaning attributed to suicidal behavior. Kleinman (1977) noted that one of the main problems of cross-cultural research is the *category fallacy*, that is, the imposition of Western categories in societies in which they lack coherence and validity. In the same way, Littlewood (1990) stressed that anthropologists cannot presume *a priori* that Western psychiatric categories such as depression, self-mutilation, or parasuicide are appropriate worldwide.

Good and Good (1982) suggested that the meaning of illness is grounded in the network of meanings that an illness has in a culture, that is, the metaphors associated with a disease, the ethnomedical theories, the basic values and conceptual forms, and the care patterns that shape the experience of the illness as well as the social reactions to the sufferer. Today, in suicidology, we make a mistake every time we apply a theory or a prevention and intervention program developed for one sociocultural setting to another setting.

As argued by Leenaars et al. (1997):

> Individuals live in a meaningful world. Culture may give us meaning in the
> world. It may well give the world its theories/perspectives. This is true about
> suicidology. Western theories of suicide, as one quickly learns from a cul-
> tural perspective, may not be shared. Suicide has different meanings for dif-
> ferent cultures. (p. 2)

Shneidman (1985) cautioned us, when making cross-cultural comparisons, to
not make the error of assuming that "suicide is a suicide." Lester (1997) too
recognized that suicidal behavior may be quite differently determined and have
different meanings in different cultures. In *Suicide in Different Cultures,* Farberow
(1975) noted that suicide is viewed very differently by different cultural groups,
and culture influences the form, meaning, and frequency of suicide. Maris
(1981) and Hendin (1965) are of the same opinion, namely, that suicide varies culturally and that differences in meaning may influence suicide. Boldt (1988) noted
also that Durkheim explicitly recognized the potential influence of cultural meanings on suicide rates, but Durkheim excluded meaning from his analysis because
he believed that Protestants and Catholics, the focus of his discussion, shared the
same meanings for suicide.

But what do we mean by *meaning* and, more specifically, by *cultural meaning*?
Strauss and Quinn (1997) defined *meaning* as the interpretation evoked in a person by an object or event at a given time and *cultural meaning* as, "the typical
(frequently recurring and widely shared aspects of the) interpretation of some type
of object or event evoked in people as a result of their similar life experiences"
(p. 6).

Along the same lines, hermeneuticists like Bracken (2002) highlighted the
importance of placing meanings in relation to the context, because meaning is
always something that exists *in relation to*, and cannot be *separated from*, the
background context of human lives.

Discourses on the meaning of suicide may be confused with discussions on the
definition of the word *suicide*, but the *meaning* of suicide, as Boldt (1988) stated,
must be differentiated from the *definition* of suicide:

> Here, I propose that the social scientific study of suicide must begin with an
> understanding of the *meaning* [italics in the original] of suicide. The prevail-
> ing definition, that is, "willing and willful self-termination," has little rele-
> vance for the decisional process of the suicidal individual. The meaning of
> suicide, on the other hand, is critical to our understanding of the individual's
> decisional process. (p. 94)

In other words, while suicidologists such as Shneidman were concerned with the definition of the act of suicide, Boldt argued that suicide research must begin with understanding the meaning of the act rather than the definition of it.

In *The Social Meaning of Suicide*, Douglas (1967) discussed our lack of knowledge of what different cultures, and also the officials in those cultures who categorize deaths, mean by the term *suicide*:

> It is not merely the cognitive meanings of suicide that very likely vary from one society to another and from one subsociety to another. The moral meanings and the affective meanings of both the term "suicide" and any actions either actually or potentially categorized as suicide almost certainly vary greatly as well. (p. 181)

Boldt (1988) stated that meaning goes beyond the universal criteria for certifying and classifying self-destructive deaths to how suicide is conceptualized in terms of cultural normative values. Boldt then listed some examples of peculiar sociocultural conceptualizations of suicide: suicide as (1) an unforgivable sin, (2) a psychotic act, (3) a human right, (4) a ritual obligation, and (5) an unthinkable act. The dominant universal definition of suicide is adequate, as Boldt noted, for a layperson's purpose and for certifications and classifications, but "the culture-specific meanings necessary for social scientific study into the origin and evolution of suicidal ideation and for development of theories of cause, prevention, and treatment are still a *desideratum*" [italics in the original] (p. 102).

Despite the number of scholars who have underlined the importance of studying what suicide means to people belonging to different sociocultural backgrounds, the study of meaning is still an unjustifiably missing area in suicide research. To date, studies analyzing this aspect are very rare, and Meng's paper (2002) on suicide as a symbolic act of rebellion and revenge for some Chinese women or Osafo and collaborators' (2011) exploration of cultural meanings of suicide in Ghana are exceptions. The writing by scholars such as Hjelmeland (who contributed the first chapter to this book) are also a rarity (see, for instance Hjelmeland et al., 2006, and Hjelmeland and Knizek, 2011).

Everall (2000), in her study of the meaning of suicide in young people noted that, despite the amount of research conducted in suicidology, surprisingly little is known about the experience of being suicidal and argued that, "while demographic variables may be useful in identifying at-risk groups, they provide little in the way of meaningful understanding of the suicidal individual" (p. 111). In a similar way, Boldt (1988) showed concern about the scarce consideration given to the study of the meaning of suicide:

Suicidologists use the term "suicide" as though there is no need to understand its meaning. This neglects the fact that meaning precedes ideation
and action, and that individuals who commit suicide do so with reference
to cultural-normative specific values and attitudes. (p. 95)

Boldt (1988) tried to find some reasons for this neglect, and he speculated that
these might depend on the following factors:

1. the observed cross-cultural commonalities in characteristics of individuals
   who die by suicide (such as depression, hopelessness, unendurable pain
   and relational problems), which lead us to assume universality and
   invariance in cross-cultural meanings;
2. our liberation from the tyranny of traditional moralistic meanings of
   suicide;
3. seduction by the assumed "scientific" credentials of the definition; and
4. the prevailing premise that suicidal individuals are irrational and, therefore,
   incapable of meaningful action.

Boldt concluded that, in the end, the main reason may reside in the frequent
error often present in science to not pay attention to fundamental things (but take
them for granted), citing a dictum from Weber's seminar about spleen: "The
spleen, he said, gentlemen, we know nothing about the spleen. So much for the
spleen." (p. 95)

The same argument was made by Douglas (1967) when he wrote that, "the
assumption that the *meanings of suicidal actions* [italics in the original] are obvious rather than problematic has most likely been the basic reason for the failure of
suicide studies to make much progress." (p. 158)

Another reason for the small number of studies to date on the cultural meaning
of suicide stems from the difficulty of this kind of study (how can we elicit and
understand meanings), not only for the researcher but for the subjects of the study
as well.

Most participants in a culture are not aware of the philosophies underlying
the meaning of suicide. They relate to the meaning of suicide reflexively
rather than reflectively. They are conditioned to conform unthinkingly to
society's normative standards and expectations. (Bold, 1988, p. 98)

I shall argue that, rather than being obvious, the meanings of suicide are very
complex and obscure, not alone to the theorists, but to the social actors
involved as well. (Douglas, 1967, p. 158)

The difficulty in fully understanding the meanings of suicide, however, is not a justification for not dedicating effort and resources to this important topic. On the contrary:

the recognition and study of the cultural relativity in the meaning of suicide is an urgent need in the present phase of suicide research. Only by differentiating as precisely as possible the culture-dependent meanings of suicide, and by systematically bringing these into a research paradigm, can the development of valid theories of causation, prevention, prediction, and treatment begin" (Boldt, 1988, p. 102).

Trying to amplify this field of knowledge, I explored the cultural meanings of youth suicide among University students aged 18–24 years old in three different countries (Italy, India, and Australia) using a combination of qualitative and quantitative methods (Colucci, 2008). Some of the findings from this study are presented later in this book (see the chapter "Cultural Meanings of Suicide").

Culture-Sensitive Suicide Prevention and Intervention[3]

Just as some scholars have emphasized the importance of studying cultural aspects of suicidal behavior, those involved in preventing suicide have suggested developing suicide prevention and intervention strategies that are more culturally differentiated. For example, De Leo (2002) stated that suicide prevention is likely to be possible when we:

[keep] in mind that we need to rephrase the WHO's slogan of "Think globally, act locally" to the more effective "Think locally and act locally." In fact, suicide prevention strategies need to be adapted to the local culture and cannot be simply exported or copied from one country to the other. (p. 29)

To this, I would add that suicide prevention strategies need to be developed from *within* the cultural milieu, rather than merely be *adapted to* the cultural milieu, that is, rather than merely making use of what has been done in one culture and trying to apply to the new culture.

Range et al. (1999), after examining suicide among African Americans, Hispanic Americans, Native Americans, and Asian Americans, declared that suicide must be

---

[3] Some important observations on the homogenization of psychiatry, which are useful to keep in mind while developing international mental health strategies including suicide prevention, have been provided by Higginbotham and Marsella (1988).

studied from all angles and that ethnic origin is one of the characteristics that must be
recognized and considered in assessing risk and designing interventions:

> Suicide prevention and intervention efforts should encourage ethnic pride,
> cultivate sensitivity to diversity, recognize how culture merges with individ-
> ual forces influencing a person, promote dialog between different cultural
> groups as well as among members of different cultural groups, facilitate
> respect for all individuals and their heritage, recognize that all individuals
> are minorities in some dimensions. (pp. 26–27)

Eshun (2003) noted that, as research and care become more global, suicide prevention programs need to be more culture-sensitive and suicide research needs to
include sociocultural variables. Cohen et al. (1997), in their study of suicidal behavior in young Israeli and Americans psychiatric patients, recognized the role of culture
for improving the understanding of suicide and contributing significant information
for suicide prevention and intervention programs. Agreement on this point comes
from Sri Lanka, where de Silva (2003) recommended that inter-sectoral programs
and interventions aimed at identifying and modifying sociocultural beliefs that promote suicidal behavior (e.g., the acceptance of suicide as a way of solving problems)
need to be developed. Similarly, the *Surgeon General's Call to Action to Prevent Suicide* (US Public Health Service, 1999) suggested that ethnic considerations are
needed before culturally-sensitive interventions can be developed and tested.

However, although various scholars and organizations (WHO, 2000) have
moved forward, as observed by Kazarian and Persad (2001), a cultural perspective
for suicide intervention continues to be in an embryonic stage, and there is much
more that needs to be done. Suggestions on the ways in which research on cultural
aspects of suicide may be improved, making research more respectful of people's
perspectives and needs and, consequently, more useful and appropriate for developing intervention strategies, are offered in the following section on methodological issues in cross-cultural studies in suicidology.

Methodological Considerations in Cross-Cultural Suicide Research

A decade ago, Watt and Sharp (2002) noted that there were relatively few cross-
cultural studies of suicide, and those that have appeared are mainly on adults.
Typically, young people are not studied separately. Following this observation,
Colucci and Martin (2007a, 2007b) reviewed cross-cultural studies on youth suicide, looking at suicide rates and methods of suicide, risk and precipitating factors,
and attitudes towards suicide.

One of the critiques made by Colucci and Martin was that the majority of the studies have been carried in Western developed countries and, in particular, in the US. We were also critical of the fact that cross-cultural research on suicide has its principal basis in the medical and positivistic paradigm. Consequently, culture and ethnicity, instead of being treated as complex constructs, are usually assessed by just one simple question. In that review, we concluded that the cultural aspects of suicidal behavior must be explored in greater depth. Most cross-cultural research on youth suicide was epidemiological and cross-national, that is, people belonging to different countries are compared without considering their own and their parents' ethnocultural background and identity. Too few studies explored ethnocultural aspects of suicide in depth and, at that point, none of them had used a qualitative approach.

Two main suggestions for future research can be made:

1. Quantitative studies should be structured in a better way and be more methodologically rigorous.

In reference to this first point, the literature review by Colucci and Martin (2007a, 2007b) identified several limitations of quantitative cross-cultural research on suicide across sites, such as the use of differing instruments, the wording of the questionnaire (suicidal ideation versus suicide plan), the style of answers (binary versus multiple choice) and time span (lifetime versus one year or one week). These limitations make cross-cultural comparisons difficult and unsound, with discordant outcomes from one study to the next. Furthermore, if "culture" is operationalized as a specific variable, a quality that a participant has or has not (e.g., country of origin), the researchers should explain the possible limitations of such approach and refer the readers to scholars who have discussed the concept of "culture."

2. There should be more qualitative research, and research should look at suicide using depth-oriented (and not size-oriented) methods.

In regard to the second point, Hjelmeland et al. (2006), in a study testing the psychometric properties of a questionnaire on attitudes towards suicide in a cross-cultural setting, stressed that cross-cultural research is essential in developing our understanding of suicide, and the way to come closer to this understanding is by using qualitative methodology and making triangulation[4] compulsory in cross-cultural studies. To force researchers to triangulate methods may not be a viable nor a desirable solution to the problem of the paucity and superficiality of

---

[4] Triangulation involves using several methodologies (such as a mixture of quantitative and qualitative methods or different qualitative methods) to explore an issue.

cross-cultural studies on suicidal behavior, but certainly increasing the number of in-depth studies of suicide will further the difficult task of understanding the cultural meaning of suicide.

Another problem noted by Colucci and Martin (2007a, 2007b) is in the selection of the ethnocultural groups under comparison. Very often the cultural groups studied are too broad, for example, cultures with different history, language, and customs such as Indians, Chinese, and Japanese, each of which consists of various subcultures, are grouped together under the label "Asians." Furthermore, too frequently the rationale for the research is not well-articulated. It seems that the ethnic or cultural groups studied are merely convenience samples, and their selection is not theoretically driven. In fact, with regard to the selection of ethnocultural groups, Kazarian and Persad (2001) noted that epidemiological research on suicide has taken an ethnic approach rather than a cultural one:

> In the ethnic approach, two or more ethnic groups are selected without a theoretical rationale for comparison purposes. In the cultural approaches, two or more ethnic groups are selected on the basis of theoretical dimensions for comparative purposes. (p. 272)

Berry (2002) also argued that cross-cultural research should be dictated by a theoretically interesting contrast between the cultures investigated, rather than by mere opportunity. He then listed what in his opinion are the only two acceptable strategies for the selection of cultures in comparative studies: (1) drawing a sample of cultures representative of all the cultures in the world or, more commonly (and, I would add, more reasonably), (2) choosing only a few cultures that clearly differ on some variables that provide a contrast of interest to the cross-cultural researcher. He called this last strategy "theory-guided selection."

Boldt (1988) also noted the lack of clarity in the relatively few research studies on suicide that specifically acknowledge cultural differences:

> They offer undefined references to "Judeo-Christian tradition," or to "national cultures," or to "religious affiliation," or to "the Western world," and so on. Such terms lack the precision required for developing testable hypotheses and theories about the influence of different cultural meanings on suicidal behavior. (p. 101)

This issue could be partially addressed if researchers restrained from grouping participants belonging to different ethnocultural backgrounds into broad categories such as "Asians" or "Blacks," and circumscribed more precisely the cultural groups under study.[5] Furthermore, Marsella (2000) recommended a pool of potential indices, dimensions, and questions useful to contextualize suicidal behavior within a sociocultural milieu that scholars might find helpful when developing research instruments.

Another matter that deserves great care in any cross-cultural research is the interpretation of contrasting results. In his analysis of cultural aspects of suicide in Britain, Atkinson (1975) wrote about the problem involved in achieving definitive conclusions about how suicide is interpreted in a cultural context:[6]

> The problem emerges because different and sometimes contradictory interpretations of some particular cultural manifestation may seem equally plausible. In other words, there is the problem of choice between competing versions of the cultural significance of suicide. (p. 136)

This impasse cannot be eliminated if is true that individuals are both agents and products of their own cultures, but what can be changed is the perspective toward this fact. Once the old vision of culture as simply consisting of shared beliefs, values, norms and attitude is abandoned, and the possibility of co-existing commonalities and differences as part of the same culture (Barrett, 2001) is accepted, what is labeled by Atkinson as a problem becomes instead a resource of great richness.

Other considerations for research that focuses on culture and ethnicity are mentioned by Okazaki and Sue (1995), who suggested:

(1) following the purpose of the study to decide if a comparison approach (e.g., African-Americans vs. Caucasian-Americans) is appropriate;
(2) matching the control groups for some aspect that the researcher believes may moderate the relationship between the variables of interest (e.g., socioeconomic status);
(3) considering the potential influence of sociocultural norms in responding to and participating in the research; and
(4) using multiple measures and multiple methods of assessments.

Another issue noted by Okazaki and Sue is the identification of the participants' ethnic identity. It should be always taken into account that, even if

---

[5] Anthropological studies are useful readings to help us uncover some of the fallacies of current (cross-) cultural mental health research.

[6] It is important to acknowledge that at the same time Atkinson indicated that literature and the arts as well as religion, law, philosophy, media, and public opinion could be analyzed to understand suicide in a particular culture.

participants may report belonging to one particular ethnocultural group, they may also identify with other cultural groups or not share a common understanding of their own ethnicity and culture. For this reason, in my cross-cultural study on the meaning of suicide (see the chapter later in this book), I asked students to describe in their own words to which ethnic group they felt they belonged, even if it was a criterion for the inclusion in the study that the participants had to be born and living in Italy (or India or Australia) and be at least second generation Italian (or Indian or Australian).

It is also important for understanding the meanings of suicidal behavior in a cultural setting to consider gender differences. For example, Brown's (1986) study of Aguaruna people in the Peruvian Amazon pointed at the subtle power struggle between men and women as determinants of suicide, which lead him to the conclusion that suicide in this community was an expression of anger and grief as well as punishment for social antagonists. Counts (1988) illustrated the ways in which a culture can determine the meaning of an individual suicidal act in her account of suicide among females in Papua New Guinea, where female suicide is a culturally-recognized way of imposing social sanctions, with political implications for the suicidal individual's kin and for those held responsible for the events driving the woman to the act. A similar study of accounts of suicidal behavior showed that Sri Lankan participants associated essentialist accounts to women's suicides and contextual accounts to men's suicides (Marecek, 1998). In particular, suicide represented a protest among these women, a channel to communicate and express unfairness and maltreatment towards them. A similar finding (suicide as a mean to express accumulated anger and frustration) emerged also among Latino women (Zayas & Pilat, 2008). Meng's (2002) work in China looked in particular at suicide patterns among women and found that the act provided a way for young women to rebel against an oppressive society and denounce the gender inequalities in China. Canetto and Lester (1998) also suggested that narratives of suicidal behavior can be examined through the lens of gender-specific cultural scripts. Thus, if the study of the cultural meanings of suicide is essential for our understanding of suicide and for the development of prevention strategies, we also need to look at what we can define as the "gendered meanings" of suicide in a particular cultural setting[7].

Marsella (2000), while recommending that sociocultural and community indices and dimensions be considered in the sociocultural assessment of suicidal behavior, pointed out that it is essential that the measurement instrument has

---

[7] Any discourse looking at gender and suicide, in my opinion, will necessarily have to deal also with issues such as domestic/family and gender-based violence, which would see suicidologists engaged with gendered meanings involved also in women rights, but this would require another chapter!

linguistic, conceptual, normative, and scale equivalence. Regarding linguistic equivalence, it is my opinion that special attention should be paid to what we desire to know from the participant and to check if the way the question is phrased is adequate for these aims. For instance, Linehan (2000) noted the "threat to validity" that derives from asking about previous suicide attempts without getting any information about the intent of this act. The issues of the way questions are phrased and which words are used are relevant in any research, but their importance is greater in cross-cultural studies. In fact, words like *suicide attempt* could have many interpretations and become even more ambiguous among different cultural groups (Kidd, 2004; Colucci, 2008).

Marsella (2000) also recommended that efforts should be made to generate the range and patterns of meanings, motivations, methods, and behaviors associated with suicidal behavior within the cultural milieu and to do so using ethnosemantic methods or other approaches that contextualize the suicidal behavior in its historical and cultural setting (for example, by using focus groups or analyzing the existing literature).

Considering the difficulties in this kind of research, Murray, Tandon, Salomon, Mathers, and Sadana (2002) proposed that the most promising and attractive strategy to enhance cross-population comparability of health measures is the use of vignettes because, in their opinion, this technique is easier to implement across a variety of settings.

A last point that needs attention in order to avoid reaching conclusions based on racial stereotypes instead of the actual research evidence is that often the differences in results tend to be evaluated negatively in disfavor of the non-Western population, as noted, among others, by Marshall and Yazdani (1999). Another risk is that the researcher may discount similarities in favor of dissimilarities whereas, as shown by Marshall and Yazdani's (1999) research on the construing of self-harm among young Asian women, it is important to explore commonalities in the accounts of the meanings of suicidal behavior across ethnocultural groups rather than starting with an expectation of cultural differences. This was criticized also by Mishara (2006) who pointed out that "Suicidology research tends to either ignore cultural differences entirely or focus upon a specific culture without examining possible commonalities across cultures" (p. 3). Therefore, Mishara argued that it is important to explore and understand the frontier between universal aspects of suicide and its cultural specificity. Leach (2006) also commented that there is overlap among cultural groups. For example, "hopelessness leading to suicide manifests itself similarly regardless of culture" (p. IX), and this has partially been confirmed also by the literature review mentioned before (Colucci & Martin, 2007a, 2007b).

Conclusions

Range and Leach (1998) remarked that research methodology in suicidology has historically developed from its philosophical roots in logical positivism and structural determinism. This has led to research based on an assumption of cause-and-effect relationships, a reductionist analysis, and a focus on the individual as the primary unit under study, which might explain why relatively little research has addressed sociocultural aspects of suicide. On the other hand, some mental health experts have recognized that culture functions as a lens through which we construct, define, and interpret reality (Marsella & Kaplan, 2002), and a growing number of scholars have underlined the need to consider the ethnocultural context during suicide risk assessment and in planning suicide prevention and intervention programs. This greater attention is reflected also in the current organization of suicide conferences, where often one session (and, in a few instances, even the conference theme) is dedicated to cultural issues. But the path to the inclusion of ethnocultural considerations in the mainstream mental health sciences and suicidology is still a lengthy and arduous one.

Kral (1998) concluded his essay with the question: "Is it time to ask different questions in suicidology?" (p. 230). My answer is "definitely, yes," and my hope is that this book will act as an invitation for a larger number of researchers, clinicians, and policy makers to consider the sociocultural milieu of their participants, clients, and communities when assessing and treating suicidal behavior.

In order to improve our ability to assess the risk of suicide it is not enough to know what the principal suicide risk factors are. As observed by Leach (2006), "it is through culture that we begin to understand personal meaning, because culture offers the lens through which suicide factors such as coping styles, buffers, emotional expressions, family structures, and identity can be viewed" (p. 3).

As has been highlighted in the chapter, we need to understand the prevailing culture-specific norms, meanings, social representations, and attitudes regarding suicide in the various cultural (and subcultural) communities of the world, even if this is a difficult task where no "true" answer should be expected and no "right" instrument should be assumed. We all, as psychologists, psychiatrists, social workers, general practitioners, nurses, educators, spiritual leaders, policy makers, and survivors, are required to understand what the act of suicide symbolizes and represents for *that* person and *that* cultural group if we really want to help to find a different way, constructive and not destructive for the individual and his or her social group(s), to express and manifest those meanings.

References

Adinkrah, M. (2012). Better dead than dishonored: Masculinity and male suicidal behavior in contemporary Ghana. *Social Science & Medicine, 74*, 474–481.

Al-Issa, I. (1982). *Culture and psychopathology*. Baltimore, MD: University Park Press.

Atkinson, M. (1975). Some cultural aspects of suicide in Britain. In N. L. Farberow (Ed.), *Suicide in different cultures*, pp. 135–158. Baltimore, MD: University Park Press.

Barrett, R. J. (2001). An introduction to sociocultural psychiatry (CD-ROM). In D. Burke & L. Newman (Ed.), *Postgraduate course in psychiatry*. Sydney, Australia: NSW Institute of Psychiatry.

Berry, J. W. (2002). *Cross-cultural psychology: Research and applications* (2nd ed.). Cambridge, UK: Cambridge University Press.

Boldt, M. (1988). The meaning of suicide: Implications for research. *Crisis, 9*, 93–108.

Bracken, P. (2002). Cultural syndromes and cognitive psychology. *Transcultural Psychiatry, 39*, 214–219.

Brown, M. F. (1986). Power, gender, and the social meaning of Aguarana suicide. *Man, New Series, 21*(2), 311–328.

Canetto, S. S., & Lester, D. (1998). Gender, culture, and suicidal behavior. *Transcultural Psychiatry, 35*, 163–190.

Cohen, Y., Spirito, A., Apter, A., & Saini, S. (1997). A cross-cultural comparison of behavior disturbance and suicidal behavior among psychiatrically hospitalized adolescents in Israel and the United States. *Child Psychiatry & Human Development, 28*, 89–102.

Colucci, E. (2006). The cultural facet of suicidal behaviour. *Australian e-Journal for the Advancement of Mental health, 5*(3), 1–13.

Colucci, E. (2008). *The cultural meaning of suicide: A comparison between Italian, Indian and Australian students*, Unpublished doctoral dissertation, The University of Queensland, Brisbane, Australia.

Colucci, E., & Martin, G. (2007a). The ethno-cultural aspects of youth suicide: Rates and methods of youth suicide. *Suicide and Life-Threatening Behavior, 37*, 197–221.

Colucci, E., & Martin, G. (2007b). The ethno-cultural aspects of youth suicide: Risk factors, precipitating agents and attitudes towards suicide. *Suicide and Life-Threatening Behavior, 37*, 222–237.

Counts, D. A. (1988). Ambiguity in the interpretation of suicide. In D. Lester (Ed.), *Why women kill themselves*, pp. 87–109. Springfield, IL: Charles Thomas.

De Leo, D. (2002). Struggling against suicide: The need for an integrative approach. *Crisis, 23*, 23–31.

de Silva, D. (2003). Suicide prevention strategies in Sri Lanka: The role of socio-cultural factors and health services. *Ceylon Medical Journal, 48*(3), 68–70.

Douglas, J. D. (1967). *The social meaning of suicide*. Princeton, NJ: Princeton University Press.

Durkheim, E. (1897). *Le suicide* [Suicide]. Paris: Felix Alcan.

Dusevic, N., Baume, P., & Malak, A. E. (2002). *Cross-cultural suicide prevention: A framework*. Sidney, Australia: Transcultural Mental Health Centre.

Eckersley, R., & Dear, K. (2002). Cultural correlates of youth suicide. *Social Science & Medicine, 55*, 1891–1904.

Eshun, S. (2003). Sociocultural determinants of suicide ideation: A comparison between American and Ghanaian college samples. *Suicide and Life-Threatening Behavior, 33*, 165–171.

Eskin, M. (1999). Gender and cultural differences in the 12-month prevalence of suicidal thoughts and attempts in Swedish and Turkish adolescents. *Journal of Gender, Culture, & Health, 4*, 187–200.

Everall, R. D. (2000). The meaning of suicide attempts by young adults. *Canadian Journal of Counselling, 34*(2), 111–125.

Farberow, N. L. (1975). *Suicide in different cultures.* Baltimore, MD: University Park Press.

Good, B. J., & Good, M. J. D. (1982). Towards a meaning-centered analysis of popular illness categories. In A. J. Marsella & G. M. White (Eds.), *Cultural conceptions of mental health and therapy*, pp. 141–166. Boston, MA: D. Reidel.

Hendin, H. (1965). *Suicide in Scandinavia.* New York: Doubelday.

Higginbotham, N., & Marsella, A. J. (1988). International consultation and the homogenization of psychiatry in Southeast Asia. *Social Science & Medicine, 27*, 553–561.

Hjelmeland, H., Kinyanda, E., Knizek, B. L., Owens, V., Nordvik, H., & Svarva, K. (2006). A discussion of the value of cross-cultural studies in search of the meaning(s) of suicidal behavior and the methodological challenges of such studies. *Archives of Suicide Research, 10*, 15–27.

Hjelmeland, H., & Knizek, B. L. (2011). What kind of research do we need in suicidology today? In R. O'Connor, S. Platt, & J. Gordon (Eds.), *International handbook of suicide prevention: Research, policy and practice*, pp. 591–608. Chichester, UK: WileyBlackwell.

Kazarian, S. S., & Persad, E. (2001). Cultural issues in suicidal behavior. In S. S. Kazarian & D. R. Evans (Eds.), *Handbook of cultural health psychology*, pp. 268–302. San Diego, CA: Academic Press.

Kidd, S. A. (2004). "The walls were closing in, and we were trapped": A qualitative analysis of street youth suicide. *Youth & Society, 36*, 30–55.

Kleinman, A. (1977). Culture and illness: A question of models. *Culture, Medicine & Psychiatry, 1*, 229–231.

Kral, M. J. (1998). Suicide and the internalization of culture: Three questions. *Transcultural Psychiatry, 35*, 221–233.

Kroeber, T., & Kluckholm, C. (1952). *Culture: A critical review of concepts and definitions.* Cambridge, MA: Papers of the Peabody Museum, Harvard University.

Leach, M. M. (2006). *Cultural diversity and suicide.* Binghamton, NY: The Haworth Press.

Leenaars, A. A., Haines, J., Wenckstern, S., Williams, C. L., & Lester, D. (2003). Suicide notes from Australia and the United States. *Perceptual & Motor Skills, 96*, 1281–1282.

Leenaars, A. A., Maris, R., & Takahashi, Y. (1997). Preface. *Suicide & Life-Threatening Behavior, 27*, 2–4.

Lester, D. (1987). The stability of national suicide rates in Europe. *Sociology & Social Research, 71*, 208.

Lester, D. (1992–1993). Suicide and culture. *Homeostasis in Health and Disease, 34*(1–2), 96–102.

Lester, D. (1994). Suicide in immigrant groups as a function of their proportion in the country. *Perceptual & Motor Skills, 79*, 994.

Lester, D. (1997). Suicide in America: A nation of immigrants. *Suicide and Life-Threatening Behavior, 27*, 50–59.

Linehan, M. M. (2000). Behavioral treatments of suicidal behavior. In R. W. Maris, S. S. Canetto, J. L. McIntosh, & M. M. Silverman (Eds.), *Review of Suicidology*, pp. 84–111. New York: Guilford.

Littlewood, R. (1990). From categories to contexts: A decade of the "new cross-cultural psychiatry." *British Journal of Psychiatry, 156*, 308–327.

Marecek, J. (1998). Culture, gender, and suicidal behavior in Sri Lanka. *Suicide and Life-Threatening Behavior, 28*, 69–81.

Maris, R. W. (1981). *Pathways to suicide: A survey of self-destructive behaviors*. Baltimore, MD: Johns Hopkins University Press.

Marsella, A. J. (2000). *Socio-cultural considerations in the assessment of suicidal behavior: In pursuit of cultural and community indices, dimensions, and perceptions.* Unpublished technical report. Geneva, Switzerland: WHO/ Mental Health.

Marsella, A. J., Dubanoski, J., Hamada, W., & Morse, H. (2000). The measurement of culture and personality. *American Behavioral Scientist, 44*, 41–62.

Marsella, A. J., & Kaplan, A. (2002). Cultural considerations for understanding, assessing, and treating depressive experience and disorder. In M. A. Reinecke & M. R. Davison (Eds.), *Comparative treatments of depression*, pp. 47–78. New York: Springer.

Marshall, H., & Yazdani, A. (1999). Locating culture in accounting for self-harm amongst Asian young women. *Journal of Community & Applied Social Psychology. 9*, 413–433.

Mayer, P., & Ziaian, T. (2002). Suicide, gender, and age variations in India: Are women in Indian society protected from suicide? *Crisis, 23*, 98–103.

Meng, L. (2002). Rebellion and revenge: the meaning of suicide of women in rural China. *International Journal of Social Welfare, 11*, 300–309.

Mishara, B. L. (2006). Cultural specificity and universality of suicide. challenges for the International Association for Suicide Prevention. *Crisis, 27*, 1–3.

Mugisha, J., Hjelmeland, H., Kinyanda, E., & Knizek, B. L. (2011). Distancing: a traditional mechanism of dealing with suicide among the Baganda, Uganda, *Transcultural Psychiatry, 48*, 624–642.

Murray, C. J. L., Tandon, A., Salomon, J. A., Mathers, C. D., & Sadana, R. (2002). New approaches to enhance cross-population comparability of survey results. In C. J. L. Murray & A. D. Lopez (Eds.), *Summary measures of population health: Concepts, ethics, measurement and applications*, pp. 421–431. Geneva, Switzerland: World Health Organization.

Okazaki, S., & Sue, S. (1995). Methodological issues in assessment research with ethnic minorities. *Psychological Assessment, 7*, 367–375.

Osafo, J. (2012). *Attitudes towards suicide: Exploring the cultural meaning(s) of suicide in Ghana.* Unpublished doctoral dissertation, The Norwegian University of Science and Technology, Trondheim, Norway.

Osafo, J., Hjelmenland, H., Akotia, C. S., & Knizek, B. L. (2011). The meanings of suicidal behavior to psychology students in Ghana: A qualitative approach. *Transcultural Psychiatry, 48*, 643–659.

Range, L. M., & Leach, M. M. (1998). Gender, culture, and suicidal behavior: A feminist critique of theories and research. *Suicide and Life-Threatening Behavior, 28*, 24–36.

Range, L. M., Leach, M. M., McIntyre, D., Posey Deters, P. B., Marion, M. S., Kovac, S. H., Baños, J. H., & Vigil, J. (1999). Multicultural perspectives on suicide. *Aggression & Violent Behavior, 4*, 413–430.

Roberts, R. E., Chen, R., & Roberts, C. R. (1997). Ethnocultural differences in prevalence of adolescent suicidal behaviors. *Suicide & Life-Threatening Behavior, 27*, 208–217.

Shiang, J. (2000). Considering cultural beliefs and behaviors in the study of suicide. In R. W. Maris & S. S. Canetto (Eds.), *Review of suicidology*, pp. 226–241. New York: Guilford.

Shneidman, E. S. (1985). *Definition of suicide*. New York: Wiley.

Strauss, C., & Quinn, N. (1997). *A cognitive theory of cultural meaning*. New York: Cambridge University Press.

Tortolero, S. R., & Roberts, R. E. (2001). Differences in nonfatal suicide behaviors among Mexican and European American middle school children. *Suicide and Life-Threatening Behavior, 31*, 214–223.

Trovato, F. (1986). Suicide and ethnic factors in Canada. *International Journal of Social Psychiatry, 32*, 55–64.

Tseng, W. S. (2001). *Handbook of cultural psychiatry*. San Diego, CA: Academic Press.

US Public Health Service. (1999). *The Surgeon General's Call to Action to Prevent Suicide*. Washington, DC: U.S. Public Health Service.

Vijayakumar, L. (2005). Suicide and mental disorders in Asia. *International Review of Psychiatry, 17*, 109–114.

Vijayakumar, L., John, S., Pirkis, J., & Whiteford, H. (2005). Suicide in developing countries (2): Risk factors. *Crisis, 26*, 112–119.

Watt, T. T., & Sharp, S. F. (2002). Race differences in strains associated with suicidal behavior among adolescents. *Youth & Society, 34*, 232–256.

WHO. (2000). *Multisite intervention study on suicidal behaviours. Supre-Miss: Components and instruments*. Geneva, Switzerland: Department of Mental Health and Substance Dependence.

Young, J. (2002). Morals, suicide, and psychiatry: a view from Japan. *Bioethics, 16*, 412–424.

Zayas, L. H., & Pilat, A. M. (2008). Suicidal behavior in Latinas: explanatory cultural factors and implications for intervention. *Suicide and Life-Threatening Behavior, 38*, 334–342.

Zonda, T., & Lester, D. (1990). Suicide among Hungarian Gypsies. *Acta Psychiatrica Scandinavica, 82*, 381–382.

The Cultural Meaning of Suicide: What Does This Mean?[1]

David Lester

Colucci (in the previous chapter) drew attention to the fact that theory and research into suicidal behavior has, on the whole, neglected the role of culture. Suicide is typically considered to be the same phenomenon throughout the world, and theories proposed in one region (such as the West) are assumed to apply to other regions. In addition, Colucci pointed out that the cultural meaning of suicide has been neglected except for rare scholars who draw attention to this issue, such as Douglas (1967) and Boldt (1988). However, there appears to be a great deal of confusion over what exactly the "meaning" of suicide refers to and, more especially, the "cultural meaning" of suicide. The purpose of the present chapter is to examine what these terms mean.

Colucci cited Good and Good (1982) who suggested that the meaning of an illness involves the metaphors associated with a disease, the ethnomedical theories, the basic values and conceptual forms, and the care patterns that shape the experience of the illness and the social reactions to the sufferer (p. 148). This encompasses many separate concepts.

The Phenomenon of Suicidal Behavior

Cultures differ in the frequency of suicidal behavior, the methods chosen for suicide, and the distribution by age, sex, and other sociodemographic variables. Many articles have appeared documenting the different suicide rates in a sample of nations, and differences in the suicide rates by age and sex from nation to nation (e.g., Levi et al., 2003). Lester (1994) found that the suicide rates of Chinese populations in China, Taiwan, Hong Kong, and Singapore and the methods used for suicide differed greatly, while sex ratio of the suicide rates and the variation over age was similar in all four nations. Lester (2006) documented great variations in suicidal behavior in the various Muslim nations of the world.

---

[1] A preliminary version of this chapter appeared as Lester (2011–2012).

These "facts" about suicide probably have little direct relevance to the meaning of suicide, either at the individual or the cultural level. However, a very high rate of suicide in a nation may make the act seem less psychopathological to the residents of the country and may become a topic of discussion in that nation. For example, Hungary had one of the highest suicide rates in the world between the two world wars and for many years afterwards, and it is interesting to note in this regard that the most famous "suicide song" *Gloomy Sunday* was written by a Hungarian (although he was living in France at the time (Stack, Krysinska, & Lester, 2007–2008).

In addition, occasionally, the most popular method for suicide may become a synonym for the act, as in "taking the pipe" in England in the 20th Century when suicide using domestic gas was the most popular method for suicide.

The Definition of Suicide

Kleinman (1977) defined the "category fallacy" as the mistake of imposing Western categories on the behavior in other cultures. Lester (2008) provided several examples of cultures that define suicide differently from scholars in the Western world. For example, according to the Mohave, a Native American tribe in the southwest of the US, a fetus which presents itself in the transverse position for birth, leading to its own death and that of its mother, is viewed as having intended to die by suicide and to murder its mother so that they can be together in the spirit world (Devereux, 1961). Medical examiners and coroners in the rest of the US would not view such a still-born infant as a suicide.

Counts (1980), who has studied the suicidal behavior of women in the Kaliai district of Papua New Guinea, noted that, in the past, elderly widows sometimes immolated themselves on their husband's funeral pyre. The German and Australian colonial governors considered this behavior to be a form of ritual murder rather than suicide, and they outlawed it. Counts, however, saw neither term (suicide or murder) as appropriate for this custom since it differed so much from what North Americans and Europeans regard as either suicide or murder. Neither term describes the behavior, the interpersonal relationships involved, or the attitudes toward the widow and those assisting in her death, nor do they predict how the community will respond to her death.

Recently, some scholars, especially in Europe, have expressed doubts that people engaging in nonfatal suicidal behavior have self-destruction as their aim, and they have begun calling the behavior "self-poisoning" or "self-injury" (e.g., Ramon, 1980). The semantic implication is that nonfatal suicidal behavior is not "suicide." Since in most cultures women engage in more nonfatal suicidal actions than do men, this renaming of nonfatal suicidal behavior as self-injury makes "suicidal behavior" less common in women than it was hitherto.

Other suicidologists, on the other hand, include a wider range of behaviors under the rubric of suicidal behavior. For example, Menninger (1938) classified behaviors such as alcoholism, drug abuse, and anorexia as *chronic suicide* since the individuals were shortening their lives by their behaviors. Menninger also classified such behaviors such as polysurgery, self-castration, and self-mutilation as *focal suicide*, a behavior in which the self-destructive impulse is focused on one part of the body. These behaviors are often gender-linked. For example, anorexia is more common in women whereas illicit drug abuse is more common in men. Canetto (1991) has speculated that adolescents may respond differentially when under stress, with girls choosing nonfatal suicidal behavior more while boys choose drug abuse more. The use of Menninger's categories would change greatly the relative incidence of nonfatal suicidal behavior in women and men.

Clearly, the definition of suicide in a culture has implications for the meaning of suicide. In a recent study, Lester and Frank (2008) found that only 59% of a sample of American undergraduate students viewed a protest suicide (such as a self-immolation carried out to protest a government decision) as suicide, and only 70% viewed a suicide bomber as suicidal. Indeed, suicide bombers are viewed as *martyrs* rather than *suicides* by many people in Muslim nations (Abdel-Khalek, 2004).

The Motives for Suicide

When we refer to the motives for suicide we are asking why people engage in the behavior. Menninger (1938) suggested three motives: the desire to escape from life ("to die"), the desire to punish oneself by committing suicide ("to be killed"), and the desire to cause pain to others ("to kill"). Farberow and Shneidman's (1961) book on attempted suicide was called *The Cry for Help*, indicating that clearly what they thought was the motive behind many acts of attempted suicide.

Several writers have proposed classifications of suicide. Reynolds and Berman (1995) examined ten proposals for a classification of suicidal acts, including those from Durkheim (1897), Menninger (1938), and Baechler (1979). They presented 484 cases of suicide from Baltimore (in the US) to judges and asked them classify each of the suicides into these ten typologies. Reynolds and Berman found a good deal of overlap between the typologies, and they identified five subtypes that described 86% of the suicides: escapist, confused, aggressive, alienated, and

depressed/low self-esteem. It would be most interesting to take any of these typologies or, better still, that identified by Reynolds and Berman, and classify samples
of suicides from different cultures. This might provide clues as to the meaning of
suicide in those cultures.

Menninger's typology focuses on what is going on in the minds of suicidal
individuals – what their desires are for engaging in the behavior. This approach
may help us understand the meaning of suicide for the individual, but it does
not help us understand the cultural meaning, unless everyone in the culture has
the same desire (or desires) for engaging in the behavior, which is very unlikely.
However, cultures may differ in the relative frequency of individual motives. In
one culture, the desire to escape may be common, whereas in another culture,
the desire for self-punishment may be common. No study has yet investigated
such cultural differences in motives.

The Precipitants for Suicide

A common answer to the question of why an individual committed suicide is to
mention the precipitating event. This person's marriage ended while this person
lost all their investments and was facing poverty. This has not been of much interest for researchers into suicide, and data on precipitants are rarely collected at a
cultural level. Japan makes an effort to categorize every suicide for the precipitant.
Lester and Saito (1998–1999) noted that, in 1990 in Japan, the precipitating event
was: 43.7% illness, 17.1% alcoholism and mental illness, 8.6% economic hard-
ship, 7.9% family problems, 7.2% job stress, 2.7% relationship problems, and
1.3% school problems. Joiner (2006) has proposed that feeling that one is a burden to others is a major causal factor in suicide, and this may account for the high
incidence of illness as a precipitant for suicide in Japan.[2]

India also attempts to classify each suicide. Using government documents,
Lester, Agarwal, and Natarajan (1999) noted that the precipitating events of suicides in India in 1990 were categorized as: dreadful disease 12.8%, quarrels with
parents-in-law 6.2%, quarrel with spouse 5.8%, love affairs 4.7%, and poverty
2.5%. However, in India, 16.2% had no known cause, and 39.0% were classified
as "other."

If these data were collected for cultures as a whole, and if standardized categories were adopted, then cultures could be compared for the relative frequency of

---

[2]   Lester (2010) has noted that feeling that one is a burden to others seems to be a factor in women
       becoming suicide bombers.

the precipitants, and this might give some clues as to the cultural meaning of suicide. For example, if almost half of the suicides in Japan are precipitated by illness, then suicide in Japan may typically be an escape from physical pain and suffering and to avoid being a burden to others.

The Psychodynamics of Suicide

Another possibility is that the meaning of suicide in a culture is related to the psychodynamics of the suicide in the culture. Hendin (1965) described the psychodynamics of suicide based on qualitative data that he obtained by visiting and interviewing people in Scandinavian countries. In Denmark, Hendin noted that guilt arousal was the major disciplinary technique employed by Danish mothers to control aggression, resulting in strong dependency needs in their sons. This marked dependency was the root of depression and suicidality after adult experiences of loss or separation. Reunion fantasies with lost loved ones were common in those committing suicide. In contrast, in Sweden, a strong emphasis was placed by parents on performance and success, resulting in ambitious children for whom work was central to their lives. Suicide typically followed failure in performance and the resulting damage to the individual's self-esteem.

The psychodynamics of suicide as described by Hendin are obviously related to the motives for suicide and to the precipitants for suicide, but they are more in-depth and meaningful. However, it might be quite difficult replicate Hendin's methodology for a larger sample of cultures.

Ethnomedical Theories

Good and Good (1982), as noted above, suggested that the meaning of an illness may be grounded in part in "the metaphors associated with a disease, the ethnomedical theories, the basic values and conceptual forms, and the care patterns that shape the experience of the illness and the social reactions to the sufferer in a given society" (p. 148). In the Western world, currently, the physiological and genetic basis of psychiatric illness is the major perspective or model. Government funding for research into this area goes primarily to physiological research. "Nature" is winning over "nurture," a major change from the 1960s when nurture ruled.

Primitive cultures, however, sometimes have very different theories of mental illness, such as soul loss, possession by evil spirits, or sins against the cultural code of conduct. Although anthropologists have documented these theories in some cultures (see Kiev, 1964), there has been no systematic study of these theories and no coding system proposed for the theories in a sample of cultures. These theories of mental illness would also be related to the differences in care patterns mentioned by Good and Good. Does treatment involve medication, counseling, expiation, or atonement for sins?

Lay Theories of Suicide

Strauss and Quinn (1997, p. 6) suggested that the meaning of a behavior is the interpretation evoked in a person by an event. The cultural meaning is the interpretation of the event evoked in people as a result of their similar life experiences. This implies that the meaning of suicide does not reside in the individual who dies by suicide, but rather in those who experience the suicides of others, that is, in the attitudes of the culture toward suicide and the lay theories of suicide present in that culture.

In her account of suicide among females in Papua-New Guinea, Counts (1988) has illustrated the ways in which a culture can determine the meaning of the suicidal act. In Papua-New Guinea, female suicide is a culturally-recognized way of imposing social sanctions. Suicide has political implications for the surviving kin and for those held responsible for the events leading women to die by suicide. In one such instance, the suicide of a rejected fiancée led to sanctions being imposed on the family which had rejected her. Counts described this woman's suicide as a political act which symbolically transformed her from a position of powerlessness to one of power. The problem with this report by Counts for the purposes of the present paper is that she did not estimate the frequency of suicide from these circumstances or to what extent the culture accepted such a sociopolitical implication of suicide.

Lester and Bean (1992) devised a questionnaire to assess whether respondents think that suicide is caused by intrapsychic, interpersonal, or societal stress. Voracek, Loibl, Egle, Schleicher, and Sonneck (2007) devised a questionnaire to explore the extent to which respondents believe that suicide is genetically caused. These lay theories of suicide would appear to tap the cultural meaning of suicide, and it would be interesting to give these questionnaires to samples of residents in different cultures. It is likely, although presently not documented, that members of a society may have several competing lay theories of suicide and, furthermore, that these lay theories may differ by sex, age, social class, ethnicity, and subculture within a society.

Some commentators see studies of lay theories of suicide as really studies of attitudes toward suicide and, indeed, there is an overlap in these two issues. However, a typical attitude toward suicide scale, for example, the Suicide Opinion Questionnaire (SOQ) (Domino & Perrone, 1993) has items about many issues and topics (such as myths about suicide) in addition to items exploring the respondent's views about the causation of suicide and, furthermore, the SOQ has no theoretical basis.

The Role of Values

Good and Good (1982) mentioned values as relevant to the cultural meaning of suicide. Kelleher, Chambers, Corcoran, Williamson, and Keeley (1998) classified 49 countries as to whether they had religious sanctions against suicide or not. They found that countries with religious sanctions against suicide were less likely to report suicide rates to the World Health Organization and, for those that did report, their suicide rates were lower than suicide rates in countries with no religious sanctions.

Stack and Kposowa (2008) used a measure of the acceptability of suicide in 31 nations, obtained through surveys of the population (Inglehart, 2000), to show that the suicide rate of those nations was positively associated with the level of acceptability of suicide in those nations. It is, therefore, possible to obtain cross-cultural measures of the acceptability of suicide.

An Illustrative Case

Meng (2002) presented the case of the suicide of a woman in rural China that she saw as throwing light on "the meaning of suicide." It also illustrates the confusion over the definition of "meaning."

Meng reported the case of Fang who killed herself by drowning at the age of 32. Her marriage was a love marriage, which is the basis for only about 13% of marriages in rural China, and her parents-in-law never accepted her. Although Fang was the wife of a first-born son, her parents-in-law gave preference to the wife of a younger son. Fang tried, but failed, to please her parents-in-law. After the birth of two sons, the couple moved to their own house in the family compound, and Fang became more hostile and confronted her parents-in-law more often. Fang's husband supported his parents and began to intervene. He hit and punished Fang for insulting his parents. Fang was socially isolated in the village, having come from a distant village, and she remained an outsider. Fang coped by seeking spiritual assistance, making friends outside of the family, converting to Christianity, and running away. After one last fight with her parents-in-law and punishment from her husband, Fang slipped away and killed herself.

The precipitating events for this suicide are quarrels with her in-laws and domestic violence. The community viewed the suicide in different ways. The in-laws viewed Fang's suicide as "a foolish act" for it cost the family a great deal in terms of cost and reputation. Fang's parents saw Fang's suicide as a "forced decision." They blamed Fang's in-laws, destroyed furniture in the in-laws' house, and demanded a very expensive funeral and headstone for Fang in her in-laws burial plot. The villagers gave Fang's suicide a mystical interpretation, believing that she was taken by a ghost, which served two functions: (1) to avoid blaming Fang or her in-laws, and (2) to escape from a sense of responsibility themselves for Fang's suicide.

Meng, however, viewed Fang's suicide as changing Fang's social status in the community. After her suicide, Fang's parents-in-law had to bow to her memory and mourn for her, that is, to accept her and treat her as they never had during her life. Thus, her suicide could be viewed as a form of symbolic revenge on her in-laws for their mistreatment of her. Only Fang's husband perhaps truly mourned his wife.

What then is the meaning of Fang's suicide? The personal meaning is unknown. The precipitating event was "family problems." Meng hypothesized that Fang's suicide was an act of symbolic revenge, but we do not know whether this was in Fang's mind at the time of her decision. Perhaps we should define the concept of "the meaning of suicide for the suicidologist"? From the details presented, including the fact that Fang ran away several times but returned because she missed her children, her suicide seems to fit Menninger's escape motive. Fang tried running away as a means of escape, but this failed. Death achieved escape for her. But, to understand the personal meaning of a suicide for the deceased individual, we need a substantial suicide note or a diary that provides insight into this meaning.

I have argued in this chapter that the cultural meaning might focus on the reactions of others to the suicide. But, in Fang's case, we have three cultural meanings – for her family, for her in-laws and for the villagers. (The commentator on the case may also perceive a different cultural meaning.) Thus, the cultural meaning for suicide is unclear. Furthermore, there has been no survey in this rural community of their theories of and attitudes toward suicide, the results of which can be compared with surveys in other communities in China and around the world.

D. Lester
The Cultural Meaning of Suicide: What Does This Mean?

55

Discussion

Of all of the possibilities discussed above, the motives for suicide seem to me to provide the best basis for the *individual meaning* of suicide. Although Menninger (1938) proposed a set of motives, the number of motives in such a classification needs to be increased, and cross-cultural studies of the frequency of these motives in different cultures would be welcome. The typology proposed by Reynolds and Berman (1995), based on ten typologies proposed by expert suicidologists, may be the best for this purpose.

Boldt (1988) stressed the importance for the understanding of suicidal behavior of conceptualizing suicidal behavior in terms of *cultural normative values*. The meaning of suicide varies from culture to culture – whether it is seen as a psychotic act, a ritual obligation or a human right, for example. The problem with this lies with the adjective "normative."

All too often sociologists and anthropologists decide *ex cathedra* what lies behind a behavior in a society or a culture. For example, Durkheim (1897) decided that the suicides of slaves are fatalistic in nature. He produced no evidence and no data to back up this assertion. Because he was an expert on the sociology of suicide, he expected us to accept his assertion. Similarly, Counts, whose analysis of female suicide in Papua-New Guinea was discussed above, asserted that it was a political act to increase the status of a low status woman. Again, since Counts is an expert, we are expected to accept this meaning of suicide without there being any data to support it. It is provocative and useful for such assertions to be made. However, it is important that such assertions be empirically tested by future researchers.

I would argue that the *cultural meaning* of suicide can be ascertained only by interviewing a representative sample of individuals in the various cultures in order to assess their attitudes toward suicide. In modern research, this has often been labeled as the study of lay theories of suicide. Furnham has studied lay theories of many behaviors (Furnham, 1988), including schizophrenia (Furnham & Bower, 1992), heroin addiction (Furnham & Thomson, 1996), and suicide (Knight, Furnham, & Lester, 2000), but so far only in Western nations. This type of research needs to be extended to other cultures.

It must be recognized that there may not be simply one cultural meaning of suicide in any given culture. Many cultural meanings may be present for any member of the culture, and different cultural meanings may exist for different subgroups of the culture, such as women and men, the young and the elderly, those of different social class, and, in multicultural societies, those of different ethnicity. The cultural meaning of suicide may change over time, and there may be different

cultural meanings for different types of suicidal acts, such as protest suicide, suicide bombers, and assisted-suicide in the terminally ill.

Some individuals behave deviantly in their culture, departing from cultural
norms. Thus, the individual meaning of a suicide may differ greatly from the cultural meaning if the suicide is a deviant in the culture. After all, Durkhem's (1897)
notion of anomic suicide is that such people are less bound by the cultural values
and norms in their society. On the other hand, those who adhere to the values and
norms of their culture often try to frame their suicide to fit into those values and
norms. Since suicides are breaking the sacred trust of life, individuals who are
going to kill themselves have to reconcile their image of a to-be-trusted person
with the fact that they are about to break that trust through their act of suicide
(Jacobs, 1967). Jacobs noted that often their suicide notes document this justification by noting their long history of distressing crises and their belief that death is
the only solution, constructing a rationalization that they are to-be-trusted people,
and making some provision that their problems will not recur after death (for
example, by stating that God will understand their choice of suicide).

Finally, as Boldt (1988) recognized, the cultural meaning of suicide may
change over time, and so longitudinal studies of lay theories of suicide must be
carried out in cultures.

References

Abdel-Khalek, A. M. (2004). Neither altruistic suicide, not terrorism, but martyrdom. *Archives of Suicide Research, 8*, 99–113.
Baechler, J. (1979). *Suicides*. New York: Basic Books.
Boldt, M. (1988). The meaning of suicide. *Crisis, 9*, 93–108.
Canetto, S. S. (1991). Gender roles, suicide attempts, and substance abuse. *Journal of Psychology, 125*, 605–620.
Counts, D. A. (1980). Fighting back is not the way: Suicide and the women on Kaliai. *American Ethnologist, 7*, 332–351.
Counts, D. A. (1988). Ambiguity in the interpretation of suicide. In D. Lester (Ed.), *Why women kill themselves*, pp. 87–109. Springfield, IL: Charles Thomas.
Devereux, G. (1961). *Mohave ethnopsychiatry*. Washington, DC: Smithsonian Institution.
Domino, G., & Perrone, L. (1993). Attitudes toward suicide. *Omega, 27*, 195–206.
Douglas, J. D. (1967). *The social meaning of suicide*. Princeton, NJ: Princeton University Press.
Durkheim, E. (1897). *Le suicide* [Suicide]. Paris: Felix Alcan.
Farberow, N. L., & Shneidman, E. S. (1961). *The cry for help*. New York: McGraw-Hill.
Furnham, A. F. (1988). *Lay theories*. Oxford, UK: Pergamon.
Furnham, A. F., & Bower, P. (1992). A comparison of academic and lay theories of schizophrenia. *British Journal of Psychiatry, 161*, 201–210.
Furnham, A. F., & Thomson, L. (1996). Lay theories of heroin addiction. *Social Science & Medicine, 43*, 29–40.

Good, B. J., & Good, M. J. D. (1982). Towards a meaning-centered analysis of popular illness categories. In A. J. Marsella & G. M. White (Eds.), *Cultural conceptions of mental health and therapy*, pp. 141–166. Boston, MA: D. Reidel.

Hendin, H. (1965). *Suicide and Scandinavia*. New York: Doubleday.

Inglehart, R. (2000). *World Values Surveys and European Value Surveys, 1981–1984, 1990–1993 and 1995–1997*. Ann Arbor, MI: Inter-University Consortium for Political & Social Research.

Jacobs, J. (1967). A phenomenological study of suicide notes. *Social Problems, 15*, 60–72.

Joiner, T. (2006). *Why people die by suicide*. Cambridge, MA: Harvard University Press.

Kelleher, M. J., Chambers, D., Corocran, P., Williamson, E., & Keeley, H. S. (1998). Religious sanctions and rates of suicide worldwide. *Crisis, 19*, 78–86.

Kiev, A. (1964). *Magic, faith and healing*. New York: Free Press.

Kleinman, A. (1977). Culture and illness. *Culture, Medicine, and Psychiatry, 1*, 229–231.

Knight, M. T. D., Furnham, A. F., & Lester, D. (2000). Lay theories of suicide. *Personality & Individual Differences, 29*, 453–457.

Lester, D. (1994). The epidemiology of suicide in Chinese populations in six regions of the world. *Chinese Journal of Mental Health, 7*(1), 25–36.

Lester, D. (2006). Suicide and Islam. *Archives of Suicide Research, 10*, 77–97.

Lester, D. (2008). Suicide and culture. *World Cultural Psychiatric Research Review, 3*(2), 51–68.

Lester, D. (2010). Female suicide bombers and burdensomeness. *Psychological Reports, 106*, 160–162.

Lester, D. (2011–2012). The cultural meaning of suicide. *Omega, 64*, 83–94.

Lester, D., Agarwal, K., & Natarajan, M. (1999). Suicide in India. *Archives of Suicide Research, 5*, 91–96.

Lester, D., & Bean, J. (1992). Attribution of causes to suicide. *Journal of Social Psychology, 132*, 679–680.

Lester, D., & Frank, M. (2008). How do American undergraduates view suicide bombers? *Psychological Reports, 103*, 713–714.

Lester, D., & Saito, Y. (1998–1999). The reasons for suicide in Japan. *Omega, 38*, 65–68.

Levi, F., La Vecchia, C., Lucchini, F., Negri, E., Saxena, S., Maulik, P. K., & Saraceno, B. (2003). Trends in mortality from suicide, 1965–99. *Acta Psychiatrica Scandinavica, 108*, 341–348.

Meng, L. (2002). Rebellion and revenge: The meaning of suicide on women in rural China. *International Journal of Social Welfare, 11*, 300–309.

Menninger, K. (1938). *Man against himself*. New York: Harcourt, Brace & World.

Ramon, S. (1980). Attitudes of doctors and nurses to self-poisoning patients. *Social Science and Medicine*, 14A, 317–324.

Reynolds, F. M. T., & Berman, A. L. (1995). An empirical typology of suicide. *Archives of Suicide Research, 1*, 97–109.

Stack, S., & Kposowa, A. J. (2008). The association of suicide rates with individual-level suicide attitudes. *Social Science Quarterly, 89*, 39–59.

Stack, S., Krysinska, K., & Lester, D. (2007-2008). Gloomy Sunday. *Omega, 56*, 349–358.

Strauss, C., & Quinn, N. (1997). *A cognitive theory of cultural meaning*. New York: Cambridge University Press.

Voracek, M., Loibl, L. M., Egle, J., Schleicher, S., & Sonneck, G. (2007). Correlates, item-sequence invariance, and test-retest reliability of the Beliefs in the Inheritance of Risk Factors for Suicide Scale (BIRFSS). *Psychological Reports, 101*, 1107–1117.

Culture and Suicide[1]

David Lester

Culture provides a set of rules and standards that are shared by members of a society. These rules and standards shape and determine the range of what is considered an appropriate behavior in a cultural setting. Culture influences the behavior of nationalities, ethnic groups, and subgroups within a nation.

The aim of this chapter is to present an overview of some of the topics and issues that are present in the interaction of suicide and culture. A major dichotomy here, of course, is the level of analysis. The interaction can be explored for the aggregate suicide rate of a culture and also for the individual suicide living in a particular society or culture. Let us first look at the interaction at the aggregate level.

Societal and Cultural Suicide Rates

It is an obvious fact that societal suicide rates differ widely over the nations of the world. As shown in Table 1, male suicide rates in 2000 ranged from 80.4 per 100,000 per year in Lithuania to 0.1 in Egypt. For females, the suicide rates ranged from 16.9 in Lithuania to 0.0 in Egypt. Knowledge of worldwide trends in suicide are limited because many African, Middle East, and Central and South American countries do not report their suicide rates to the World Health Organization.

For all the nations shown in Table 1, the male suicide rate is higher than the female suicide rate. The lone exception was China, where women have a higher suicide rate than men.[2] However, China documents suicide fatalities for only a small percentage of the nation, and so the suicide rates are not accurate for the nation as a whole.[3]

---

[1] A modified version of this chapter appeared as Lester (2008).
[2] Phillips, Liu, and Zhang (1999) reported suicide rates of 33.6 per 100,000 per year versus 24.2 for the 1990–1994 period for women and men, respectively. In recent years, the rates have converged and now the male suicide rate is slightly higher than the females suicide rate (Michael Phillips, personal communication, April, 2011).
[3] Suicide rates for China in 2000 were not available from the World Health Organization.

Table 1. Suicide rates around the world for men and women per 100,000 for 2000 (from www.who.int)

	Male	Female
Albania	2.4	1.2
Argentina	12.3	2.9
Armenia	2.5	0.7
Australia	19.8	5.2
Austria	29.3	10.4
Azerbaijan	1.2	0.4
Belarus	63.6	9.5
Brazil	6.4	1.6
Bulgaria	25.2	9.1
Canada	18.4	5.2
Chile	16.8	2.7
Costa Rica	10.7	1.5
Croatia	32.9	10.3
Cuba	23.4	9.6
Czech Rep.	26.0	6.7
Ecuador	6.0	2.6
Egypt	0.1	0.0
Estonia	45.8	11.9
Finland	34.6	10.9
France	27.9	9.5
Germany	20.3	7.0
Georgia	4.8	1.2
Greece	5.5	1.5
Hong Kong	16.1	10.1
Hungary	50.7	15.1
Ireland	20.3	4.3
Italy	10.9	3.5
Japan	35.2	13.4
Kazakhstan	51.7	9.7
Kuwait	1.6	1.6
Kyrgyzstan	17.2	3.9
Latvia	56.6	11.9
Lithuania	80.4	16.9
Macedonia	10.3	4.5
Mauritius	18.8	5.2
Mexico	6.0	1.1
Moldova	26.7	4.1
Netherlands	12.7	6.2

(Continued)

Table 1. Continued.

	Male	Female
New Zealand	19.8	4.2
Norway	18.5	5.8
Panama	8.4	1.3
Paraguay	3.9	1.7
Poland	25.9	4.9
Portugal	8.5	2.0
Puerto Rico	15.2	1.4
Romania	21.2	4.5
Russia	70.6	11.9
Singapore	12.5	6.4
Slovakia	22.6	4.9
Slovenia	45.2	15.2
South Korea	18.8	8.3
Spain	13.1	4.0
Sweden	18.3	7.3
Switzerland	27.8	10.8
Thailand	13.5	3.7
Ukraine	52.1	10.0
United Kingdom	11.3	3.2
US	17.1	4.0
Uruguay	29.0	5.5
Uzbekistan	11.8	3.8
Venezuela	8.8	1.5

These differences in national suicide rates are large and generally stable over time. For example, in Table 2 the suicide rates for 16 nations in 1901, 1950, and 1990 are shown and, despite fluctuations, the rates in one year are positively associated with the rates in other years.

Suicide rates also vary widely over the different geographic regions of a nation (for example, over American states and Canadian provinces, suicide rates increase toward the west, Lester, 1985) and over the different social groups within a nation (for example, some groups of both Native Americans and Native Canadians have very high suicide rates, Lester, 1997a).

An obvious explanation of such variations in the aggregate suicide rate is that the reporting and counting of suicides in different nations and cultures differ greatly in accuracy (Douglas, 1967). Indeed, it has been easy to document serious official under-reporting of suicides, for example, in Newfoundland (Malla & Hoenig, 1983) and Native Americans in Alaska (Hlady & Middaugh, 1988).

Table 2. Suicide rates per 100,000 in 1901, 1950, and 1990

	1901	1950	1990
Australia	11.9	9.3	12.9
Belgium	12.7	12.9	19.0
England/Wales	9.6	10.2	7.8
Finland	6.1	15.6	30.3
Germany	20.8	18.8*	17.5
Ireland	2.9	2.6	9.5
Italy	6.2	6.5	7.6
Netherlands	5.8	5.5	9.7
New Zealand	10.2	9.2	13.5
Norway	5.5	7.4	15.5
Portugal	4.3	10.1	8.8
Scotland	5.3	5.3	10.5
Spain	2.0	5.4	7.5
Sweden	13.1	14.9	17.2
Switzerland	22.4	23.5	21.9
US	10.4	11.4	12.4
Correlations			
1901	–	0.87	0.47
1950		–	0.73
1990			–

Sources: www.who.int and WHO (1956).
*This rate is for West Germany.

Nevertheless, it is very unlikely that completely accurate reporting of suicides would eliminate the national and cultural differences. The suicide rates of immigrant groups moving both to the US and to Australia are strongly associated with the suicide rates in the home nations from which they arrived (Sainsbury & Barraclough, 1968; Lester, 1972; Voracek & Loibl, 2008). For example, the Irish had a relatively low suicide rate in 1959, 2.5 per 100,000, and Irish immigrants to the US in 1959, where they encountered the same medical examiners as other immigrant groups, also had the lowest suicide of all immigrants groups from European countries, only 9.8 (Dublin, 1963).

The distribution of suicide rates by age varies with the level of economic development of the nation (Girard, 1993). Male suicide rates increase with age in most nations of the world. For the wealthy nations, such as the US and Sweden, female suicide rates tend to peak in middle age. For poorer nations, such as Venezuela, suicide rates are higher for elderly women, while for the poorest nations, such as Thailand, the peak shifts to young women (Girard, 1993).

Explaining National Differences in Suicide

The association of sociodemographic and economic variables with national suicides has been best analyzed using factor analysis. Conklin and Simpson (1987) identified two clusters of variables that appear to be associated with national suicide rates: one cluster had the highest loading from the Islam religion and the second cluster assessed economic development. Lower suicide rates were found for nations with less economic development and where Islam was the dominant religion.

In a similar study of cross-national suicide rates in 72 countries, Lester (1996) identified thirteen independent orthogonal factors for the social variables, only one of which was associated with suicide rates. This factor was economic development, with high loadings from such social variables as low population growth and high gross domestic product per capita.

Physiological Differences

One possible explanation for differences in national suicide rates is that different nationalities differ in their physiology. For example, there are clear differences in the frequency of genes in the people from the different nations of Europe (Menozzi, Piazza, & Cavalli-Sforza, 1978). Thus, different nations and cultures may differ in their genetic structure. Current research on identical twins and adopted children has shown that psychiatric disorders have a strong genetic basis. These differences in inherited psychiatric disorders, particularly affective disorders, or in brain concentrations of serotonin, the neurotransmitter believed to be responsible for depression, may be responsible for the differences in the suicide rates of nations and cultures.

One study has attempted to demonstrate an association between physiological factors and suicide rates at the cross-national level. Lester (1987) found that the suicide rates of nations were associated with the proportion of people with Types O, A, B, and AB blood – the higher the proportion of people in the nation with Type O blood, the lower the suicide rate. However, few studies have explored the role of physiological differences in accounting for national differences in suicide rates.

Psychological and Psychiatric Differences

The major psychological factors found to be associated with suicidal behavior are depression, especially hopelessness, and psychological disturbance, such as neuroticism, anxiety, or emotional instability. Psychiatric disorder appears to increase the risk of suicide, with affective disorders and alcohol and drug abuse leading the list (Tatarelli, Pompili, & Girardi, 2007). Nations may differ in the prevalence of these conditions, and such differences could account for the differences in suicide rates. For example, nations certainly do differ in their consumption of alcohol (Adrian, 1984), as well as their rates of depression (Weissman & Klerman, 1977).

Social Composition

Moksony (1990) noted that one simple explanation of national differences in suicide rates is that the national populations differ in the proportion of those at risk for suicide. For example, typically in developed nations, suicide rates are highest among the elderly, especially elderly males. Therefore, nations with a higher proportion of elderly males will have a higher suicide rate.

Societal Differences

The most popular explanation of the variation in national suicide rates focuses on social variables. These social variables may be viewed in two ways: (1) as direct causal agents of the suicidal behavior, or (2) as indices of broad social characteristics which differ between nations.

Durkheim (1897) hypothesized that the suicide rate is related to the level of social integration (the degree to which the people are bound together in social networks) and the level of social regulation (the degree to which people's desires and emotions are regulated by societal norms and customs). According to Durkheim, *egoistic* and *anomic* suicides result from too little social integration and social regulation, respectively, while *altruistic* and *fatalistic* suicides result from too much social integration and social regulation, respectively. Later sociologists have argued that altruistic and fatalistic suicide are rare in modern societies. Therefore, suicide rarely results from excessive social integration or regulation. As a result, suicide in modern societies seems to increase as social integration and regulation *decrease* (e.g., Johnson, 1965).

Studies of samples of nations have found that suicide rates are associated with such variables as low church attendance, the amount of immigration and interregional migration, and divorce (e.g., Stack, 1983). Some investigators view these associations as suggesting a positive relationship between broken relationships and suicidal behavior. For example, divorce may be associated with suicide at the societal level because divorced people have a higher suicide rate than those with other marital statuses.

A major issue here has been raised by Moksony (1990) and Taylor (1990) concerning whether *specific* social variables are directly related to social suicide rates or whether these specific social variables are measures of more basic, abstract, and broad social characteristics which determine social suicide rates. Lester (2004) proposed that the strong associations between social variables argues for the importance of basic broad social characteristics. For example, in the US, interstate migration, divorce, church nonattendance and alcohol consumption all intercorrelate highly, supporting the importance of a social characteristic, perhaps best called *social disorganization*, as a determinant of societal suicide rates. In this case, regions of the world with high rates of divorce would have high rates of suicide for those in all marital statuses. This is found for the US where states with higher divorce rates have higher suicide rates among the single, the married, the divorced, and the widowed (Lester, 1995a).

Lester (2005) entered percentage Type O blood type, alcohol consumption, percentage elderly, divorce rate, and birth rate into a multiple regression for 17 industrialized nations. The multiple R was 0.85. He then used the regression equation to predict the suicide rate of seven other European nations, and the Spearman rank correlation was 0.89. However, using the regression equation to predict the suicide rates in seven non-European nations gave a rank correlation of zero! Thus, the predictors (and, therefore, the possible causes) of suicide rates in non-Western nations may be quite different from those for European nations.

Comment

There is clearly much more research needed to compare and contrast these competing explanations for differences in national suicide rates.

Cultural Influences on the Motives for Suicidal Behavior

Suicidal behavior is differently determined and has different meanings in different cultures, as demonstrated by Hendin's (1964) study of suicide in Scandinavian countries. In Denmark, Hendin noted that guilt arousal was the major disciplinary technique employed by Danish mothers to control aggression, resulting in strong dependency needs in their sons. This marked dependency was the root of depression and suicidality after adult experiences of loss or separation. Reunion fantasies with lost loved ones were common in those who died by suicide.

In Sweden, a strong emphasis was placed by parents on performance and success, resulting in ambitious children for whom work was central to their lives. Suicide typically followed failure in performance and the resulting damage to their self-esteem when they are adults.

At the time Hendin conducted his study in Norway, the suicide rate was much lower than that found for Denmark. Although Hendin found strong dependency among the sons on their mothers in both countries, Norwegian children were less passive and more aggressive than Danish children. Alcohol abuse was more common among the Norwegians, and Norwegian men were more open about their feelings – able to laugh at themselves and cry more openly. Norwegian boys strove to please their mothers by causing no trouble, and they did not worry unduly about failure, typically blaming others for their personal failures and retreating into alcohol abuse.

In her account of suicide among females in Papua-New Guinea, mentioned also in the previous chapter, Counts (1988) has illustrated the ways in which a culture can determine the meaning of the suicidal act. In Papua-New Guinea, female suicide is a culturally-recognized way of imposing social sanctions. Suicide also holds political implications for the surviving kin and for those held responsible for the events leading women to commit suicide. In one such instance, the suicide of a rejected fiancée led to sanctions being imposed on the family that had rejected her. Counts described this woman's suicide as a political act which symbolically transformed her from a position of powerlessness to one of power.

Cultures also differ in the degree in which suicide is condemned. It has been argued that one explanation for the low suicide rate in African-Americans is that suicide is a less acceptable behavior for African-Americans (Early, 1992). Murder rates are much higher in African-Americans, both as murderers and as victims, and a larger proportion of the murders involving African Americans are victim-precipitated, that is, the victim played some role, conscious or unconscious, in precipitating their own demise (Wolfgang, 1957). African-American culture appears to view a victim-precipitated murder as a more acceptable method of dying than suicide (Gibbs, 1988; Early & Akers, 1993).

Choice of Method for Suicide

The methods chosen for suicide differ between cultures. DeCatanzaro (1981) documented culturally unique methods for suicide, such as hanging by tying a noose around one's neck and running to another part of the house in Tikopia. Sati, which is suicide by burning on the husband's funeral pyre, is a common form in India, while seppuku, which is ritual disembowelment, is common in Japan. These well-known examples of cultural influences on suicide methods also have culturally determined motives (grief and shame, respectively).

Firearms are the most common method for suicide in the US and Canada presently, while in Switzerland, whose residents typically own firearms as part of their participation in the civilian militia, hanging is the most common method for suicide. As mentioned in an earlier chapter, a method may come to symbolize the act of suicide, as in England earlier this century when "to take the pipe" meant to commit suicide by inhaling toxic domestic gas since the gas was brought into houses by means of pipes and this was the most common method for suicide. (After the 1960s, domestic gas became less toxic as a result of the switch from coal gas to natural gas.) Burvill and his colleagues (1983) found that immigrants to Australia shifted over time from using the most common methods of suicide in their home nations to those most common in Australia.

Research indicates that increased availability of a method for suicide is associated with an increase in its use for suicide (Clarke & Lester, 1989). For example, Killias, van Kesteren, and Rindlisbacher (2001) found that, in nations where a large proportion of the population owned guns, a higher number of suicides used guns. However, ownership of guns had no association with the *total* suicide rate. This suggests that, if guns are not freely available, people use guns less often for suicide but switch instead to other methods for suicide, such as poisons, hanging, stabbing, jumping, and drowning.

Related to this is the proposal for preventing suicide by limiting access to lethal methods for suicide (Clarke & Lester, 1989). Kreitman (1976) documented how detoxification of domestic gas in England and Wales led to a virtual elimination of domestic gas for suicide and a reduction in the overall suicide rate. Lester (1995b) studied this phenomenon in six other nations and found that detoxification of domestic gas reduced the use of domestic gas for suicide in all of the nations and, in those nations where suicide by domestic gas was more common initially, reduced the overall suicide rate as well. More recently, restricting access to pesticides has proved to be of some use in reducing their use for self-harm in Sri Lanka. (For a recent review of this method for preventing suicide, see Lester, 2009.)

Suicide in One Culture: The Chinese

Studies by Lester (1994a, 1994b) on suicidal behavior in Chinese people illustrate the role of culture, a culture of particular interest because the Chinese are native to many nations (such as mainland China and Hong Kong) and have emigrated in large numbers to nations such as America.

The suicide rates of Asian Americans are relatively low compared to Whites in the US. For example, in 1980, the suicide rates were 13.3 per 100,000 per year for Native Americans, 13.2 for White Americans, 9.1 for Japanese Americans, 8.3 for Chinese Americans, 6.1 for African Americans, and 3.5 for Filipino Americans (Lester, 1994b).[4]

Lester noted that the patterns of suicide also differed for these ethnic groups. The ratio of the male to female suicide rates was much larger for Whites and African Americans than for Asian Americans, for whom the suicide rates of men and women were more similar. In addition, suicide rates increased with age for Asian Americans, whereas the suicide rates peaked in young adulthood for African Americans and Native Americans. Asian Americans used hanging for suicide much more often than Whites and African Americans, and they used firearms relatively less often.

Lester concluded that the epidemiology of suicide in Asian Americans in America showed similarities to the results of epidemiological studies of suicide in their home nations, indicating that cultural factors have an important influence on the circumstances of suicidal behavior.

Lester (1994a) then examined the epidemiology of suicide in Chinese people in Hong Kong, Singapore, Taiwan, mainland China, Hawaii, and the US as a whole. A couple of examples here will illustrate the results. The ratio of the male to female suicide rates in 1980 were 1.2 for Chinese Americans, 1.2 for Hong Kong residents, 1.2 for Taiwanese residents, and 1.2 for Singaporean Chinese, identical gender ratios. Suicide rates peaked in the elderly in all the nations: for those 65 and older in Chinese Americans, 75 and older in Hong Kong and Taiwan, and 70 and older in Singapore Chinese.[5]

However, the methods used for suicide did differ for the different groups of Chinese people: jumping was more common in the Chinese in Singapore and Hong Kong, hanging in Chinese Americans, and poisons in Taiwan, probably a result of the difference between the nations in the availability of methods for suicide.[6] Furthermore, the suicide rates differed: in 1980 the suicide rates were

---

[4]   Whites have higher suicide rates than Blacks in the US (13.0 per 100,000 per year versus 6.8 in 1992) and also in African nations which report suicide rates such as Zimbabwe (17.6 versus 6.9 in 1983–1986) and South Africa (18.4 versus 3.0 in 1984) (Lester, 1998).
[5]   The nations used different classifications by age.
[6]   For example, Lester (1994c) showed that the use of jumping for suicide in Singapore was strongly associated with the development of high rise apartments.

13.5 in Singapore and Hong Kong Chinese, 10.0 in Taiwan, and 8.3 for Chinese Americans.

Thus, the gender and age patterns in Chinese suicide seem to be affected strongly by culture, while the absolute suicide rates and methods used are affected by the nation in which the Chinese dwell.

Culture, Linguistics, and Suicide

As Douglas (1967) pointed out, a shared linguistic terminology for suicidal behavior is associated with shared meanings of the behavior, and there are also shared associated terms and phrases, such as despair, hopelessness, and "life isn't worth living." Douglas emphasized that these terms are not the phenomenon itself but rather are adopted by members of the culture (or subculture) to construct meanings for suicidal behavior. However, since the terms are rarely clearly defined or detailed and since there is often disagreement among commentators on their meaning, it follows that the meaning of suicide is ambiguous. Furthermore, since the terms are used to construct meanings for suicidal behavior, then estimates of the incidence and circumstances of suicidal behavior are, in part, a social construction. This was illustrated in the previous chapter with examples from the Mohave, a group of Native Americans, in their classification of still-born infants (Devereux, 1961) and from women in Papua New Guinea who engage in sati (Counts, 1980).

Other examples in the previous chapter included relabeling attempted suicide as self-injury (Ramon, 1980), which narrows the definition of suicidal behavior, and Menninger's (1938) enlargement of suicidal behavior by defining chronic suicide (such as alcoholism) and focal suicidal (such as self-blinding).

The Study of Culture Can Challenge Myths

Many theories of human behavior, including suicidal behavior, are based on physiological factors. Cultural anthropology helps challenge such theories by showing, for example, that behaviors which we consider gender-specific are not found in every culture. As we have noted above, in the US and in European nations, nonfatal suicidal behavior appears to occur at a higher rate in women than in men and, as a result, it is has come to be viewed as a "feminine" behavior by the general public (Linehan, 1973) and by suicidologists as well. Other cultures, however, provide examples where nonfatal suicidal behavior, often carried out in front of others, is more common in men rather than women. The Nahane (or Kaska), a Native Canadian tribe located in British Columbia and the Yukon, provide a good example of this.

> ... observations and communications agree that attempted suicide by men is of frequent occurrence and very likely to appear during intoxication. There is a general pattern for such attempted self-destruction. In the two cases of the sort observed during field work, the weapon selected was a rifle. As he brandishes the weapon the would be suicide announces his intention in an emotional outburst. This becomes the signal for interference to block the deed. One or more men leap forward to wrest the gun from the intended suicide's possession and toss it out of sight. The would be victim is now usually emotionally overwhelmed by his behavior. This pattern is illustrated by Louis Maza's behavior during intoxication. Several times during the afternoon, Louis had manifested aggression toward himself, crying: "I don't care if I'm killed. I don't care my life." After several hours of such emotional outbursts interspersed with quarreling and aggression toward his companions, he seized his large caliber rifle and threatened to kill himself. Old Man threw himself on the gun and as the two men grappled for the weapon, Louis succeeded in firing one wild shot. John Kean and the ethnographer ran to the camp and together wrenched the gun from the drunken man. John fired the shells in the chamber and Old Man tossed the gun half-way down the cutbank. No punishment or other discrimination is reserved for attempted suicides. The individual is comforted and in the future, while intoxicated, he is watched lest he repeat the attempt. (Honigmann, 1949, p. 204)

Among the Washo, located in Nevada and California, nonfatal suicidal behavior seems to be equally common in men and women.

> In one case, a man had been having difficulty with his wife; she was interested in another man. The husband ate wild parsnip, but was saved. As a result his sons brought pressure on the wife and made her behave. The couple stayed together until the husband died. Pete also says that men attempt suicide more than women, who just leave home when interpersonal difficulties arise. The destruction of the self is an ultimate, and the fact that men are more likely to invoke it than women indicates a lack of male authority in Washo culture. (D'Azevedo et al., 1963, pp. 50–51)

The Washo man is described as lacking authority and lacking in self-confidence, perhaps because the Washo man has had more difficulty adapting to the changing culture in this century than has the Washo woman. Interestingly, the explanation provided by these Western anthropologists for the occurrence of nonfatal suicidal behavior among Washo men may be generalizable to societies where nonfatal suicidal behavior is more common in women. It may be that nonfatal suicidal behavior is not simply a "feminine" behavior, but rather a behavior found more commonly in those who are oppressed in a society, perhaps because the oppressed have fewer options for expressing their discontent.

The Impact of Culture Conflict

An issue that has become important in recent years is the impact of the pervasive Western culture on the suicidal behavior of those living in less modern cultures. The high suicide rates in some Native American and Canadian groups and in some Micronesian islands has made this an issue of grave concern rather than mere academic debate (Rubinstein, 1992).

Cultures often come into conflict. For example, the conflict between the traditional Native American culture and the dominant American culture has often been viewed as providing a major role in precipitating Native American suicide. May and Dizmang (1974) noted that there were three major sociological theories which have been proposed for explaining the Native American suicide rate. One theory focuses on *social disorganization*. The dominance of the Anglo-American culture has forced Native American culture to change and has eroded traditional cultural systems and values. This changes the level of social regulation and social integration, important causal factors for suicide in Durkheim's (1897) theory of suicide.

A second theory focuses on *cultural conflict* itself. The pressure from the educational system and mass media on Native Americans, especially the youth, to acculturate, a pressure which is opposed by their elders, leads to great stress for the youths. A third theory focuses on the *breakdown of the family* in Native American tribes. Parents are often unemployed, substance abusers, and in trouble with the law, and divorce and desertion of the family by one or more parents is common.

Acculturation occurs when a culture encounters a dominant alternative culture. The resulting pressure from the dominant culture leads to a variety of changes in the nondominant culture (Berry, 1990): physical changes (such as type of housing, urbanization and increasing population density), biological changes (resulting from changing diet and exposure to new diseases), political changes (such as loss of autonomy for the nondominant culture), economic changes (such as changes in type of employment), cultural changes (in language, religion, education, and the arts), changes in social relationships (both within the culture and between the two cultures), and psychological changes at the individual level (in behavior, values, attitudes, and motives).

Berry noted that four possibilities are open to the nondominant culture: *integration* – maintaining relations with the dominant culture while maintaining cultural identity; *assimilation* – maintaining relations with the dominant culture but not maintaining cultural identity; *separation* – not maintaining relations with the dominant culture but maintaining cultural identity; and *marginalization* – not maintaining relations with the dominant culture and not maintaining cultural identity. It would be of great interest to categorize the different Native American tribes as to which strategy appears to have been chosen and to examine the different consequences for the society and for the individuals in the society.

Research on Acculturation

Supportive results for the influence of acculturation on suicide in Native Americans comes from Van Winkle and May (1986) who examined suicide rates in three groups of Native Americans in New Mexico (the Apache, Navajo, and Pueblo) and attempted to account for the differences in terms of the degree of acculturation. Overall, the crude suicide rates were 43.3 per 100,000 per year for the Apache, 27.8 for the Pueblo, and 12.0 for the Navajo.

The Jicarilla and Mescalero Apache of New Mexico were originally nomadic hunters and gatherers, organized into self-sufficient bands whose leaders held limited power. Their religion had no organized priesthood and was not a cohesive force in their lives. Individualism was a highly valued characteristic. Today they live in homes scattered about the reservation or in border towns. They raise livestock, cut timber, or work in tribally-owned businesses. Formal tribal governments have been established, but religion remains unimportant. Individualism is still valued. However, the raiding parties which formerly provided some degree of social integration have been eliminated. The Apache appear, therefore, to have few integrating forces in their culture, and Van Winkle and May saw their high suicide rate as a direct result of this lack of integration. The Apache have been in close contact with Whites. Their reservations are small and surrounded by White communities. Indeed many Apache live in mixed communities. Thus, the Apache have high acculturation in addition to their low social integration.

The Pueblo traditionally lived in compact towns and engaged in agriculture. Religion permeated their lives and was a strong integrating force. There was an organized priesthood and religious societies, which took care of religious and civil matters. Individualism was discouraged and conformity valued. Thus, the Pueblo were the most integrated group, and Van Winkle and May found their intermediate suicide rate a puzzle. They tried to explain the Pueblo suicide rate using the role of acculturation. The Pueblo have had increasing contact with Whites since 1959. Many of the Pueblos are near large cities such as Albuquerque and Santa Fe. Thus, they have high social integration and moderate but increasing acculturation. For the larger Pueblo tribes, Van Winkle and May compared the suicide rates of those tribes that had acculturated and those which had remained traditional and found a clear tendency for the acculturated and transitional tribes to have the higher suicide rates.

The Navajo, who have the lowest suicide rate, were nomadic hunters and gatherers who later settled down and turned to agriculture. They are organized into bands, and matrilineal clans exert a strong influence. Although religion is important in their lives, they have no organized priesthood. Individualism is valued but not as strongly as among the Apache. Thus, their social integration appears to be intermediate between that of the Apache and that of the Pueblo. However, the Navajo were the most geographically and socially isolated from Whites of the three groups until the 1970s when mineral exploration increased on their reservations and some Navajo began to take wage-earning jobs.

Van Winkle and May's explanation of the suicide rates in the three groups can be summarized as follows:

	Social Integration	Acculturation	Suicide Rate
Apache	low	high	high
Pueblo	high	moderate	moderate
Navajo	moderate	low	low

It can be seen that acculturation performed better than social integration as an explanation for the differing suicide rates.

In contrast, however, Bagley (1991) found in Alberta that it was those native Canadian reservations that were more isolated (and, incidentally, poorer) that had the higher suicide rates. In Taiwan also, Lee, Chang, and Cheng (2002) found that the less assimilated aboriginal groups had higher suicides rates than those groups that were more assimilated in the mainstream culture.

These studies indicate that when different cultures encounter each other, the problems of acculturation can result in stress and its consequences, including increased rates of suicidal behavior, especially in the less dominant cultural group. But acculturation may not always lead to an increased incidence of suicide (and other disturbed behaviors). In the future, anthropologists may be able to identify which cultural characteristics enable some cultures to acculturate with few social and personal problems while other cultures develop many problems.

The Assumption of Cultural Invariability

Investigators often assume that a research finding found in one culture will apply to other cultures. It is, therefore, important to replicate research findings in cultures other than the one in which the results were first obtained to check on this assumption. For example, at the sociological level, Lester and Yang (1991) found that females in the labor force and the ratio of divorces to marriages predicted suicide rates in the US and Australia from 1946 to 1984, but the associations were in opposite directions for the two nations. While in the US the ratio of divorces to marriages was positively associated with the suicide, the association was negative in Australia.

Stack (1992) found that divorce had a deleterious effect on the suicide rate in Sweden and Denmark, but not in Japan. Stack offered four possible reasons: the divorce rate may be too low in Japan to affect the suicide rate, Japanese family support may be strong enough to counteract the loss of a spouse, ties between couples may be weak in Japan, and the cultural emphasis on conformity in Japan may suppress suicidal behavior.

At the individual level, Lester, Castromayor, and Icli (1991) found that an external locus of control was associated with a history of suicidal preoccupation in American, Philippine and Turkish students, but the association was no longer found for American students once the level of depression was controlled. In a comparison of depression and suicide in mainland China and the US, Chiles et al. (1989) found that suicidal intent was predicted better by depression for Chinese psychiatric patients and better by hopelessness for American psychiatric patients. De Man and his associates (for example, De Man et al., 1987) have published a number of studies of suicidal behavior in French-Canadians in order to explore the replicability of research findings originally identified for English-speaking cultures.

It is important, therefore, for researchers to identify which findings have cross-cultural generality (and to which cultures) and which are specific to one culture.

Subcultures

Cultures are not uniform, and often many subcultures co-exist side-by-side within a culture. Wolfgang and Ferracuti (1967) examined the role that a subculture of violence plays in producing high murder and assault rates. For example, Gastil (1971) argued that such a subculture of violence pervaded the southern portion of the US, and Marks and Stokes (1976) used this to account for the greater use of firearms for suicide in southern states as compared to the rest of America.

Platt (1985) suggested that electoral wards in Edinburgh (Scotland) differed in their rates of attempted suicide and had different norms for suicidal behavior, thereby differing in their *subculture of suicide*. Those living in wards with the highest rate had more intimate contact with suicidal individuals and had different values about life, such as having a greater expectation that married couples would quarrel and that men would fight in public. However, Platt was unable to find to his satisfaction that the wards differed in the proposed subculture of suicide.

Suicide Among Indigenous Peoples

In some nations there has been a good deal of research on and speculation about suicidal behavior in indigenous peoples, in some countries labeled as aborigines. A great deal of research has been conducted on Native Americans in the US, and some on aborigines in Australia and Taiwan and on the Inuit in Canada and Greenland.

What is noteworthy, however, is that many nations have indigenous peoples, yet we hear little about their suicidality and other self-destructive behaviors. For example, in Central and South America, almost every nation has an indigenous population: 71% in Bolivia, 66% in Guatemala, 47% in Peru, 38% in Ecuador, 14% in Mexico, 8% in Chile, 2% in Colombia, 1.5% in Paraguay, 1% in Venezuela, and 0.4% in Brazil (Anon, 2004). In recent years, these indigenous peoples have become organized politically. They have begun to protest against the governments of their nations, often toppling governments (as in Bolivia and Ecuador) and in some cases assuming power (as in Bolivia and Peru).

Even in developed nations, the oldest inhabitants are often ignored. In suicide statistics from the UK, data from England and Wales are reported together. A report on suicide in Wales (Lester, 1994d) was rejected by reviewers for the *British Journal of Psychiatry* as being of no interest![7] The UK has ethnic groups in Wales and the county of Cornwall who predate the Roman, Danish, and French invaders and who have their own languages and ethnic identity. Yet their suicidal behavior has received no attention.

---

[7]   It is no wonder that there is a Welsh liberation movement!

In Africa, the situation is odd in a different way. Setting aside the remnants of the European colonialists, all of the peoples there can be considered indigenous. Yet, when data on suicide are reported, they are reported for the artificial nations that the colonial rulers established with no regard for the tribal groups in each country. For example, suicide rates have been reported for Zimbabwe (Rittey & Castle, 1972; Lester & Wilson, 1988), yet Zimbabwe has two major ethnic groups, the Shona (the dominant ethnic group) and the Ndebele. It would make much more sense to explore and compare suicide in these two ethnic groups.

Some nations are only now beginning to organize their mortality-reporting procedures and structures. In many of these, it will be important to take into account the various indigenous groups in the country, such as China, which has a multitude of ethnicities within its borders.

Comparisons of Indigenous Peoples Within a Nation

In a couple of nations, it has been possible to compare different ethnic groups within a nation. Lester (1997a) reviewed all of the studies on Native American suicide and summarized the suicide rates by tribe and by era (see Table 3). It can be seen that there was a slight tendency for the suicide rates to rise during the 20th Century and for the tribes to differ greatly in their suicide rate, ranging in the 1970s from 149 per 100,000 per year in the Kwakiutl and 73 in the Sioux to 7 in the Pima and 9 in the Lumbee.

Cheng (1995, 1997) compared suicide in Taiwan in two aboriginal groups (the Atayal and the Ami) with suicide in the dominant Han Chinese. The Atayal had a suicide rate of 68.2 per 100,000 per year, the Ami 15.6 and the Han Chinese 18.0. The suicides in all three groups had a similarly high incidence of psychiatric disorder, and the high suicide rate in the Atayal was attributed by Cheng to their high rate of alcoholism and earlier onset of major depressive disorders.

We need many more studies comparing the different groups of indigenous peoples within a nation, not simply the crude suicide rates, but also the circumstances, motives, and meanings of suicide in these different groups.

The Human Relations Area Files

Anthropologists have typically studied historical societies or societies that have been relatively less influenced by modernization, often called preliterate, nonliterate, or primitive societies, societies composed of whom we would now call indigenous peoples.

Table 3. Tribal suicide rates per 100,000 in America (from Lester, 1997a)

Tribe	1910s	1920s	1930s	1940s	1950s	1960s	1970s	1980s
Aleut							16	
Apache					26	18	40	
Blackfoot						125		
Cherokee							23	
Cheyenne	22	21	13	6	40	48		
Eskimo							42	
Kwakiutl						40	149	
Lumbee							9	
Navajo					8	13		
Ojibway					6		56	
Papago						100		
Pima						40	7	
Pueblo					10	55		
Pueblo (Hopi)					8	13	30	17
Shoshoni							38	
Shoshoni-Bannock						98		
Shoshoni-Paiute					113			
Sioux							73	31
Tlingit							30	
Yaqui						30		

There is a superb source of data on indigenous peoples in the Human Relations Area Files (HRAF). The headquarters for this project are at Yale University, but microfiche copies of the results of the project are available at other major universities in the US and around the world. The staff of the project has collected reports from visitors to these cultures as far back as they can and from all kinds of visitors (such as missionaries, colonial administrators, and anthropologists). The content of the reports is coded for topic and, for example, in order to read what has been written about suicide in these cultures, the code for suicide is ascertained from the codebook (it is 762), and then the section for 762 can be located for each culture in the HRAF. There are about 330 cultures represented in the HRAF. The files are now available on a CD-ROM, and there is a website for the HRAF (www.yale.edu/hraf/collections.htm).

The files are updated and enlarged continually. To give some examples of the source material, in 1994, the Ainu in Japan had 1,573 text pages from 11 sources that had been coded, the Lapps in Finland 3,284 text pages from 16 sources, the Yoruba in Nigeria 1,637 text pages from 45 sources, and Delaware Indians in the US 1,733 text pages from 15 sources.

Several projects on suicide can be devised from the HRAF. For example, some investigators have read the files on suicide for a sample of societies and tried to estimate the suicide rate for each society. Masumura (1977) had two judges rate 35 nations for the frequency of suicide by having them read the suicide entries in the HRAF, and his ratings are shown in Table 4.[8] From this group of cultures, it would appear that, among Native American groups, the Kwakiutl have a relatively high suicide rate and the Pomo a relatively low suicide rate. In a research study on this sample, Masumura found that the estimated suicide rate was *positively* associated with a measure of social integration in opposition to a prediction from Durkheim's (1897) classic sociological theory of suicide.

Ember and Ember (1992) drew attention to the fact that the materials on suicides in the HRAF come from very different time periods. Therefore, they urged that it was important to specify the year from which the data were derived. For example, they rated the Creek suicide rate as 1.74 (on a scale of 0–8) *in 1800* and the Omaha as 1 *in 1860*.

Case Studies

On occasions, anthropologists who have studied particular cultures write specifically on suicide. For example, Bohannan (1967) edited a book on suicide in Africa in which the contributors looked at suicidal behavior in several tribes from Uganda and Kenya. Bohannan noted first that earlier investigators had differed greatly in whether they thought that suicide in primitive societies was rare (Cavan, 1928) or common (Steinmetz, 1894). It is more reasonable to conclude that the range for the incidence of suicide in primitive societies may be as great as in modern societies (Westermarck, 1908). Not only may the rate of suicide vary from one primitive society to another, but these differences may be stable even after emigration, forced as a result of slavery or freely chosen. For example, Bastide (1952) noted that Mina, Dahomeans, and Yoruba slaves in Brazil tended more often to assault and kill their slave owners, whereas Fulani slaves and those from Gabon and Mozambique tended more often to kill themselves.

As an anthropologist, Bohannan was not so much interested in the individual motives that people had for killing themselves in a society (he viewed what was in the mind of the suicide as unknowable), but rather he was interested in the causes ascribed to the suicide by members of the society. These popular ideas about suicide tell us something about the culture.

---

[8] Each judge rated the suicide rate of each society on a scale of 0–4, and their ratings were summed.

Table 4. Estimates of relative suicide rates for 35 nonliterate societies by Masumura (1977)

Group	Suicide score (range 2–8)
Ainu	6
Andamanese	2
Araucanians	5
Ashanti	6
Bakongo	6
Banks Islanders	7
Bushmen	6
Chippewa	7
Chukchee	8
Creek	6
Crow	6
Dahomeans	6
Fang	6
Hottentot	6
Iban	7
Iroquois	5
Jivaro	7
Kazak	6
Kutenai	4
Kwakiut	8
Lango	8
Maori	8
Navajo	2
Norsemen	5
Omaha	4
Pomo	2
Rwala	7
Samoan	8
Sema Naga	6
Semang	2
Toda	6
Trobrianders	8
Tuareg	4
Vedda	4
Yahgan	2

For example, Fallers and Fallers (1967) examined suicide among the Busoga of southeastern Uganda. The Busoga view suicide as an irresponsible and foolish act, probably impulsive. Thus, suicide, like homicide, is an act which must be punished. The body of a suicide used to be burnt, along with the tree from which the person hung himself, and buried in waste land or at a crossroads. For the period from 1952 to 1954, the official suicide rate for the society was 7.0 per 100,000 per year, which the Fallers thought was a slight underestimate.

Taking one hundred cases of suicide, the Fallers found that 86 percent hung themselves, in most cases impulsively. Sixty-nine percent were men. The most common motive was disease (31%) followed by quarrels with spouse, lover, or kinsman (23%). Quarrels with a spouse were present in 48% of the homicides and 21% of the suicides, suggesting that marriage was full of conflict. The patrilineal nature of the society meant that spouses had divided loyalties. The wife, in particular, felt drawn back to her family, and wives who felt oppressed by their husbands (which was not uncommon) often fled back to their father. The Fallers noted that the breaking down of the cultural traditions had decreased the incidence of suicide and homicide, probably as a result of the weakening of intergenerational family ties, which in turn reduced marital conflicts.

In commenting on this and other reports, Bohannan (1967) noted that domestic institutions were responsible for the greatest number of the suicides. Women killed themselves as wives – they were unable to play the role of wife or mother because of conflict with husbands or fathers, co-wives, or fate. Men, to a lesser extent, killed themselves as husbands, but impotence and loss of status played roles too. Suicide was consistently viewed as irresponsible and evil, and rituals involved destruction of the suicide's possessions and ritual cleaning. Bohannan felt that the suicide rates were moderate to low, though accurate estimates were mostly absent.

It should be noted that historical studies of indigenous peoples may become more important as indigenous peoples cross-marry with the dominant cultures. For example, at the present time in New Zealand, there are no "pure" Maoris. All surviving Maoris have at least one White ancestor.

Theories of Suicide

There has been one theory of suicide, proposed by Naroll (1962, 1963, 1969), which was based on a study of these nonliterate societies and tested using data from the societies rather than data from modern nations, the basis for Durkheim's (1897) theory of suicide. Naroll proposed that suicide occurred in those who were *socially disoriented*, rather than in those who lack or lose basic social ties. But since all of those who are in this condition do not commit suicide, there must also be a psychological factor involved, that is, the individual's reaction to *thwarting disorientation contexts*. Thwarting disorientation contexts are those in which the individual's social ties are broken or weakened and those in which another person thwarts the individual and prevents him or her from achieving desired and expected satisfactions or in which they experience frustration. This thwarting must be interpersonal and not impersonal. Storm damage to one's dwelling is not thwarting but, when another person sets fire to it and destroys it, it is thwarting. The widow is not thwarted, but the divorced spouse is thwarted. Under the conditions of thwarting disorientation, individuals are more prone to suicide in such a way that it comes to public notice, that is, *protest suicide*. Naroll felt that this theory, better than other theories, explained suicide in indigenous peoples.[9]

Jeffreys (1952) felt that Durkheim's (1897) categories of suicide, based on the concepts of social integration and social regulation, were not sufficient to explain cases of suicide he found in African tribes. He described suicide in order to revenge oneself on those one is angry at – a type of suicide he called "Samsonic suicide" after the story of Samson in *The Bible*. Revenge can be obtained in two ways. In some societies, the belief is that one's ghost can return and harm those at whom one is angry, as among the Herero of South West Africa (Vedder, 1928). Alternatively, the societal laws demand that those who provoked a suicide must pay some penalty, usually a fine and, in some societies, death. The payment of a heavy fine by the person who provoked a suicide is customary, for example, among the Bavenda (Stayt, 1931) and the Kassena (Cardinall, 1920).

Lester (1997b) noted that the Mohave have a clearly specified theory of suicide – namely that suicide in their people is increasingly due to a breakdown in ties to the community and tribe as a whole and to an increasing dependence on a primary relationship with a lover or spouse. Lester tested this hypothesis that suicide would be common in nations with higher levels of individualism, and the results confirmed this hypothesis.

It can be seen that examples of suicide behaviors, customs, and attitudes in indigenous peoples can challenge traditional Western theories of suicide.

Comment

There has been a failure of suicidologists to study suicidal behavior in many indigenous peoples. On occasions they ignore indigenous peoples completely, such as the Welsh and Cornish peoples in the UK or the Basques in France and Spain. On other occasions, as in Africa, they study suicide in the artificially-created nations (created by the colonial rulers) rather than in the more meaningful ethnic groups.

---

[9]   Lester (1995c) has compared and contrasted Naroll's theory with those of Durkheim (1897) and Henry and Short (1954).

Occasionally, when suicide is studied in these nations, the investigators omit to
mention the ethnic background of the people (e.g., Sefa-Dedeh & Canetto, 1992).

Second, this section has drawn attention to the Human Relations Area Files
(HRAF) with its rich source of data on indigenous peoples, including suicide.
Data from the HRAF were used to illustrate how suicide rates can be estimated
and how the data can be used to test theories of suicide.

Finally, examples were given of theories of suicide which derive from studies
of suicide in indigenous peoples rather than from studies of suicide in Western
nations.

Psychotherapeutic Implications

All of this scholarly discourse is important at the theoretical level, but it may be
asked whether there are implications for counseling and psychotherapy. It is sometimes argued that only "like" can counsel "like," that is, that only homosexuals
can counsel homosexuals, women counsel women, ex-addicts counsel addicts,
and so on. Is the same true also for different cultures? The majority of counselors
and psychotherapists deny this, claiming that a good counselor or psychotherapist
can counsel any kind of patient. However, to counsel someone very different in
background from oneself may require that the counselor learn about the background and culture from which the individual comes. Sue and Sue (1990)
addressed the issues that psychotherapists of one culture must confront when
counseling clients from different cultures, such as racism and cultural differences
in verbal and nonverbal communication styles.

Zimmerman and Zayas (1995) illustrated this point in their discussion of treating the suicidal adolescent Hispanic female. They noted that, in New York City,
the values of the adolescent Latina often clash with those of her more traditional
mother. Both mother and daughter experience problems in communication and a
rupture in their relationship. Thus, the problem of acculturation exacerbates the
normal adolescent turmoil. The Latina's mother wants her daughter to succeed
in this new culture, yet she also wants her daughter to maintain traditional cultural
attitudes and roles. The adolescent Latina feels overwhelmed by this conflict and,
in extreme cases, makes a suicide attempt in an effort to reduce the tension felt in
this conflict. After a suicide attempt, the psychotherapist must explain the conflict
to the mother and daughter and help them find ways to re-establish mutual understanding and empathy.

It is possible, of course, that psychotherapists could identify the nature of the
problems confronting suicidal people and their families each time they encounter

such a family, but the psychotherapeutic process is facilitated if psychotherapists have some notion of the cultural issues that they are likely to encounter.

Sue and Sue (1990) presented the case of Janet, a Chinese-American female college senior majoring in sociology, who came to the college counseling center complaining of depression, feelings of worthlessness, and suicidal thoughts. She had difficulty identifying the causes of her depression, but she seemed quite hostile to the psychotherapist who was also Chinese-American. Discussion of this revealed that Janet resented being seen by a Chinese psychotherapist, feeling that she had been assigned to one because of her own race. Janet disliked everything Chinese, including Chinese men whom she found sexually unattractive. She dated only White men, which had upset her parents. However, her last romance had broken up partly because her boyfriend's parents objected to him dating a Chinese woman. Janet clearly had difficulties stemming from her continuing denial of her Chinese heritage. She was being forced to realize that she was Chinese since she was not fully accepted by White America. Initially she blamed the Chinese for her dilemma, but then she turned her hostility toward herself. Feeling alienated from her own culture and rejected by the White culture, she was experiencing an identity crisis with a resulting depression.

The psychotherapist in such a case must deal with cultural racism and its effects on minorities. Positive acculturation must be distinguished from rejection of one's own cultural values, as well as typical adolescent rebellion from one's parents. Psychotherapists can work with such a client more effectively if they are conversant with the cultural history and experiences of Asian-Americans.

Does Cultural Conflict Cause Suicide?

Although the problem of acculturation has been proposed as one of the major causes of depression and suicidal behavior among Native Americans, the majority of research reports on Native American individuals who attempt or complete suicide mention precipitating causes such as grief over loss and quarrels with relatives and friends. Rarely is cultural conflict listed among the precipitating causes. Of course, it may be that the problems of acculturation raise the stress level of individuals so much that stressors, which under ordinary circumstances would not precipitate suicide, now do so.

A few brief case histories have been published that illustrate the problems of acculturation and culture conflict. For example, Berlin (1986) described the case of a bright young Native American woman who completed undergraduate school and qualified as a teacher and who was admitted to graduate school. Her clan, however, told her that she was required to teach on the reservation. Her desire to go to graduate school was seen as striving to be better than her peers, and this was unacceptable and forbidden. The young woman had a psychiatric breakdown and was hospitalized. In a similar situation, the tribe and another family could not decide whether to let a young woman go to graduate school for an MBA after she obtained her undergraduate degree and, during the long wait for a decision, she attempted suicide.

In this latter case, the young woman, whom Berlin called Josie, had alcoholic parents who frequently sent her and her brothers and sisters to live with relatives while they went on drinking sprees. A teacher realized Josie's potential and received permission for Josie to live with her. With this teacher's help, her academic performance improved, and she went to college. Josie now resented that her parents, who had neglected her, were involved in decisions about her life. The clan leadership and tribal council were relatively enlightened about the issues and eventually gave permission for Josie to attend graduate school. While at graduate school, Josie underwent psychotherapy to deal with her depression and anger and other personal problems. After graduation, she returned to the tribe to manage their business office, marrying a young man who had fought a similar battle in order to obtain an MSW degree.

Westermeyer (1979) provided cases of Native Americans seen at the University of Minnesota Hospitals for whom trying to live in the mainstream American culture had presented problems. Westermeyer felt that identity problems were perhaps no more common in Native Americans than in Whites, but that Native Americans did show a unique type of identity problem, namely, ambivalent or negative feelings about their ethnic identity. Westermeyer presented cases of urban Native Americans who illustrate this problem.

Five of the patients, ranging in age from 12 to 23, had identity crises – they experienced conflict about their Native American identity and about what being "Indian" meant. All were students and economically dependent upon others. For example, one young girl, who was seen after a suicide attempt, had her Indian mother die two years earlier. She then lived with her White father and six siblings for a year. The father had trouble supporting them and sent the children to live with their Indian maternal grandmother. The patient began to use drugs and had problems with her White teachers at school. Eventually a White welfare worker sent her to a White foster home, at which point she attempted suicide. In the hospital, she said, "I'm the only Indian here and I hate everybody like they hate me." She had a recurrent dream in which she gave birth to baby girl with blue eyes who she loved but who she also wanted to injure.

Five of the cases were judged to have a negative identity. These were older than the patients with identity crises, and all were males. They were estranged from their Indian family members, and they lived as lower class individuals on the periphery of the White society. One patient was admitted with hallucinations and paranoid delusions after a drinking binge. He had a record of multiple psychiatric admissions. Although he supported the idea of Indian activism, he felt estranged from Indians, had little respect for them and avoided them. He had joined a Jewish student activist group that he admired, and he wondered whether his Indian tribe might be a lost tribe of Israel. He identified himself as a Zionist.

Conclusions

There are large cultural differences in the incidence of suicidal behavior, and culture also influences the methods used for suicide and the reasons for doing so. Although these cultural differences may be a result of physiological differences between the members of the different cultures, the more plausible explanations involve psychological and social variables, such as the abuse of alcohol and the level of social integration and regulation. When competing cultures interact, there may be increased stress (and, as a result, an increase in suicidality) in the less dominant culture.

It should be noted also that, in societies that are culturally heterogeneous, such as the US, Canada, and Australia, it cannot be assumed that suicides from the different cultural groups are similar in rate, method, motive, and precipitating factors. Those working to prevent suicide in such societies must take these cultural influences into account (Sue & Sue, 1990; Zimmerman & Zayas, 1993).

This chapter has attempted to raise and briefly discuss several of the issues involved in the interaction of culture and suicide. These issues should not be viewed as problems, but rather as opportunities to plan and execute innovative and exciting research and to work more effectively with suicidal clients from diverse cultures.

References

Adrian, M. (1984). International trends in alcohol production, trade and consumption, and their relationship to alcohol-related problems, 1970 to 1977. *Journal of Public Health Policy, 5,* 344–367.

Anon. (2004). A political awakening. *The Economist, 370*(8363), 35–37.

Bagley, C. (1991). Poverty and suicide among native Canadians. *Psychological Reports, 69,* 149–150.

Bastide, R. (1952). Le suicide du nègre brésilien [Suicide in Braslian Blacks]. *Cahiers Internationaux de Sociologie, 7*(12), 79–90.

Berlin, I. N. (1986). Psychopathology and its antecedents among American Indian adolescents. *Advances in Clinical Child Psychology, 9,* 125–152.

Berry, J. W. (1990). Acculturation and adaptation. *Arctic Medical Research, 49,* 142–150.

Bohannan, P. (Ed.) (1967). *African homicide and suicide.* New York: Atheneum.

Burvill, P., McCall, M., Woodings, T., & Stenhouse, N. (1983). Comparison of suicide rates and methods in English, Scots and Irish immigrants in Australia. *Social Science & Medicine, 17,* 705–708.

Cardinall, A. W. (1920). *Natives of the northern territories of the Gold Coast.* London: G. Routledge & Sons.

Cavan, R. S. (1928). *Suicide.* Chicago: University of Chicago.

Cheng, A. T. A. (1995). Mental illness and suicide. *Archives of General Psychiatry, 52,* 594–603.

Cheng, A. T. A. (1997). Personality disorder and suicide. *British Journal of Psychiatry, 170,* 441–446.

Chiles, J. A., Strosahl, K., Ping, Z. Y., Clark, M., Hall, K., Jemelka, R., Senn, B., & Reto, C. (1989). Depression, hopelessness and suicidal behavior in Chinese and American psychiatric patients. *American Journal of Psychiatry, 146,* 339–344.

Clarke, R. V., & Lester, D. (1989). *Suicide: Closing the exits.* New York: Springer-Verlag.

Conklin, G. H., & Simpson, M. E. (1987). The family, socioeconomic development and suicide. *Journal of Comparative Family Studies, 18,* 99–111.

Counts, D. A. (1980). Fighting back is not the way: Suicide and the women on Kaliai. *American Ethnologist, 7,* 332–351.

Counts, D. A. (1988). Ambiguity in the interpretation of suicide. In D. Lester (Ed.), *Why women kill themselves,* pp. 87–109. Springfield, IL: Charles Thomas.

D'Azevedo, W. L., Freed, S. A., Freed, R. S., Leis, P. E., Scotch, N. A., Scotch, F. L., Price, J. A., & Downs, J. F. (1963). *The Washo Indians of California and Nevada.* Salt Lake City, UT: University of Utah.

De Man, A. F., Balkou, S., & Iglesias, R. I. (1987). A French-Canadian adaptation of the scale for suicide ideation. *Canadian Journal of Behavioural Science, 19,* 50–55.

DeCatanzaro, D. (1981). *Suicide and self-damaging behavior.* New York: Academic Press.

Devereux, G. (1961). *Mohave ethnopsychiatry.* Washington, DC: Smithsonian Institution.

Douglas, J. D. (1967). *The social meanings of suicide.* Princeton, NJ: Princeton University.

Dublin, L. I. (1963). *Suicide.* New York: Ronald.

Durkheim, E. (1897). *Le suicide* [Suicide]. Paris: Felix Alcan.

Early, K. E. (1992). *Religion and suicide in the African-American community.* Westport, CT: Greenwood.

Early, K. E., & Akers, R. L. (1993). "It's a white thing": An exploration about beliefs about suicide in the African-American community. *Deviant Behavior, 14,* 277–296.

Ember, C. R., & Ember, R. (1992). Warfare, aggression, and resource problems. *Behavior Science Research, 26,* 169–226.

Fallers, L. A., & Fallers, M. C. (1967). Homicide and suicide in Busoga. In P. Bohannan (Ed.), *African homicide and suicide,* pp. 65–93. New York: Atheneum.

Gastil, R. (1971). Homicide and a regional culture of violence. *American Sociological Review, 36,* 412–427.

Gibbs, J. (1988). Conceptual, methodological, and sociocultural issues in black youth suicide. *Suicide and Life-Threatening Behavior, 18,* 73–89.

Girard, C. (1993). Age, gender, and suicide. *American Sociological Review, 58*, 553–574.

Hendin, H. (1964). *Suicide and Scandinavia*. New York: Grune & Stratton.

Henry, A. F., & Short, J. F. (1954). *Suicide and homicide*. New York: Free Press.

Hlady, W. G., & Middaugh, J. P. (1988). The underrecording of suicide in state and national records, Alaska, 1983–1984. *Suicide and Life-Threatening Behavior, 18*, 237–244.

Honigmann, J. J. (1949). *Culture and ethos of Kaska society*. New Haven, CT: Yale University Press.

Jeffreys, M. D. W. (1952). Samsonic suicide or suicide of revenge among Africans. *African Studies, 11*(3), 118–122.

Johnson, B. D. (1965). Durkheim's one cause of suicide. *American Sociological Review, 30*, 875–886.

Killias, M., van Kesteren, J., & Rindlisbacher, M. (2001). Guns, violent crime, and suicide in 21 countries. *Canadian Journal of Criminology, 43*, 429–448.

Kreitman, N. (1976). The coal gas story. *British Journal Preventive & Social Medicine, 30*, 86–93.

Lee, C. S., Chang, J. C., & Cheng, A. T. A. (2002). Acculturation and suicide. *Psychological Medicine, 32*, 133–141.

Lester, D. (1972). Migration and suicide. *Medical Journal of Australia, 1*, 941–942.

Lester, D. (1985). Variation in suicide and homicide rates by latitude and longitude in the US, Canada and Australia. *American Journal of Psychiatry, 142*, 523–524.

Lester, D. (1987). National distribution of blood groups, personal violence (suicide and homicide), and national character. *Personality & Individual Differences, 8*, 575–576.

Lester, D. (1994a). The epidemiology of suicide in Chinese populations in six regions of the world. *Chinese Journal of Mental Health, 7*, 21–24.

Lester, D. (1994b). Differences in the epidemiology of suicide in Asian Americans by nation of origin. *Omega, 29*, 89–93.

Lester, D. (1994c). Suicide by jumping in Singapore as a function of high-rise apartment availability. *Perceptual and Motor Skills, 79*, 74.

Lester, D. (1994d). Predicting the suicide rate in Wales. *Psychological Reports, 75*, 1054.

Lester, D. (1995a). Explaining the regional variation of suicide and homicide. *Archives of Suicide Research, 1*, 159–174.

Lester, D. (1995b). Effects of the detoxification of domestic on suicide rates in six nations. *Psychological Reports, 77*, 294.

Lester, D. (1995c). Thwarting disorientation and suicide. *Cross-Cultural Research, 29*, 14–26.

Lester, D. (1996). *Patterns of suicide and homicide in the world*. Commack, NY: Nova Science.

Lester, D. (1997a). *Suicide in American Indians*. Commack, NY: Nova Science.

Lester, D. (1997b). Note on a Mohave theory of suicide. *Cross-Cultural Research, 31*, 268–272.

Lester, D. (1998). *Suicide in African Americans*. Commack, New York: Nova Science.

Lester, D. (2004). *Thinking about suicide*. Hauppauge, NY: Nova Science.

Lester, D. (2005). Predicting suicide in nations. *Archives of Suicide Research, 9*, 219–223.

Lester, D. (2008). Suicide and culture. *World Cultural Psychiatry Research Review, 3*(2), 51–68.

Lester, D. (2009). *Preventing suicide: Closing the Exits revisited*. Commack, NY: Nova Science.

Lester, D., Castromayor, I. J., & Icli, T. (1991). Locus of control, depression, and suicidal ideation among American, Philippine, and Turkish students. *Journal of Social Psychology, 131*, 447–449.

Lester, D., & Wilson, C. (1988). Suicide in Zimbabwe. *Central African Journal of Medicine, 34*, 147–149.

Lester, D., & Yang, B. (1991). The relationship between divorce, unemployment and female participation in the labour force and suicide rates in Australia and America. *Australian & New Zealand Journal of Psychiatry, 25*, 519–513.

Linehan, M. (1973). Suicide and attempted suicide. *Perceptual and Motor Skills, 37*, 31–34.

Malla, A., & Hoenig, J. (1983). Differences in suicide rates. *Canadian Journal of Psychiatry, 28*, 291–293.

Marks, A., & Stokes, C. S. (1976). Socialization, firearms and suicide. *Social Problems, 23*, 622–629.

Masumura, W. T. (1977). Social integration and suicide. *Behavior Science Research, 12*, 251–269.

May, P. A., & Dizmang, L. H. (1974). Suicide and the American Indian. *Psychiatric Annals, 4*(11), 22–28.

Menninger, K. (1938). *Man against himself.* New York: Harcourt, Brace & World.

Menozzi, P., Piazza, A., & Cavalli-Sforza, L. (1978). Synthetic maps of human gene frequencies in Europeans. *Science, 201*, 786–792.

Moksony, F. (1990). Ecological analysis of suicide. In D. Lester (Ed.), *Current concepts of suicide*, pp. 121–138. Philadelphia, PA: Charles Press.

Naroll, R. (1962). *Data quality control.* New York: Free Press.

Naroll, R. (1963). *Thwarting disorientation and suicide.* Unpublished discussion paper, Northwestern University;Evanston, IL.

Naroll, R. (1969). Cultural determinants and the concept of the sick society. In S. C. Plog & R. B. Edgerton (Eds.), *Changing perspectives in mental illness*, pp. 128–155. New York: Holt, Rinehart & Winston.

Phillips, M. R., Liu, H., & Zhang, Y. (1999). Suicide and social change in China. *Culture, Medicine & Psychiatry, 23*, 25–50.

Platt, S. D. (1985). A subculture of parasuicide? *Human Relations, 38*, 257–297.

Ramon, S. (1980). Attitudes of doctors and nurses to self-poisoning patients. *Social Science & Medicine, 14A*, 317–324.

Rittey, D. A. W., & Castle, W. M. (1972). Suicides in Rhodesia. *Central African Journal of Medicine, 18*, 97–100.

Rubinstein, D. H. (1992). Suicide in Micronesia and Samoa. *Pacific Studies, 15*, 51–75.

Sainsbury, P., & Barraclough, B. M. (1968). Differences in suicide rates. *Nature, 220*, 1252.

Sefa-Dedeh, A., & Canetto, S. S. (1992). Women, family and suicidal behavior in Ghana. In V. P. Gielen, L. L. Adler, & N. A. Milgram (Eds.), *Psychology in international perspective*, pp. 299–309. Amsterdam, The Netherlands: Swets & Zeitlinger.

Stack, S. (1983). The effect of religious commitment on suicide. *Journal of Health & Social Behavior, 24*, 362–374.

Stack, S. (1992). The effect of divorce of suicide in Japan. *Journal of Marriage & the Family, 54*, 327–334.

Stayt, H. A. (1931). *The Bavenda.* Oxford, UK: Oxford University Press.

Steinmetz, S. R. (1894). Suicide among primitive peoples. *American Anthropologist, 7*, 53–60.

Sue, D. W., & Sue, D. (1990). *Counseling the culturally different.* New York: Wiley.

Tatarelli, R., Pompili, M., & Girardi, P. (Eds.). (2007). *Suicide in psychiatric disorders.* Commack, NY: Nova Science.

Taylor, S. (1990). Suicide, Durkheim, and sociology. In D. Lester (Ed.), *Current concepts of suicide*, pp. 225–236. Philadelphia, PA: Charles Press.

Van Winkle, N. W., & May, P. A. (1986). Native American suicide in New Mexico, 1959–1979. *Human Organization, 45*, 296–309.

Vedder, H. (1928). The Herero. In C. H. L. Hahn (Ed.), *The native tribes of South West Africa*, pp. 153–211. Cape Town, South Africa: Cape Times.

Voracek, M., & Loible, L. M. (2008). Consistency of immigrant and country-of-birth suicide rates. *Acta Psychiatrica Scandinavica, 118*, 259–271.

Weissman, M. M., & Klerman, G. L. (1977). Sex differences and the epidemiology of depression. *Archives of General Psychiatry, 34*, 98–111.

Westermarck, E. (1908). Suicide. *Sociological Review, 1*, 12–33.

Westermeyer, J. (1979). Ethnic identity problems among ten Indian psychiatric patients. *International Journal of Social Psychiatry, 25*, 188–197.

Wolfgang, M. E. (1957). Victim-precipitated criminal homicide. *Journal of Criminal Law, Criminology & Police Science, 48*, 1–11.

Wolfgang, M. E., & Ferracuti, F. (1967). *The subculture of violence*. London, UK: Tavistock.

Zimmerman, J. K., & Zayas, L. (1995). Suicidal adolescent latinas. In S. Canetto & D. Lester (Ed.), *Women and suicide*, pp. 120–132. New York: Springer.

Research on Culture and Suicide

Cultural Meaning(s) of Suicide: A Cross-Cultural Study[1]

Erminia Colucci

No one who kills himself does so without reference to the prevailing normative standards, values and attitudes of the culture to which he belongs (Boldt, 1988)

Overall, the suicide rates of nations tend to be stable over time and very different from one another, and these differences are maintained when people migrate to a new country (Voracek & Loibl, 2008). These observations raise the question of what impact culture and ethnicity have on people's suicidal behavior. While we have considerable knowledge about the prevalence of suicidal behavior and about risk factors (such as depression, anxiety, drug and alcohol dependence, and physical and sexual abuse), we still have little understanding of cultural influences on suicide. For instance, Eskin (1999, p. 188) noted that, "although the prevalence of youthful suicidal mortality varies widely, suicidological investigations have often failed to adopt a cross-cultural perspective ... Further cross-cultural work is needed to unpack the effects of culture on a seemingly very personal act like suicide."

This is particularly true for youth suicide (Tomori, Kienhorst, de Wilde, & van den Bout, 2001). Colucci and Martin (2007a, 2007b) reviewed 82 cross-cultural studies on youth suicide and noted the lack of both quantitative and qualitative cross-cultural studies. Most of the research had been conducted in the US, mainly addressing differences between Blacks, Whites and Hispanics, and few studies had explored ethnicity in depth. In almost all the research, race and ethnicity were

[1] This research is part of the doctoral dissertation: Colucci, E. (2008b). *The cultural meaning of suicide: A comparison between Italian, Indian and Australian students.* The University of Queensland, Brisbane. I would like to acknowledge Harry Minas, Anthony Marsella, Robert Schweitzer, and Graham Martin for the supervision provided in this project. Project funded by Australian IPRS, UQ Travel Award and Zonta Memorial Prize.

just two of many demographic variables analyzed and not the central focus of the study. A major limitation of the research was the categorization of people into one "racial" group, ignoring the fact that one race (e.g., Asians) may actually include many diverse ethnic groups (such as Chinese, Indians, and Vietnamese), and there was also a neglect of subcultures. Some studies found ethnicity not to be related to suicide risk (e.g., Garrison, Jackson, Addy, McKeown, & Waller, 1991), while others found it to be important (e.g., Tortolero & Roberts, 2001). Thus, more studies are needed to clarify the impact of culture on suicide, as argued also by Borowsky, Ireland, and Resnick (2001, p. 485) who stated, "A better understanding of factors that predict and protect against suicidal behaviors among racial/ethnic groups of adolescents is needed to identify modifiable factors and develop culturally responsive prevention and intervention strategies."

The Neglected Area of Cultural Meanings of Suicide

As discussed in the present book, relatively few studies in suicidology have addressed culture or ethnicity as an important dimension impacting upon the decision to kill oneself. In particular, we have little understanding of the variation of a key aspect of suicide that differs across cultures, namely the *meaning* of suicide. Culture provides the context in which people interpret and negotiate the meaning and the (perceived) meaninglessness of their lives. Thus, as argued in earlier chapters, the study of the cultural meanings of suicide is necessary if we want to fully understand suicidal behavior and, through this, develop culturally adequate and relevant suicide prevention strategies.

The cultural meaning of suicide is a heterogeneous construct (shared and contested) of which people are not necessarily aware. Almost half a century ago, Douglas (1967) recognized this. "The meaning of suicide is by no means unidimensional, universally agreed upon, or unchanging among the various societies of Europe – and certainly not beyond the cultural boundaries of Europe" (p. 178).

The present chapter reports a study of the meanings of suicide among university students, 18–24 years old, in three different countries (Italy, India, and Australia), using a combination of qualitative and quantitative methods.

While suicide has been looked at in Italian, Indian, and Australian cultures (e.g., De Leo & Meneghel, 2001; Farber, 1975; Martin, 1996; Venkoba Rao, 1975), the topic of cultural meanings and social representations in these cultures and between these cultures remains largely unexplored. Although samples are often chosen on the basis of convenience (in the present case, I am Italian, I love Australia, and I am fascinated by Indian culture), the samples for the present study were also selected on the basis of theoretical concerns. The first strategy for the selection was what Berry, Poortinga, Marshall, and Dasen (2002) called a "theory-guided selection": "Cultures should be selected which differ on the postulated independent variable that is the focus of research" (p. 299). With youth suicide being the topic of this project, the first interesting point of comparison is that, historically, Australia, India, and Italy have different rates of youth suicide: quite high in Australian young men, high in young Indians, especially young women in some regions, and low in young Italian men and women (Joseph et al., 2003; Meneghel et al., 2004; WHO, 2012;). Secondly, these countries show some similarities and differences on important sociocultural dimensions.

One simple categorization of cultures is between "Western" and "Eastern" cultures. Laungani (2001) reported the main differences between these two (over-arching) cultures and, in his discussion, focused on the English and Indian cultures. The main differences identified by him were as follows:

Western Cultures	Eastern Cultures
Individualism (emphasis on high degree of self-control, personal responsibility and self-achievement)	*Communalism* (dependence on elders or other family members, emphasis on collective responsibility and achievement)
Cognitivism (emphasis on rationality and logic, on work and activity, feelings and emotions kept in check)	*Emotionalism* (emphasis on feelings and intuition, on relationships; feelings and emotion expressed freely)
Free will (emphasis on freedom of choice, proactive, self-blame as a consequence of failure)	*Determinism* (limited freedom of choice, reactive, no guilt attached to failure because success or failure related to one's karma)
Materialism (the world is real, physical; rejection of contradictory explanations of phenomena; reality is external to the individual)	*Spiritualism* (the world is illusory, co-existence of contradictory explanations, reality is internal to the individual)

Certainly, this is a general description and does not describe all Western and Eastern societies. For example, Laungani (2001), writing about cognitivism-emotionalism, noted that some Western societies such as Italy allow more psychological space for the expression of emotions in the context of familial and friendship bonds. Furthermore, Eckersley and Dear (2002), describing some qualities that are thought to characterize Western culture, made the point that cultures are not monolithic and do not exert a uniform effect on everyone. Individuals are not cultural sponges, passively absorbing cultural influences, but rather they interact actively with them. Despite these caveats, the broad categorization of Western and Eastern is historically important and constitutes a first "lens" through which to read the data emerging from anthropological works.

Some researchers have offered other dimensions to distinguish Western and Eastern societies. Barrett (2001), referring specifically to Hindu culture, observed that the anthropological literature shows that small-scale agrarian communities, as well as large-scale civilizations that are based on the Hindu concept of reincarnation, are pervaded by a cyclical notion of time. In contrast, modern Western societies are characterized by a "straight line" concept of time.

Another concept central to the differentiation between cultures is that of the self. For example, Shweder and Bourne (1982) identified two different concepts of person: egocentric and sociocentric. The egocentric concept refers to people who are individualistic, with an identity that emphasizes a uniqueness derived from their distinct biographies. This is present in Western cultures, and the authors traced its origins back to ancient Greece. The sociocentric concept is of a person embedded in context, whose identity derives from his/her social affiliations (with caste, clan, kin group, or family). The sociocentric person is defined in terms of membership of the social group to which he/she belongs. This is found in small-scale societies and large-scale non-Western cultural traditions such as in India.

Based on what has been presented so far, some basic variables distinguishing the three cultures that form the focus of the present study can be summarized as follows:

ITALY	INDIA	AUSTRALIA
Suicide an elderly problem	Suicide mostly a youth problem (in some instances, more females)	Suicide a youth problem (especially males)
Religious (mainly Catholic)	Religious (mainly Hindu, Islam, Christian)	Less strongly religious, many agnostics/atheists
Collectivism	Collectivism	Individualism
Education toward independence and interdependence	Education toward interdependence	Education toward independence
Part of Ancient World	Part of Ancient World	Part of the New World
Modern and traditional society	Traditional society, often in conflict with modernization	Modern society

On the basis of these differences the following "hypotheses" were developed:

(1) There will be commonalities and differences across countries and within countries on the meanings, opinions, and beliefs about youth suicide among Italian, Indian, and Australian students;

(2) There will be differences in the attitudes toward suicide especially in the beliefs about the causes of youth suicidal behavior, with Indian students endorsing more negative attitudes (as suggested by studies reviewed in Colucci and Martin, 2007a, 2007b);

(3) Indian and Italian students, belonging to more collectivistic societies, will refer more often to the role of family when talking about suicide;

(4) Indian and Italian students will be more influenced by and will attribute more importance to religion and religious beliefs;

(5) Australian students will have more knowledge on the topic (because of the presence of an active national suicide prevention program, including education on suicide).

This research, driven by a phenomenological and constructivist approach, aimed to elicit constructs and meanings about suicide among young people from these three backgrounds (Italian, Indian, and Australian). In particular, I explored the similarities and differences in students' suicide explanatory models, spiritual beliefs regarding suicide, attitudes towards youth suicide, and opinions on deterrent and protective factors, help-seeking behavior, and youth suicide prevention. In this project, I also investigated feelings towards death, the cultural meanings of the words *suicide* and *suicide attempt*, and the mental representations and stereotypes of suicidal youth (considering also gender issues).

The following section describes the epistemology (phenomenology) and theoretical models (personal and social constructivism and symbolic interactionism) that informed and framed this explorative process.

Methodology

There are many approaches to categorizing scientific knowledge, and a common dichotomy is that between positivism and phenomenology (Taylor & Bogdan, 1984). *Positivism* is mainly focused on research for facts and causes. Positivism leads researchers to utilize methods allowing for the quantification of observations using replicable procedures in order to find the rules, patterns, and causal relationships of social life and human behavior (Ambert et al., 1995). It assumes there is an orderly, material world that is independent of the observed (McGrath &

Johnson, 2003). Positivism has dominated scientific inquiry. However, an alternative conception of knowledge (and method) has challenged the traditional view of what research entails, namely phenomenology. Taylor and Bodgan (1984) noted that the phenomenologist is committed to understanding phenomena from the subject's own perspective. *Phenomenology* looks at the subject as the starting point, the central point of inquiry. Reality is what people perceive. In the phenomenological framework, several different schools of thought have developed (Hein & Austin, 2001), two of which are symbolic interactionism and constructivism (personal and social).

Symbolic interactionism focuses on the social meanings people attach to the world around them. Blumer (1969) stated that symbolic interactionism rests on three basic premises:

(1) People do not simply respond to stimuli or follow cultural scripts. People attach meanings to things, and these meanings determine the way they relate to them and act.

(2) Meanings are social products that arise during interaction. People's worldviews are not independent from other people's worldviews. People learn from other people how to see the world.

(3) Social actors attach meanings to situations, settings, things, others, and themselves through a process of interpretation; that is, people individually, on the basis of a specific situation and their own experience, select, check, interpret, suspend, reconstruct, and transform meanings.

This active role of individuals in constructing meanings and understandings is one of the key points of *Constructivism*. As Schwandt (2000, p. 197) stated, "We are all constructivist if we believe that the mind is active in the construction of the knowledge." In this sense, constructivism means that human beings do not "find" or "discover" knowledge, but "construct" it. People formulate concepts, models, schemes, and theories to make sense of their experiences, and these constructions are ceaselessly tested and modified in the light of new experiences ("constructive alternativism"). Kelly (1955) presented this view of the human being as a scientist in his personal construct theory, arguing that people attempt to understand, predict, anticipate and control events and, as scientists, formulate hypotheses that are successively tested against reality. In this process, people differ from each other, and the construction of events is idiosyncratic.

While Kelly emphasized the individual process of constructing reality, other authors argued that people do not construct interpretations in isolation but refer to a background of shared understandings, from which comes social constructionism, as illustrated in Carr, Marsella, and Purcell (2002). This conceptualization applies to the research process itself as well. As Koch (1999, p. 25) underlined, "A constructivist epistemology asserts that the inquirer and the subject of inquiry are interlocked in such a way that the findings of an investigation are the literal creation of the inquiry process." A key point of constructivism is the holistic approach. A complete understanding depends on the investigation of connections and interactions between various aspects of the system and not on an analysis of isolated elements. Central to a constructivist view is the possibility of alternative explanations and the idea that different types of phenomena may require different kinds of explanation (Thakker et al., 1999).

Quantitative and Qualitative Research: Opposite or Complementary?

Positivists and phenomenologists have long traditions in different categories of method, positivists opting mainly for methods that produce data amenable to statistical analysis (questionnaires, tests, inventories, etc.) and phenomenologists seeking understanding through methods such as participant observation and indepth interviews (individual and group). Although some scholars think that the *triangulation* of qualitative and quantitative method is impossible because the epistemologies characterizing these methodologies are incompatible, there is no reason to view qualitative and quantitative methods as opposed and, thereby, miss the chance to appreciate the way in which they can complement each other. In fact, many anthropologists and sociologists combine questionnaires and ethnographic interviews in their research (Bernard, 1995).

Qualitative methodology[2] incorporates a variety of methods of which participant observation and individual interviews are among those predominantly used. Focus group discussion is a qualitative method that possesses elements of both these techniques while maintaining its own peculiarity and uniqueness as a distinctive research method (Morgan, 1996). Various definitions have been proposed for focus groups, which have in common the following points:

(1) Focus groups are a method of research to collect data.
(2) The source of data collection is the group, and it uses group interaction as part of the method.

---

[2]   In this regard, I must point out that the typology of research is not defined by the data collected and the methods chosen for the data collection. What makes a research qualitative is the epistemology that informs "each" stage of the research project: the key question(s), sample selection, method of data collection, data analysis, and data report.

(3) Researchers have an active role in generating and coordinating the group discussion.
(4) The questions that participants are asked to answer aim to elicit their opinions, views, beliefs, and attitudes on the topic under investigation.
(5) Although focus groups usually provide qualitative data, they can have different degrees of structure.
(6) Focus groups are always "focused," which means that even the least structured group has a well-defined purpose and topic.

Although focus group discussions have infrequently been used in suicide research, some scholars have employed this technique to build and validate questionnaires or surveys. For example, Pinzon-Perez and Perez (2001) in their study of suicide-related behaviors among Colombian youth, needed to translate the Youth Risk Behavior Survey (YRBS) from English to Spanish. The language appropriateness and question listing was determined through focus groups.

Other studies have used focus groups to collect qualitative data on various aspects of suicidal behavior. For instance, Coggan, Patterson, and Fill (1997) organized focus groups with young people (16–24 years old) within the Auckland region (New Zealand) with the aim of enhancing the knowledge of ways in which to address youth suicide. Three themes were perceived by participants as being warning signs of a suicidal friend: personality changes, risk-taking behavior, and unusual actions. An important finding for suicide prevention was that young people would either cope alone or turn to a friend if they were feeling suicidal because they did not see health professionals as a useful resource. Finally, a lack of knowledge was identified as the major barrier to the use of existing services and resources. The authors concluded: "The use of focus groups with young people has provided valuable insights into ways to address youth suicide. We urge other researchers to incorporate similar methodologies" (p. 1563).

Focus groups are often implemented in health research to inquire about needs, complaints, and experiences of service providers and users of these services. Examples of this use for focus groups are also available in suicide research. Vrale and Steen (2005) interviewed expert nurses – individually and in focus groups – to describe how they perform constant observation of patients with suicidal ideation. The interviews showed how, in the beginning, preventing the patient from self-harm is the most important aspect, while the relationship between patient and nurse later develops into a therapeutic relationship.

The above are a just a few examples of the application of focus groups (in multi-method or free-standing approaches) in some areas of suicide research which, as stated earlier, are quite infrequent.[3] However, although this method is already seldomn used in suicidology, it is almost completely lacking in cross-cultural studies on suicide. In fact, in spite of the evidence of the benefits and advantages of conducting studies on sociocultural aspects with focus group discussions (see Marsella, 2000; Colucci, 2008a), cultural and cross-cultural research on suicide has neglected this method, as further discussed below.

Focus Groups in Cultural and Cross-Cultural Research on Suicidal Behavior

To date only a few studies addressing cultural aspects of suicide have used focus groups (e.g., Chew-Graham et al., 2002; Burr, 2002), and the neglect of focus groups is almost total in cross-cultural research. An exception is the study by Braun and Nichols (1997) with the purpose of exploring cultural variations in response to the process of dying and grieving among four Asian American populations (Chinese, Japanese, Vietnamese, and Filipino). Key informants and focus group interviews were conducted with adult members of these ethnic groups, and significant differences between, and within, groups were found. Although this was not the focus of the study, one of the areas explored was suicide.

Chinese Americans stated that suicide is considered wrong among their people. However, in traditional Chinese culture, suicide may be acceptable for women who have been raped or want to avoid being raped, people captured by enemies during war, and government officials whose good advice was refused. The burial service was the same as for Chinese dying by other means, although the family of a person who died by suicide may attempt to cover up the suicide because of shame, and they would likely mourn privately.

Vietnamese Americans thought that suicide is wrong and taught this to their children at a very young age. An exception is in war. A military man who dies by suicide instead of surrendering to the enemy is said to go to a higher plane in the afterlife. However, most suicides go to Suicide Land where they are very unhappy because they have not paid back their Karma, and so it will follow them.

---

[3] This resistance to using focus groups might be justified by the misconception that focus groups are not suitable for sensitive topics, which has been challenged by several authors such as Wellings, Branigan, and Mitchell (2000) and Phan and Fitzgerald (1996). Bloor and colleagues (2001) suggested that focus groups are an ideal environment for researching sensitive topics because participants may feel more relaxed and less inhibited in the co-presence of others, and they might feel empowered and supported in the co-presence of those similarly situated to themselves. In this regard, the study by Chew-Graham, Bashir, Chantler, Burman, and Batsleer (2002) is of particular interest. Community group leaders suggested that, in safe groups, women would discuss the topic of suicide, and this convinced the authors to use group interviews instead of individual interviews for their research on self-harm in South-Asian women.

They referred to the case of a person who dies by suicide at age 30, but was supposed to live until age 80. In this case his soul will live in Suicide Land for 50 years to make up the difference. Vietnamese people were afraid of suicides because they believe that the unhappy ghost of the person will return to bother the living. The funeral service is the same for a person who dies by suicide as for those dying from other kinds of death, but mourners feel more sorrow for the surviving family members.

Japanese Americans felt that there are two ways to look at suicide. One is that people are given life by their parents and ancestors and should take care of it and not hurt their ancestors. In addition, the taking of any life is wrong, even one's own. However, although they believe that suicide "is not good," it is sometimes the only solution for a bad situation. It does not matter how a person dies because Buddha is compassionate and embraces all beings without discrimination. In the same way, the participants felt it is best to have a compassionate and nonjudgmental view of suicide.

Filipino Americans agreed that suicide is not acceptable. A Catholic nun explained that suicide goes against the Fifth Commandment – "Thou shall not kill." If a person dies by suicide, the priest will refuse to perform a funeral service and will not allow the body to be buried in the Catholic cemetery. Therefore, the person will not go to heaven and will not be forgiven.

The focus group approach was chosen as the main method for the research presented in this chapter for several reasons. First of all, it is able to access "meanings." Phan and Fitzgerald (1996, p. 13) observed: "Focus groups provide the opportunity to explore the reasons behind or the meaning of human phenomena." Focus groups are appropriate tools in situations in which the research aims to answer "why" and "how" rather than "what" and "how much" questions (e.g., Schilder et al., 2004). Hughes and DuMont (1993) observed that focus groups more readily facilitate exploration rather than hypothesis testing, and the centrality of the interaction between participants in this method and its sensitivity to cross-cultural differences make focus groups appropriate for the study of sociocultural dimensions (Colucci, 2008a). Lastly, as observed above, focus groups are indicated by some authors as adequate for the study of sensitive topics (Wellings et al., 2000), such as suicidal behavior.

However, in the spirit of the triangulation of methods advocated above, meant not for validation purposes but as a way to enrich and reflect the complexity of people's understanding/construction, in this project, in addition to focus group discussions, I also used a questionnaire with structured and semi-structured (open-ended) sections.

The Sampling

The samples investigated, young university students, are not only samples of convenience, but samples for whom suicide represents an epidemiological reality. In their "Call to Action," Westefeld et al. (2006) labeled college student suicide an issue of major concern requiring a strong response. Moreover, research on youths who are not psychiatric patients is needed because research in the past has focused principally on psychiatric patients or young people using emergency services due to self-harm (Perkins & Hartless, 2002). This restriction to a specific section of the youth population will also make the data more comparable between the three countries. The minimum age was limited to 18 (the minimum age to finish high school in Italy) and the maximum to 24, given that for WHO the age range for "youths" is 15–24 years.

Apart from the age range, other sampling criteria were that students had to be born in the country under study (e.g., Italy) and had both parents of the same nationality (e.g., Italians). Therefore, participants had to be at least second generation in the country where they were living. The subjects involved in this research were university students 18–24 years old from the University of Padua (Italy) and various colleges in the city of Bangalore (India) and Brisbane (Australia). In order to make the samples more similar, students were selected from comparable cities and colleges (inasmuch as this can be possible). The University of Queensland and Queensland University of Technology, the two universities from which the Australian sample was taken, are situated in Brisbane, a city with a high rate of literacy and a good quality of life in terms of the education and health system. The Italian sample belonged to the University of Padua situated in North Italy. Although some southern Italians are part of the final sample, North Italy is comparable to the Australian sample for standard of living and literacy. Having chosen these two samples, it was important to select a sample of Indian students not too different in these basic aspects. Bangalore, where classes are usually taught in English, is a cosmopolitan and relatively modern city that attracts students from every corner of India. Several colleges (diverse in terms of religious connotation and social class) were involved in order to guarantee the presence of a broad range of Indians – for religion (Catholic and non-Catholic colleges), SES (lower class and higher classes), and residency (resident and not-resident in the college).

Students were enrolled on a volunteer basis, mainly through the help of academics working in the respective universities. In the classes where lecturers agreed, I usually introduced the study to the students and distributed envelopes containing the questionnaires and forms to those who were interested and matched the sampling criteria. Some of the questionnaires were also distributed directly to students around the campus and the same instructions were given to students in both situations (i.e., group and individual recruitment).

Table 1. Survey sample

			Mean Age	Range
ITALY	100 Males	124 Females	21.3	19–24
INDIA	113 Males	125 Females	20.9	18–24
AUSTRALIA	96 Males	125 Females	20.1	18–24

Two hundred has been identified as the "critical sample size" for some statistical analyses (see Marshall et al., 2007). Therefore, I aimed for 200–250 students in each country. Furthermore, the samples had to be equally divided into males and females so that I could have a representation of opinions and ideas equally distributed by sex[4] and could make some exploratory comparisons based on this variable. Of the 794 questionnaires returned, 686 questionnaires met the criteria for inclusion in the study (see Table 1).

The focus group sample followed the suggestion of Bloor et al. (2001). Where focus groups are used in conjunction with a survey, respondents can be drawn from the survey sample to then participate in focus groups. For this reason, together with the participant information sheet, questionnaire consent form and questionnaire, students received a consent form for the focus group. After explaining focus group aims and procedure, I invited interested students to leave their contact details and sign a consent form in order to be contacted.

For each country, 4–5 groups were organized using *systematic sampling,* that is, randomly selecting participants from a larger group to eliminate bias in the selection process (Morgan & Scannell, 1998). Generally groups met for two sessions of 1.5–2.0 hours each (including a break). Eight participants is a commonly used size for group interviews (Bernard, 1995) and, to reach this number, 10 students were invited for each group since 1–2 participants generally tend to withdraw. A way to investigate the effects of group composition is the *mix-and-match* design (Morgan, 1997): some groups are composed of a mix of different categories of participants, whereas other groups match the participants to assure homogeneity. To control the effect of discussing the sensitive topic of suicide with students of the opposite sex, in each country at least two groups mixed by gender, a group of females only and a group of males only were organized.

In summary, 4 groups in Italy (35 students), 5 in India (41 students) and 4 in Australia (20 students) were organized for a total of 96 students and 24 group sessions. More details on the samples are reported in Table 2.

---

[4] Throughout the chapter, the terms "sex" and "gender" will be used interchangeably, although sex refers to the biological distinction between males and females whereas gender to the social constructions.

Table 2. Focus groups samples

	N	Mean Age	Range
ITALY			
Males	15	20.3	19–23
Female	20	21.0	19–24
INDIA			
Males	25	19.6	18–24
Females	16	21.3	19–24
AUSTRALIA			
Males	8	20.3	18–23
Females	12	19.9	18–24

The Questionnaire

After an extensive literature search (see Colucci, 2006; Colucci & Martin, 2007a; 2007b), I was unable to find an instrument that suited my research questions, and so I built a questionnaire entitled "Exploring the Meaning of Suicide." This included questions about reasons for attempting and completing suicide, a suicide attitude questionnaire, questions about exposure to suicide and a history of suicidal ideation and behavior, case scenarios, a "Cultural Identification Battery," and some open-ended questions exploring suicide meanings and mental constructions and suggestions for youth suicide prevention.

To investigate the students' beliefs about the reasons for youth suicide attempts, participants were asked "In your opinion, when a young person makes a suicide attempt, what are the reasons?" and were offered seven possible reasons to be scored on a 5-point Likert scale from the highest disagreement ("no") to the highest agreement ("yes"). The question about reasons for youth suicide was a ranking order task: participants were provided with 14 categories of possible reasons for young people to kill themselves which they had to rank from the most important (rank 1) to the least important (rank 14). Participants could use the same number more than once if they thought some reasons had the same importance. For each item, two variables were created: one was the mean score for that item (i.e., the exact number the student wrote) and the second considered the items that were placed in the first three highest positions (ranking 1, 2, or 3) and the lowest one. This variable was created because, at times, participants did not start with number 1 or did not finish with the number 14. Reasons written in the blank spaces were also considered for the ranking. Lists of reasons for both questions were extracted from suicide attitude scales and from the literature on suicide. In both questions, participants were offered the option to write other reasons in the blank space provided at the bottom of the list of possible answers.

Questions on attitudes toward suicide were based on existing literature and tests including Domino, Moore, Westlake, and Gibson's Suicide Opinion Questionnaire (SOQ; 1982), Diekstra and Kerkhof's Suicide-Attitude Questionnaire (SUIATT; 1989) and the Salander Renberg and Jacobsson's The Questionnaire on Attitudes towards Suicide (ATTS; 2003). A 21-item Attitudes Towards Youth Suicide scale (AtYS) was built, with a 5-point Likert-scale from "Strongly agree" to "Strongly disagree." The majority of the questions referred to youth suicide.

Next, there was a word association task ("When you think about suicide, what are the first three words that immediately come into your mind?") and open-ended questions, which addressed topics similar to those later examined in the focus groups. Before presenting these questions, participants were asked again to express their beliefs and opinions. Two questions examined the cultural meaning of the words "suicide attempt" ("What do you mean by attempted suicide?") and suicide ("What do you mean by suicide?"). Their mental representations and stereotypes were further explored by inviting them to describe in their own words what kinds of youths attempt suicide ("What words would you use to describe a young person who made a suicide attempt?") or kill themselves ("What words would you use to describe a young person who killed him/herself?"). Another question investigating the same topic asked if there are differences in the suicidal behaviour of young males and females ("Are there differences between males and females in youth suicide? If yes, what are the differences?"). Feelings towards death were also explored ("What do you feel when you think about death?") with the aim of comparing the responses of participants at lower risk of suicide (no ideation, plan, or attempt) with those of participants at higher risk (previous suicidal behavior).

To explore what participants believed keeps many youths alive in spite of life difficulties (i.e., deterrents and protective factors), they were asked "Why would you not suicide (or what would stop you from doing it) even if your life was horrible?" Other questions inquired about youth suicide prevention, opinions about how much is done in their country to prevent youth suicide ("In your opinion, how much is done about youth suicide prevention in India [or Italy or Australia]?), in what ways could youth suicide be prevented ("What should be done to prevent youth suicide in India [or Italy or Australia]?") and what can family and friends do to prevent youth suicide ("In which ways could the family and friends help to prevent the suicide of a young person?"). A final question asked more directly if they would ask for help if they were suicidal and, if so, to whom (i.e., help-seeking behavior). Participants were asked to indicate a first option ("If you were thinking about taking your own life, with whom would you speak about this?") and a second option if that person was not available ("If he/she was not available, with whom would you subsequently speak?"). This kind of investigation is essential because, as Coggan and Patterson (1998) noted, while there is an extensive literature in the area of youth suicide, there were no qualitative studies incorporating young people's views on ways to address the issue.

The case scenarios section invited participants to construct a case vignette of a peer who they thought was very likely to kill him/herself and then, in contrast, a case vignette of another peer very unlikely to kill him/herself, in order to explore the stereotypic ideas of situations and circumstances that lead to or protect someone from suicide as well as the participants' mental constructions and representations of a suicidal peer.

The participants were next asked personal questions about previous experience and exposure to suicidal behavior. The questions about suicide ideation, plan, and attempt were posed referring to the intention "to kill oneself" (e.g., "Did you ever think about killing yourself?"). Questions about suicide ideation, plan, and attempt were multiple-answer questions, that is, participants could check one or more answers from a list of options related to the time-frame (from "never" to "more than one year ago"). In the statistical analyses, the affirmative answers to each of these questions were coded as "yes" (even if the student gave more than one answer) whereas the answer "never" was coded as "no," creating a binomial variable, and the answers related to the time-frame were analyzed separately. From the answers to the questions about previous suicide ideation, plan, and attempt, a score on a suicide risk scale was derived, where a value of 1 means the presence of suicide ideation and a value of 8 represents presence of suicide ideation, plan, and repeated and recent (less than one month) suicide attempts.

Following Bernard's (1995) suggestion that general socioeconomic and demographic questions be placed at the end of the questionnaire in order to diminish the respondents' fear of being identified, the questions about gender, age, year of study, religion/spirituality, mother's and father's occupation, and the country of birth of participants, their parents and their grandparents were in the final section. The profession of the participants' fathers was used as an (approximate and limited) index of the participants' socioeconomic status. The answers provided were collapsed into three categories: lower class (e.g., farmers, unemployed, working class, or "blue-collar"), lower-middle class (e.g., "white-collar" and small business), and upper-middle class and upper (e.g., big business, doctors, engineers, self-employed, wealthy landowners or entrepreneurs). Answers not classifiable because participants wrote "retired" or "deceased" (without any specification) or unknown acronyms were grouped in an "unclassifiable" category. This category, however, was excluded from the analysis because it was too broad. A contingency table was produced to document the distribution of those five categories among the three countries and, given that some cells had very few cases in two of the three countries, the lower-low and upper-low class were collapsed into a more generic lower class, and the few upper class participants (totaling 14 in the three countries) were aggregated with the upper-middle class.

Participants were simply asked to answer "yes" or "no" to a question inquiring if they were religious/spiritual persons. Those who answered positively were then asked what their religious preferences were at the time of the study. They had the option to tick several religious denominations (e.g., "Hindu") or the item "other," which had a blank space in which to specify the answer. The answers given to the category "other" were then divided into three groups: "Christian (non-Catholic)," which incorporates the answers given to the "Anglican" option, the category "spiritual beliefs" (also labeled "spiritual"), which includes answers such as "personal religion" or "spirituality," and the category "other," which contains answers that were not possible to include in the existing categories or answers that, although not inserted in the "spiritual" category, might in fact consist of generic/nonreligious spiritual beliefs (e.g., "autonomous" or "humanity"). For this reason, these two latter categories (i.e., spiritual beliefs and other) are likely to be partially overlapping.

To verify the participants' ethnocultural background, they were requested to write their country of origin and that of both their parents and all their grandparents. Participants were also asked to describe in their own words the ethnocultural group to which they felt they most belonged.

The construct of ethnic identity has been seen as central by several authors (e.g., Roberts, 2000; Yamada, Marsella & Atuel, 2002). I investigated ethnic identity using a modified version of the "Cultural Identification Battery" (Yamada et al., 2002). The Attitudinal Index of the scale is divided in two sections, making it a short but comprehensive instrument: Ethnic Affiliation, which assesses the degree of attachment one feels towards one's cultural background, and the Impact of Ethnic Identity, assessing the influence and role of one's ethnocultural identity in one's life. Participants were asked to express their answer (depending upon the question) on a 5-point or 7-point Likert-scale, where 0 or 1 was the lowest score and 4 or 7 the highest, for a maximum possible score on the index of 50.

Focus Groups to Elicit the Meanings of Suicide

The focus group interview schedule operated as a flexible guide rather than a structured protocol, and the content (and questions) of the sessions were greatly determined by the participants' answers.

Overall, the focus group questions were similar to the open-ended questions included in the questionnaire, and the aim of the focus groups was to go into those issues in more depth (i.e., spiritual beliefs, suicide deterrents and protective factors, youth suicide prevention and help-seeking behavior). The session design followed a funnel pattern (Morgan, 1996), beginning with a fixed set of core questions and then proceeding to a variable set of issues specific to the group. This has the advantage of maintaining comparability across groups for part of each discussion while allowing other sections of each session to vary according to the specific issues that emerge in the group. Therefore, the questions included were only an indication of relevant topics, and not all of them were asked, nor in exactly the same wording. Moreover, some of the answers given in the questionnaire inspired additional topics to be addressed during the group discussions (e.g., warning signs, friends as important resource of help, and gender issues).

The focus group agenda also included some activity-oriented questions (Colucci, 2007). For the exercise called *Stick Figure*, I drew a stick figure and told participants that he/she represented a young person who was on the verge of attempting suicide (but did not die). Participants were asked to describe what they believed this person would think, communicate and feel before engaging in this act. In the *News Bulletin* exercise, participants had to write a news article on a young person of their age who killed him/herself, describing the person, the act and the reasons. I then asked questions to find out more about their beliefs about "suicidal youths" and for which reasons some youths kill themselves. During the second session, a few of these news articles were selected, and participants were asked to propose what could have been done to prevent the suicide of the young person in the news who killed him/herself. I wrote on a whiteboard the suicide prevention strategies suggested by the participants and, when they agreed that the list was complete, I asked each of them to choose the most and the least effective strategy.

At the end of the second session, participants completed a focus group feedback form (where they were also given the opportunity to add answers they were unable or unwilling to give during the sessions) and, afterwards, received a small surprise from one of the other two countries involved in the study, accompanied by a small leaflet containing help-services contacts.

The questionnaire was originally written in English and back-translated. I then compared the original and the two back-translated versions and discussed the discrepancies with the translators. A final version was produced and tested with a sample of Italian, Australian, and Indian participants, separately, in a pilot study.

Data Analysis

For the questionnaire, two bilingual psychology trainees and myself separately coded the answers written in the blank spaces at the end of the structured questions into categories. After discussion, a list of categories was defined, which underwent additional modifications after this first attempt to code the answers (e.g., some categories had too few cases or were too big). Analyses were supported with the software for qualitative analysis ATLAS.ti 5.6. The open-ended questions investigating sociodemographic variables (such as the parents' occupation, ethnicity and grandparents' origins) were categorized and then statistically analyzed, as for the structured questions, using statistical software SPSS 14.0.

The focus group data analysis and explication used three sources: co-moderators notes, field notes written by the moderator, and *verbatim* transcriptions of the tape-recorded sessions. The analytical framework that shaped the focus groups analysis is phenomenological, in congruence with the epistemology that informed this study. In particular, the interpretative phenomenological analysis (IPA) presented and exemplified by Smith, Jarman, and Osborn (1999) and Smith and Osborn (2003) was applied. However, the IPA epistemological orientation is aimed at understanding the individual, and so this approach had to be adapted to look into similarities and differences between groups of individuals from different countries. This multi-layered analytical process was also supported by ATLAS.ti 5.6.

The following section presents the results from the structured and open-ended sections of the questionnaires followed by the key themes emerged in the focus groups.

Results from the Structured Questions[5]

The analyses were performed on 686 questionnaires (224 Italians, 238 Indians, and 221 Australians), which, following the sampling criteria, were almost equally distributed by gender. There was a statistically significant difference in the three samples' mean age perhaps because undergraduate degrees in Italy begin two years later than in Australia and India.[6]

All participants had to be at least second generation citizens of the country under study to take part in the project and, for 88% of participants, the four grandparents, were also from the same country – 98% of the Italians and 96% of the Indians were third generation compared to only 70% of the Australians.

The Australian participants were of higher social class than the Indian participants who, in turn, were of higher social class than the Italian participants. For

---

5   For ease of reading, the results of many of the statistical tests of significance have been omitted.
6   The possible effect of age was checked through analyses of variance for relevant variables (e.g., suicidal ideation and behaviors), and the differences between countries do not seem to be a result of differences in the students' mean ages.

example, more participants in Italy and India belonged to the lower classes (33% and 24%) compared to only 13% in Australia, whereas in India and Australia almost half of the sample belonged to the upper-middle and upper class compared to 26% in Italy.

When asked if, at the present time, they would define themselves as being religious/spiritual persons, although overall 68.8% of the participants answered positively, there were some differences between countries ($p < .001$). The most religious were Indians (83.5%) followed by Italians (68.2%), whereas Australians were the least religious (53.5%). There were no differences by gender in India and Australia, but in Italy more females reported being religious or spiritual than males (76.4% vs. 57.7%, $p < .005$).

Participants from the three countries had different religious affiliations ($p < .001$). The majority of the Italian religious participants selected Catholicism as their preference (83.4%). In India, 66.2% of the participants chose Hindu, followed by 16.2% Catholic and 8.1% Islam. In Australia the religious sample was divided mainly into two groups: 40.5% Christians and 39.7% Catholics. There were statistically significant differences by gender ($p < .005$). For instance, in both Italy and India, more females identified themselves as Catholics compared to males. In India more males were Hindu whereas more females were Muslims.

Prevalence of Suicidal Behavior

More than half of the 686 participants across the three countries (52.8%) answered affirmatively to the question "Have you ever thought about killing yourself?," but there was a statistically significant difference between samples ($p < .001$). While 61.6% of the Italian participants and 62.6% of the Australian participants reported suicidal ideation, only 35.3% of the Indians did so.

While 10% of Australian participants reported suicidal ideation in the month before the survey, only 4.5% of Italians and 5.5% of Indians did so ($p < .05$). Similarly, 18.3% of Australian participants reported ideation in the last 12 months compared to 13.4% of Italian and 10.2% of Indian participants ($p < .05$), and 46.9% of Italians did so more than one year before, compared to 37.9% of Australians and 21.7% of Indians ($p < .001$).

There were also differences in the distribution by gender. In Australia there was a similar percentage of male and female participants who had thought about suicide (59.1% vs. 64.5%) whereas, in Italy, significantly more males had thought about suicide (69% vs. 55.6%, $p < .05$). In contrast, suicide ideation was more common in Indian females (46.4% vs. 22%, $p < .001$).

The prevalence of previous suicide plans was similar among participants from the three countries, with an overall percentage of 17.7% participants reporting a plan. However, there were some statistically significant differences concerning the time when the plans were made ($p < .05$). Only 0.4% of Italian and 1.4% of Australian participants had made a plan in the month before, compared to 3.4% of Indian participants. There was a significant difference in India and a trend towards significance in Australia for distribution by gender: more females than males made a plan in India (27.2% vs. 11.7%) and in Australia (21.8% vs. 12.6%).

The final question asked if they had ever tried to kill themselves. Overall, 10.7% of participants reported a previous suicide attempt, but there were statistically significant differences between the three countries ($p < .005$). The country with the lowest percentage was Italy (4.9%), followed by Australia (12.2%) and India (which was the country with the lowest percentage of suicide ideation) at 14.8%.

No Italian student reported a suicide attempt in the month or year before the survey compared to 1.7% and 1.4%, respectively, of Indian and Australian participants who did so in the month before, and 3.0% and 2.7% in the year before ($p < .05$). Of the 4.9% Italian participants who tried to kill themselves, all did so more than one year before, compared to 9.7% of Indians and 9.5% of Australians, but the difference was not significant. Twice as many Indian females had attempted suicide compared to males (20.8% vs. 8.2%, $p < .01$), whereas in Italy and Australia there was a similar distribution (6% men vs. 4% women in Italy, and 10.5% men vs. 12.9% women in Australia). Gender also had a significant influence ($p < .05$) on the time-frame in India, where the majority of the female participants had suicidal thoughts or made a suicidal plan or an attempt one year or more before the survey.

Table 3 illustrates that Australian participants had the highest suicide risk scores, followed by Indian participants and Italian participants ($p < .001$). In India and Australia, there were more participants at higher risk (i.e., a score on the scale equal to or higher than 6, which represents the presence of suicidal ideation, plan, and attempt). Nineteen Indian participants and 20 Australian participants scored 6 compared to only nine Italians. Furthermore, seven participants in India and four in Australia, compared to zero in Italy, made more than one recent suicide attempt.

There were also differences by gender. Overall, female participants from the three countries had higher scores on the suicide risk scale compared to the men (1.36 vs. 1.03, $p < .05$), but the pattern changed when the mean scores were considered separately for each country. While scores were higher for Indian females as compared to males (1.67 vs. 0.72, $p < .001$), in Italy there was a tendency towards the opposite (1.25 vs. 0.92, $p < .10$) and in Australia there was no significant gender difference (1.15 in men vs. 1.50 in women).

Table 3. Suicide risk

	Total	Italy	India	Australia
Suicide risk				
Mean scores (min 0-max 8)	1.21	1.07	1.23	1.35
Males	1.03	1.25	0.72	1.15
Females	1.36	0.92	1.67	1.50

Data were also analyzed for the association between socioeconomic status and suicidal ideation and behavior.[7] Overall and within countries, there were no statistically significant differences for suicidal ideation but, in Australia, almost twice as many participants from the upper-class (52.6%) made a suicidal plan compared to 23.7% for participants from the lower and lower middle class ($p < .05$). Suicide attempts showed a trend toward significance overall and for India ($p < .10$). Overall, 56.5% of the participants who made a suicidal attempt belonged to the upper-class, 25.8% to the lower-middle and 17.7% to the lower class. In India, only 7.1% of the attempted suicides were lower-class, compared to 28.6% in the lower-middle and 64.3% in the upper-class. These differences by social class were also reflected in the suicide risk scale scores, where Indians in the lower-class showed a trend for lower scores ($p < .10$).

Previous Exposure to Suicide and Association with Suicidal Ideation and Behavior

Participants from the three countries had differences in their exposure to suicide attempts ($p < .001$). Overall, 41.5% of the participants reported that someone close to them had made a suicide attempt, but many more reported this in Australia (52.3%) than in Italy or India (33.6% and 38.9%, respectively). The suicide attempt was more often made by a family member in Australia (13.5%) than in Italy or India where 5.8% and 7.1% of the participants, respectively, reported that someone in their family had tried to kill him/herself ($p < .01$). The exposure to completed suicide was similar across countries (the overall percentage was 27.8%).

Having been exposed to the suicide of a close friend or relative is known to be an important risk factor for suicidal behavior. In the overall sample, there was an association between participants' suicidal ideation and previous exposure to a

---

[7] Although students' suicidal behavior showed some differences based on socioeconomic status, the utility of investigating SES without consideration of the actual social context and social meaning of this factor is questionable, and so these data must be viewed with caution.

suicide attempt ($p < .05$): 45.5% of participants with suicidal ideation knew someone close to them who tried to kill him/herself versus 36.8% of those without ideation. On the other hand, exposure to suicide attempts had different effects across cultures. A similar percentage of the Italian participants with suicidal ideation and of those without ideation knew someone who tried to take his/her own life (30.4% vs. 38.8% respectively), whereas in India a greater number of those who had suicide ideation had been exposed than those with no ideation (47.0% vs. 34.2%, $p = .05$). In Australia, the difference was even greater (59.9% vs. 39.5%, $p < .005$). Exposure to completed suicide did not have a statistically significant impact on the suicidal ideation of the participants overall or separately for any of the three countries. When the answers to the questions about previous exposure to suicide attempt and death were combined into one, previous exposure of any kind had a statistically significant difference both overall (54.5% of students with ideation had been exposed vs. 44.7% of those without ideation, $p < .05$) and, more specifically, in the Indian (56.6% vs. 41.4%, $p < .05$) and Australian samples ($p < .01$) but not in the Italian sample.

Similar findings were found for the associations between exposure to a suicide attempt and having made plans for one's own suicide, having made a suicide attempt, and the suicide risk score. In regard to the latter, exposure of any kind (combined) was associated with higher scores on the suicide risk scale in the total sample ($p < .001$), and for the Indian ($p < .05$) and Australian samples ($p < .001$), whereas it did not impact the Italian sample score.

Religiosity/Spirituality and Suicidal Behavior

Overall, participants from the three countries who were nonreligious had more suicidal thoughts than religious/spiritual peers (60.9% vs. 48.5%, $p < .005$) but, by country, this was significant only for the Indian participants ($p < .05$). Here, 32.3% of participants who defined themselves as religious thought about suicide compared to 50% of those who were nonreligious. In Italy and Australia the percentages were similar for both religious and nonreligious participants (respectively, 59.3% vs. 64.3% in Italy and 61.6% vs. 62.6% in Australia).

Going into more depth, in Italy, Catholics had a lower incidence of suicidal ideation than non-Catholic Christians and those choosing "spiritual beliefs" (54.8% versus 75% and 87.5%, respectively, $p < .05$). The effect of religious denomination was not significant in India or Australia. There were no statistically significant differences (overall or by country) with regard to a suicide plan. For suicide attempts, significant differences were found only in India. Indian participants who saw themselves as nonreligious/nonspiritual attempted suicide more

Table 4. Religious affiliation and suicide risk scores

	Christian Non-Catholic	Catholic	Islam	Hindu	Buddhist	Spiritual	Other Beliefs
Italy	1.50	0.87	–	–	2.20	2.00	1.25
India	0.25	1.56	2.12	0.96	0.00	2.00	2.71
Australia	1.37	1.26	–	–	0.00	2.00	2.33

often than religious/spiritual participants did (26.3% vs. 12.5%, $p < .05$). The specific religion was also related to suicide attempts. In India, 42.9% of participants who selected "other," 29.4% of Muslims and 20.6% of Catholics made a suicide attempt compared to 0% of Christians and Buddhists and 10.3% of Hindus ($p < .05$).

Similar results emerged when scores on the suicide risk scale were analyzed (see Table 4). In the overall sample, the highest scores (indicating more suicidal ideation and behavior) were found among participants who were Muslim (mean = 2.12), closely followed by those reporting more generic "spiritual beliefs" (2.00) and those belonging to the category "other" (2.08). The lowest scores were found for those who were Hindu (0.96), Catholics (1.07) and Buddhists (1.10), ($p < .05$).

In Italy, the lowest scores were among Catholics (0.87), whereas Catholics had a high score in India ($p < .05$). This suggests that belonging to a minority religious denomination may be more stressful than belonging to the majority religious denomination.

Reasons for Youths to Attempt and Complete Suicide

A section of the questionnaire investigated the participants' beliefs about the reasons why young people attempt suicide and kill themselves. There were statistically significant differences on six of the seven listed reasons for attempting suicide (Table 5). For example, Indians scored higher (mean = 2.26) on the item "To force others to do what he/she wants to do" (which may indicate a perception that a suicide attempt has manipulative aims, but also that it may be a means to be heard) than Italians (1.38) and Australians (1.26). In India and Australia there was more agreement that youths who attempt suicide are mentally ill (respectively, 2.65 and 2.72 compared to 1.68 in Italy), whereas Italians had a higher mean score on the reason "To get attention" (2.82 vs. 2.18 in India and 2.42 in Australia).

Table 5. Reasons for young people to attempt suicide

	Italy	India	Australia
To force others to do what he/she wants	1.38	2.24	1.26*
To make others notice how big his/her problems are	2.72	2.37	2.59*
Because he/she wants to die	2.25	2.23	2.61*
Because he/she is mentally ill	1.68	2.65	2.72*
To get attention	2.82	2.18	2.42*
To get emotional support from others	2.62	2.69	2.52
To escape from problems	3.08	3.49	3.49*

*statistically significant differences (p between $< .05$ and $< .001$)

The participants were given the option of adding other reasons. Of particular note are the answers provided by those participants at higher risk of suicide (i.e., with a score on the suicide risk scale of 5 or higher). In Italy those participants wrote that some youths attempt suicide: to escape from the "falling world," because he/she is tired of the real world, for something that makes him/her feel uneasy but is not able to confide to anyone, for sentimental problems, because he/she feels powerless in front of the problems he/she must face, to not feel powerless and for feelings that are "too strong." In India, the answers were: no self-esteem, love failure (twice), lack of support or family support, being harassed by family members, loneliness (twice) and lonely, being fed up with their environment, depression, no acceptance by society, fear of society, uncaring society, worthless, not happy and revenge (to teach the other person a lesson). In Australia participants at highest risk added: low self-esteem, poor self-view, media-stimulated solution, pain distraction, lack of other options, feelings of worthlessness, to make others feel bad, because he/she is structurally oppressed, self-hatred, and loneliness, lack of belonging, and social discrimination.

The second question was about reasons for completing suicide and was a ranking task. The participants ranked the fourteen reasons from 1 to 14. Overall, the three most important reasons (that is, those that were most often ranked first) across the countries were "mental disease/depression/anxiety" (36%), "loneliness/interpersonal problems" (33%) and "physical or sexual abuse" (16%). The least important (most often ranked last) were "revenge/punish someone" and "to protect self/family honor."

The rankings were different between countries for each of the 14 reasons (p between $< .05$ and $< .001$). In Italy the three most important reasons were "loneliness/interpersonal problems" (43%), "mental disease/depression/anxiety" (32%), and "incurable illness/severe chronic pain/becoming severely disabled" (23%), and the least important was "protect self/family honor." In India the most important reasons were "financial problems (e.g., unemployment, gambling, dowry, bankruptcy)" (35%), "mental disease/depression/anxiety" (26%) and "physical or sexual abuse" (25%), and the least important was "revenge/punish someone." In Australia "mental disease/depression/anxiety" was chosen as the most important reasons by more than half of the participants (51%), followed by "loneliness/interpersonal problems" (35%) and "physical or sexual abuse" (14%), whereas the least important reason was "protect self/family honor," the same as for the Italians. Fewer students added to the list of reasons why some youth kill themselves. However, participants at higher suicide risk indicated: stealing and discovered robbery (in Italy), loss of self-respect, lack of love from family, not being cared for by parents, forced to follow unjust decisions, change of caste, religious concerns, lack of support for education, and extreme negative views of present situations (in India), and persecution on the basis of sexuality, sexuality issues, drug overdose and structured oppression (in Australia).

There were also statistically significant differences on the basis of sociodemographic characteristics, both in the overall sample and for each country (p between $< .05$ and $< .005$). To cite some examples, in the overall sample, women agreed more than men that some young people attempt suicide because they want to die, get emotional support from others and escape problems. Regarding completed suicide, women ranked reasons related to infertility/illegitimate pregnancy, interpersonal and family problems, physical/sexual abuse, failure at school, and death of a loved one as more important than did men. Males ranked "cowardice/weak personality" as slightly more important (p between $< .05$ and $< .001$). However, there were differences between countries. For instance, Italian females gave more importance to family problems ($p < .001$) compared to Italian males. In India, females ranked physical/sexual abuse higher than did males ($p < .001$), whereas Australian males ranked cowardice/weak personality as more important compared to females ($p < .01$).

Participants belonging to a different socioeconomic status ranked the reasons for suicide differently (p between $< .05$ and $< .005$). In Italy, for instance, participants from the lower class agreed more that some youths attempt suicide to escape problems. In India, the lower class participants showed a trend toward less agreement that youths attempt suicide to get attention. Italians from different socioeconomic classes did not show any significant difference for the reasons youths complete suicide. Indians from the middle class gave more importance to infertility and illegitimate pregnancy, whereas those from the lower class gave the least importance to this. In India, participants from the upper classes ranked the death of a loved one as a more important reason for youth suicide, whereas in Australia this reason was ranked higher by participants from the lower classes.

Identifying oneself as being religious/spiritual had an effect on the reasons for suicide attempt and suicide (p between $< .05$ and $< .01$). For example, overall, religious/spiritual participants saw financial problems, protecting self/family honor and exam/school failure as more important reasons for youth suicide than loneliness/interpersonal problems compared to nonreligious/spiritual participants. When analysed by country, the only statistically significant differences were in Italy.

In the overall sample, participants with suicidal ideation agreed more that young people who attempt suicide do so because they want to die or to get attention ($p < .05$). Some differences emerged also analyzing the results in each country. Participants with suicidal ideation from the three countries saw reasons for some youths to complete suicide as partially different (p between $< .05$ and $< .001$): in Italy they saw an incurable illness, chronic pain, or severe disability as a less important reason for youth suicide than students without ideation, whereas in India they ranked loneliness/interpersonal problems, family difficulties, and the protection of honor as more important, and in Australia only exam failure/lack of success at school was seen as more important.

Some differences in reasons why some youths attempt suicide or kill themselves emerged, overall and by country, also in relation to participants who had previously made a suicidal plan or attempt, and on the suicide risk scale. For instance, Italians at higher risk of suicide attributed more importance to the belief that suicide might be a rational decision for an unsolvable problem ($p < .05$) whereas Indians gave more importance to the protection of self/family honor ($p < .05$). Participants in the three countries who had previously been exposed to suicidal behavior also saw reasons for suicide attempt and completed suicide as partially different from those who had not been exposed.

Attitudes Towards Youth Suicide

The Attitudes Towards Youth Suicide Scale (AtYS) included 21-items, each composed of a 5-point scale, from "strongly disagree" (0) to "strongly agree" (4). As AtYS is a new scale, the items were subjected to a (principal component) factor analysis to see if they formed clusters, and four clusters were identified: (1) negative attitudes (e.g., In general, suicide is an act not to be forgiven), (2) belief in the preventability of suicide (e.g., Youth suicide can be prevented), (3) acceptability/normality (e.g., People do have the right to suicide), and (4) belief in signs for suicide (e.g., Youths who talk about suicide do not suicide).

The participants from the three countries differed on all four scales (see Table 6) and showed statistically significant differences on 20 of the 21 items

Table 6. Differences between the participants on the AtYS

	Italy	India	Australia
Negative attitude	6.01	11.95	7.73*
Preventability	12.39	12.64	13.07*
Acceptability	11.34	10.49	11.75*
Risk signs	5.54	6.11	5.16*

($p < .001$ and $< .01$). Higher values mean higher agreement and lower values mean higher disagreement. The scores indicated a more negative attitude in India and Australia than in Italy. Australian participants also had a stronger belief that suicide is preventable and that it is possible to help suicidal people more than did Italians and Indians. Italians and Australians showed more acceptability and a greater tendency to normalize suicide than did Indians. On the last factor, lack of belief in the signs of suicide (e.g., lack of belief that youth who threaten or talk about suicide might kill themselves), Indians scored higher, followed by Italians and then Australians.

The attitudes towards suicide of the participants were analyzed by gender. Men had a more negative attitude towards suicide but were also more accepting of suicide and had a stronger belief that there are signs of suicide risk, whereas women had a stronger belief that suicide is preventable (p between $< .05$ and $< .001$). As before, men and women differed somewhat by country (e.g., Indian and Australian males had more negative attitudes and Italian males were more accepting than females). There were also differences in attitudes toward suicide by age, religiosity/spirituality, and religious affiliation, overall and within the samples from each country. For instance, there were no statistically significant differences in India between religious/spiritual and nonreligious/spiritual participants whereas, in Italy and Australia, religious/spiritual participants agreed less that suicide is acceptable ($p < .05$ and $p < .01$, respectively). Scores on the subscales were also analysed looking at the specific religious affiliations, which significantly impacted the scores on each of the four attitude subscales.

With regard to the relationship between the attitude subscales and previous suicidal ideation and behavior, the most consistent associations for the total sample and for each country separately were with the "negative attitude" and the "acceptability/normality" subscales. Participants with previous suicide ideation and behavior had less negative and more accepting attitudes towards suicide (p between $< .05$ and $< .001$).

Similarly, for the total sample and for each country separately, there was a statistically significant negative correlation between suicide risk and the negative attitude subscale and a positive correlation between suicide risk and acceptability of suicide. In other words, Italian, Indian, and Australian participants who were at greater risk of suicide had less negative attitudes towards suicide and considered suicide as more acceptable and normal ($p < .001$). Furthermore, Australian participants at greater risk believed more in the existence of possible signs of suicide risk ($p < .005$).

With regard to the participants' exposure to attempted and completed suicide, no association reached statistical significance in the total sample, and only few did so in the individual countries ($p < .05$). In Italy, participants who knew someone who had attempted or completed suicide believed more in the existence of signs of suicide (i.e., believed that a person talking and threatening suicide might actually suicide) than participants not previously exposed to suicide. In India, participants who knew someone who died by suicide agreed less that suicidal behavior is acceptable/normal. There were no statistically significant associations in Australia.

The Cultural Identification Battery

Participants were asked to write down the ethnic group(s) to which they felt they most belonged, and they had to complete the Attitudinal Index of the Cultural Identification Battery, which is divided into two subscales: Ethnic Affiliation and Impact of Ethnic Identity. The majority of the participants in each country identified their ethnic group(s) with their country/nationality, but significantly more Italians (57%) and Australians (61%) did so than Indians (45%, $p < .001$). Others listed a region of the country, a religion, or a language. On the Ethnic Affiliation and Impact of Ethnic Identity scales, the Indian participants obtained the highest scores ($p < .001$).

It is interesting to note that in the total sample, participants who defined themselves as religious/spiritual obtained higher scores on the Ethnic Affiliation and Impact subscales ($p < .001$). This association was also significant in each country, suggesting that participants who are more connected to "traditions" are more connected on several levels, including religiosity/spirituality.

Participants' scores on this scale were also associated with their suicidal ideation, plan, and attempts. The overall total score was negatively correlated with suicide risk ($p < .05$) but the negative correlation both with the Affiliation subscale and the total score was significant only for Australian students when data were analyzed by country ($p < .05$).

In the overall sample, participants who scored higher on the Ethnic Affiliation and Impact subscales had more negative attitudes towards suicide and less belief in signs of suicide ($p < .001$), but the correlations differed somewhat by country. For example, the correlation of ethnic identity with negative attitudes toward suicide was significant only for Italian participants ($p < .05$). However, other correlations appeared. For instance, in the Indian participants, higher scores on the affiliation subscale were associated with a greater belief in the preventability of suicide but less of a belief in the existence of signs for suicide ($p < .05$).

Summary

The analyses of the structured part of the questionnaire showed the presence of differences (and similarities) between Italian, Indian and Australian participants. For example, regarding the prevalence of suicidal ideation and behavior, the former was more common among Italian and Australian participants and the latter among Indians, followed by Australians. A more negative attitude was endorsed more by Indians and, to a lesser extent, Australians than by Italians. Australian participants also believed more that suicide is preventable and that it is possible to help suicidal people than did Italians and Indians. Italians and Australians showed greater acceptance and tendency to normalize suicide than did Indians. On the lack of beliefs in signs of suicide, Indians scored higher, followed by Italians and then Australians. In regard to reasons for youth suicide, Italian participants indicated "loneliness/interpersonal problems," "mental disease/depression/anxiety," "incurable illness/severe chronic pain/becoming severely disabled" as the three most important reasons, Indians indicated "financial problems," "mental disease/depression/anxiety" and "physical or sexual abuse," and Australians indicated "mental disease/depression/anxiety" (which was chosen as one of the most important reasons by more than half of the participants), followed by "loneliness/interpersonal problems" and "physical or sexual abuse."

Several associations between these variables were statistically significant. For instance, religion/spirituality was associated with the participants' suicidal ideation and behavior, and these were linked to the participants' beliefs pertaining to reasons for youth suicide. There were also some differences by gender. For example, men reported slightly more negative attitudes towards suicide compared to women.

What is notable was that, in addition to differences by country and sex, there were also differences by religion and social class, as well as by past experiences (such as their own suicidal behavior and that of friends and family). The complexity of the beliefs and attitudes measured in the structured questionnaire cannot be underestimated. For each association identified in the total sample of participants, it was rare that the association was found for the participants of each country.

Open-Ended Questions

Defining Suicide

As indicated by Kidd (2004), a suicide attempt can have many meanings, and this becomes more ambiguous among different cultural groups. The participants were asked to describe what they understood by the terms "attempted suicide" and "suicide." The data collected showed that the definitions of these terms vary, not only between groups, but also within groups, particularly for the term *attempted suicide* that often resulted in confused or unclear definitions. Overall, most participants defined a suicide attempt in a generic way, as an attempt to kill oneself or take one's own life or trying to suicide. Often participants added that the attempt fails. In Italy the majority of participants provided details about the intentionality, lethality, or the reason why it failed. More specifically, quite a few participants believed that, in a suicide attempt, the person intends or wants to die, but a similar proportion of participants included situations in which there is low or no intention to die. However, often the two things (intention to die or not) were mentioned together, for example:

> *An act through which a person intends, to a high or low degree of intentionality, to take his/her own life. An act with an unsuccessful outcome* (IT92f).[8]

A small number of participants also added their own personal comments or experiences with suicide attempts. For example, a participant who had been exposed to the suicide of an uncle and an acquaintance (in both cases preceded by a suicide attempt) commented:

> *A suicide attempt is a failed suicide, which however must not be underestimated because it expresses pain, suffering, a request of help, and a potential relapse* (IT117f).

While in Italy the majority of participants added some details about the intentionality, lethality, or reason for the failure, both in India and Australia the very generic definition of suicide attempt (i.e., as an attempt to kill oneself or take one's own life or try to suicide) was the most frequent response. The majority of Indian participants wrote responses similar to the following examples: "*It means when a*

---

[8] The code after the extracts (e.g., IT128f) indicates the country (IT for Italy, IN for India, and AU for Australia), the number of the questionnaire or the focus group and participant' sex.

person has tried to commit suicide but did not die" (IN6f) or "*A person tries to kill himself unsuccessfully*" (IN16m). However, many Indians appeared confused and unsure about the term. This is expressed by a student who clearly stated her uncertainty: "*I am not sure but I think it means making an effort to commit suicide.*" A few participants also wrote some negative judgments about the person, such as "*It is a cowardly act*" (IN133m), "*It is foolishness*" (IN144f). In Australia, approximately a third of participants added some details about lethality, intentionality, or the reason for the failure of the attempt.

The word suicide was generally defined in a "correct way," but quite a few times the description was ambiguous and, taken as a whole, less than one-third of participants clearly stated that suicide is voluntary, intentional, or deliberate or that it is a self-initiated act, implying that it is the person who does it to him/herself. Almost half of the Italian participants provided some details about the intention and self-determination of suicide. For example: "*The voluntary act to put an end to one's own life*" (IT37f) and "*The voluntary renunciation of living*" (IT141m).

However, even when some details were provided, it was not always clear which cases participants saw as suicide and which they did not (e.g., passive suicide, risky behaviors, self-induced homicide, etc.). Two participants stated that it is suicide also when performed by someone else (e.g., "*To be voluntarily killed,*" IT180m), and a few others included risky behavior or "slow" deaths, for example:

Taking one's own life but also those behaviors (like taking drugs or drinking excessively or letting yourself die by starvation) which are not evident/obvious deaths (IT54f).

An act through which the person takes his own life immediately or later in time (IT160f).

Even though the participants sometimes described suicide in a way that clearly distinguished this from a suicide attempt (e.g., "*I distinguish suicide from parasuicide. Suicide is without concealed motives, to take one's own life,*" IT75m), a few participants did not differentiate suicide from a suicide attempt (e.g., "*When a person succeeds in taking his own life or at least succeeds in doing what he had in his mind [to kill himself] even if he is then saved by someone,*" IT25f).

In India most participants defined suicide correctly, although sometimes vaguely, as "killing oneself," and only few participants added some details like intentionality and self-determination. A larger number of participants expressed some negative judgment or suggested reasons and aims for suicide. Besides the generic definition of suicide without any detail, suicide was occasionally described as a premature or unnatural death. The following is an example: *"Suicide is a term used for killing one self before the actual death or natural death"* (IN34f).

As noted above, some of the descriptions about suicide appeared to be referring more to attempted suicide. There is always the possibility that the participants meant something else (and this is a limitation in doing research with a questionnaire), but this might suggest that some participants have no clear understanding of what the two terms mean, for example: *"An attempt to end one's own life"* (IN14f) and *"A person who tries to kill himself"* (IN121m).

As already mentioned, quite a few participants suggested reasons for suicide and the aims of the act but, compared to Italy, where many participants believed that the person who dies by suicide cannot see or does not have another solution, this hypothesis was postulated by fewer Indian participants. Quite a few participants expressed negative judgments, usually saying that suicide is a cowardly, foolish, and stupid act, and some others mentioned the shame of it (e.g., *"Suicide means an act which cannot be justified. It is something which is unforgivable,"* IN60f) and made critical comments (e.g., *"A mockery of life!!!,"* IN157f).

The majority of Australian participants, like Italians and Indians, wrote generic definitions about suicide like "taking one's life" or "killing oneself." However, Australian participants, more than Indians but less than Italians, also added some details about intentionality and/or self-initiation (e.g., *"Deliberately killing oneself,"* AU94f). These two categories (i.e., generic or with details about intentionality or self-induced) represented most of the answers. Some Australian participants (but fewer than participants from India or Italy) wrote about reasons for a suicide and a few about the aims, such as:

> *"Wanted to terminate own life for reasons such as problems impacting on ability to have satisfaction in life: inability to find answer to help some problems"* (AU25f).

Compared to Italian and Indian students, Australian answers seldom included some sort of comment.

To summarize, suicide was described in generic ways but, overall, quite straightforwardly across cultures. Italians and Australians often provided more details, specifying that it is a voluntary or self-induced act. Italians and Indians also quite often wrote possible reasons for the act. Indians more frequently included negative judgments and used words similar to those used for a suicide attempt.

The majority of the participants gave a generic definition of attempted suicide. However, this was particularly true in India and Australia. In Italy, more than half of the participants provided some details about lethality, intentionality, or reasons for the failure of the attempt. One third of Australians also did so, but only a small proportion of the Indian participants did so. Since I used a self-administered questionnaire, it was not possible to ask further questions about their answers, but it appears that some participants, especially in India, were unclear about attempted suicide and included suicide ideation, suicidal plans, and self-harm. In India, quite a few participants did not seem to differentiate between attempted and completed suicide. Furthermore, a considerable proportion of the participants, in all three countries, seemed confused about these terms or included death-related behaviors that are not normally defined as suicide by experts.

Death

When asked about what they feel when they think about death, the majority of participants expressed negative feelings, but there were some similarities and differences between cultures about the types and contents of such feelings. Among Italian participants, the negative feeling associated with death was usually fear, but quite often they also expressed sadness and emptiness. Some examples are:

> The idea [of death] scares me. I do not have religious convictions and I do not believe in life after death. I believe it [death] is something that puts an end to everything. Consequently, I hope to delay it as much as possible (IT20f).

> A feeling (not very pleasant) to have someone who has "fixed in his personal diary" an unavoidable appointment without a come-back road and without a date (IT98m).

At times a negative thought towards death was seen as an incitement to live life at its fullest and best, such as:

> I value the importance of living well each moment of life because death, then, annuls and deletes everything (IT191m).

Quite often Italian participants also indicated that these negative feelings represented what their loved ones would feel if they died or what they felt when they thought of their loved ones' death. Related to this was a differentiation, mentioned by just a few participants, between what they felt when they thought about their own death versus about other people's death. For instance, a student, who reported suicidal ideation and plan, wrote, "*Fear for other people's death, much less for mine*" (IT48f). Another differentiation was related to the kind of death and at which moment in life and in what circumstances the death took place (in old age, because of sickness, etc.).

A few Italian participants, similar to Indian and Australian participants, reported positive feelings towards death, associated sometimes with religious thoughts, such as peace, serenity, and hope. In particular, quite a few of the "at-risk" youths wrote positive remarks (constituting half of the group of participants who reported this sort of feeling). For instance, three participants who reported suicidal ideation, plans, and attempts wrote:

Peace – no sensation (IT21f).
Lightness: an idea of death as natural, a transition from a state of being to another (IT52m).
Tranquility, peace, at the end is the most normal thing of life in general (IT189m).

In India, negative feelings towards death (particularly fear, but also loneliness, pain, etc.) were most prevalent, but to a lesser degree than in Italy and Australia, and these feelings were mentioned almost as often as feelings of acceptance and resignation to death. Although some Italian and Australian participants reported an acceptance that death is part of life, this was much more evident among Indian participants. Acceptance and resignation towards death was expressed in various ways, sometimes as an inducement to live life at its fullest. For instance:

Everyone has to die one day, death doesn't scare me, live life to the fullest and when the time comes I am ready to go (IN29f).
Ironically, the only certain element of life (IN30f).
Nothing special, it will happen [in] its own time (IN83m).

Similar to Italian participants and, to a lesser degree, Australian participants, Indians sometimes reported feelings related to other people (e.g., a loved ones' death or the pain felt by other people for the individual's death).

A few Indians manifested positive feelings about death, sometimes clearly linked to religious beliefs. More than two-thirds of these positive feelings were expressed by Indians who had suicidal ideation, plans and, in a few cases, also suicide attempt(s), such as *"Freedom"* (IN26f) or *"It's a new beginning"* (IN191f). Albeit gender issues were not the focus of this research, it is worth mentioning that the mixed feelings and positive feelings were expressed mainly by female participants.

Some participants differentiated their feelings towards natural death and suicide, sometimes expressing negative opinions towards the latter, for example:

Inevitable but scary when caused by accident and foolish when suicide (IN35f).
Death is something that cannot be prevented, however suicide can be" (IN95m).

The majority of Australian participants showed negative feelings towards death (e.g., *"Miserable. I don't believe in an afterlife, so death makes me pretty miserable,"* AU174m), usually fear and sadness and, at times, those feelings were related to the death of other people or the idea of leaving them. Also in Australia, a few participants differentiated between their death and other people's death and between different kinds of death (e.g., in young or old age).

Some participants manifested both positive (in some cases more acceptance) and negative feelings towards death and more than a quarter of these reported suicidal ideation and plan and, at times, also attempt. Of those people who expressed positive feelings, almost a third reported suicidal ideation, plan, and/or attempt. Examples of mixed or positive feelings from such participants are:

Scared but reassured, probably more frightened of how death comes about than death in itself (AU37f).
Sometimes I get upset when I think about others' deaths, especially those I'm close to. When I think of my own death, I usually feel peace (AU123f).
I feel an eclectic mix of emotions: fear, joy, religious, sanctimonious (AU171m).
I don't want to die, but it feels like it might be a place without pain. It makes me feel solemn, but not upset or worried (AU108m).

Australian students seldom expressed some negative opinions towards death by suicide or made a comparison between suicide and other deaths.

To summarize, although negative feelings were the most prevalent feelings in all three cultures, these were much more present among Italian and Australian participants than among Indian participants where there was often a feeling of acceptance and resignation towards death. Similarly, although mixed feelings (positive/acceptance and negative) were reported quite often by participants in all countries, Italians did so more than Australians and much more than Indians (e.g., fear and peace/hope/curiosity). Acceptance and resignation toward death were often mentioned by Indian participants and, to a lesser degree, by Australian and Italian

participants. Indian participants also expressed negative feelings about death by
suicide relatively more often as, to a lesser extent, did the Australians. A few participants in all three cultures showed positive feelings towards death (e.g., freedom, peace, end of suffering, etc.). Therefore, although overall feelings towards
death appeared to be similar across cultures, death was usually experienced more
negatively by Australians, followed by Italians (who also reported more mixed
feelings) and Indians (who reported acceptance more often). Participants who
reported suicidal ideation, plans, or attempts had relatively more positive feelings
or mixed feelings and this was a constant across cultures.

Word Association

In the word association task, participants were asked to list three words that come
into their mind when they think about suicide. For the Italian participants, the
most frequent words were loneliness/alone (33%), pain/suffering (30%), death
(27%), despair/desperation (17%), and fear (10%). For the Indian participants,
the most frequent words were coward/cowardice (16%), family/parents, other negative judgments (e.g., wrong, immoral, stupid) and, problems/causes (all at 14%),
pain/suffering (12%), and death/die (11%). For the Australian participants, the
most frequent words were pain/suffering (27%), sad/sadness (24%), depression/
depressed (23%), death/dying/dead (21%), and loneliness/alone (18%). Thus,
the responses of the Indian participants were very different from those of the participants in Italy and Australia. The Indians participants mentioned cowardice and
negative judgments much more often and also words relevant to the family.

It is worth noting that both Italian and Australian students mentioned pain and
suffering the most frequently and death, die, and dying as the third most frequent
words. However, whereas in Italy the second most frequent word was lonely,
loneliness or alone, referring to social and interpersonal factors, in Australia it
was depression or depressed, referring to an individual internal state. If depression
and depressed are put together with sad and sadness, this new category including
depression and sadness becomes very strongly represented in the Australian
sample, with a total frequency of 110. This result is quite different from Italy
(where the two categories together totaled 41 and India 21, showing a greater
association of suicide with depression and sadness in Australia. This might partly
be the effect of suicide prevention strategies in Australia that have often proposed
an association between suicide and depression.

It is interesting that some words appeared in one or two countries but not in the
other(s), such as words that relate to crime (i.e., crime, offence and murder), which
were mentioned only in India where suicide is still a criminal offence. Despair and

desperation had the fourth highest frequency, percentage, and score in Italy but were absent in India and less frequent in Australia. Words related to loss/lost were rare in Italy but were cited sometimes in India and even more often in Australia.

There were also some patterns of words that tended to be presented together. For example, in Italy, often the same participant wrote together (in various orders): loneliness, suffering and death/die; in India death/die was often linked to pain, suffering, or sorrow; whereas in Australia the co-occurrence of sad/sadness and loss/lost was more typical.

Opinions about Gender Differences

Across all the three countries, the majority of participants reported having an opinion about gender differences, at times correct and at other times incorrect. Most of Italians (both women and men) believed incorrectly that there are no differences in youth suicide by gender in Italy. In India participants reported no differences, and this might reflect an awareness of the fact that, in India, female and male rates of suicide are, in reality, similar. The majority of Australian female participants were aware that suicide rates are higher in males, whereas about half of the males thought that there are no differences.

In addition, many of the participants specified what the differences between genders were. Italian males and females specified fewer causes of youth suicide than Indians and Australians but, when they did so, they usually suggested that females are more sensitive, emotional, and weaker (although at other times these attributes were conferred on men). Social expectations and roles were also seen as different among the sexes, although only rarely. Indian females and males often saw differences in the reasons for suicide, usually financial problems and inability to meet expectations for males and various forms of harassment (including rape and by in-laws), unmarried pregnancy, dowry, lack of freedom and independence for females. For instance:

> *Yes, females face more problems than males – Indian women are tied to various bonds and are forced to do things, They have no life of their own. Their life is ruled by others which makes them commit suicide whereas males do suicide coz of ego problems, financial, or home problems* (IN38f).

Some participants expressed the view that females kill themselves more because in general they have to face more difficulties (e.g. *"Female rate is higher since they have more to cope with because of just being female,"* IN17f), and some males indicated that females are weaker and more emotional. India was

the only country where, although infrequently, participants indicated that females
might be forced to kill themselves (e.g., *"Yes, females: lack of interest, pressure
on her for her death,* IN2f; *"Females are forced more to commit suicide than
males. May be dowry or other lots of problems"* IN194f).

Australian males and females mainly indicated the impact of social expectations, particularly the expectation that men should not show their emotions and
feelings, while it was more acceptable for women to ask for (and receive) help
(e.g., *"Males commit probably because the male gender role does not accommo-
date talking as normal as female gender role does,"* AU46m). Italian and Australian females also identified differences in method (more violent and lethal in
males), but males rarely did so.

Characteristics of Young People Who Attempt or Complete Suicide

Overall Italian participants, although at times they expressed negative comments,
were generally nonjudgmental of suicidal youth and were more often empathic
than were Indian and Australian participants. This was evident in the attempt
made by many participants to "be in the suicidal person's shoes," to try to see
the way he or she sees and thinks, and to consider what might be his or her emotional state (i.e., highlighting the way the youth interpreted problems or perceived
suicide as the only or last option, and that the youth was desperate and in pain and
suffering). For instance:

> *Assaulted by gloomy thoughts; it is like there was a black, imperturbable veil
> between the suicidal person and the world* (IT99f).
> *He/she is a person in whom the hope of a better reality is extinguished and,
> with it, his/her soul* (IT1f).

The needs of the suicidal youth were quite often discussed with an empathic attitude. Furthermore, although intrapersonal attributions were given slightly more
often than interpersonal ones, in the majority of cases, participants "involved" other
people in the description of a suicidal person, affirming that he/she was alone, had
been abandoned, was not understood, or that people did not help or listen to him/
her, such as *"He/she was a person who felt alone, not understood, fragile, who could
not find sufficient reasons to keep living because, for him/her, life is a worthless
suffering"* (IT50m). This more compassionate attitude, together with a greater
"involvement" of other people in the suicidal act (which was sometimes expressed
as blame on the social context for the act, especially for not having helped, listened
to, or understood the person) was what most differentiated Italian participants from
Australians and, even more, from Indians. Fewer Italian participants mentioned

problems, but they usually focused on the person's perception of the problem rather than the problem itself, or on the lack of capacity, desire, or courage to face it (which was also frequently mentioned by Indian participants). The suicidal person was seldom described as mentally ill/depressed, and negative judgments were occasionally expressed. Youths who attempt suicide and those who kill themselves were generally described very similarly, and the few differences usually concerned the degree of certainty in the act (e.g., confused, insecure vs. determined), "intensity" of the emotions or thoughts (for instance, low hope vs. no hope; alternative vs. no alternative) and satisfaction of his/her needs (e.g., needs help vs. has not been helped; needs to be listened to vs. has not been listened to).

Compared to the Italian participants (who in a few instances used positive or empathic expressions), Indian participants generally used negative judgments to describe suicidal youths and made intrapersonal attributions (with many of these being equally judgmental). A few of these negative opinions involved "other people," but this was in reference to the person's responsibilities towards family and society. Examples are:

Coward, cannot face life, did not complete his responsibility due to his family and society (IN23f).
He is a very cruel man (IN86m).
Already I hate that person (IN179f).

Problems and difficulties were also mentioned, but usually in reference to the person's inability or lack of courage when facing life's problems. While it is true that this represented the majority of answers, a few Indian participants expressed more neutral opinions or more empathy, showing an attempt to understand the dynamics of suicide and to feel sorrow for the suicidal youth (e.g., *"Poor person, sympathy,"* IN28f; *"Dear friend do not suicide, I'm here! You don't worry,"* IN218m). Indian participants usually used the same attributions for the young person who attempted suicide and the one who died by suicide. The main difference was that usually the latter was seen even more (at times much more) negatively.

Australian participants were similar to Italians in some aspects and more similar to Indians in others. Like Italians and Indians, Australians mainly used intrapersonal attributions and, similarly to Italians, generally these were accompanied by interpersonal attributions and the aims and needs of the act (although, in Italy, interpersonal attributions were given more frequently). However, in Australia, similar to India, there was rarely an emphasis on the role of other people in the suicidal act. In fact, although quite a few participants wrote about aims and needs, these generally were given for an individual who attempted suicide (quite often "a cry for help" or "attention-seeking") and not for an individual who completed suicide. Only occasionally were "others" mentioned for the effects that suicide has on them or because the suicidal person did not ask or seek help from them (rather than not receiving help as for Italians), such as "*Someone who needed help of some sort, and should have asked for help*" (AU176m). Although these answers were rare, this also differentiated Australians from those few Indians who blamed others for not having helped. Australians were the only participants to often use words related to mental problems, such as depressed and mentally ill/disturbed. A few Australian participants also expressed negative judgments (slightly more than Italians but much less than Indians), especially when describing a youth who killed him/herself (e.g., "*Crazy, silly, troubled, stupid*," AU135m). However, some Australian participants expressed some sort of empathic remarks about the person or the act (usually "unfortunate"), such as "*Sad, sorry for them that they thought that was the only way out*" (AU49f). Usually similar attributes and themes were used by the same participant to describe a youth who attempts or completes suicide. The differences were generally about the "intensity" of the condition/feeling or the youth who died was described more negatively. In some instances, participants stated that the person who died did not ask for or did not see help.

What Keeps Young People Alive in Spite of Difficulties

Participants from all three countries indicated similar motivations to stay alive even when their lives are difficult. These motivations referred to the value of and love for life, loved ones (i.e., because family and friends love them, and they would not want to hurt them), and the belief that they can face the problem and that difficulties are a part of life and can be overcome. However, there were also differences.

First of all, the frequency of some answers was different. In India, for instance, God (expressed often as the belief that life is God's and God has a plan for each person) was mentioned more often as a deterrent than in Italy and Australia. Italians rarely expressed negative judgments towards suicide (such as suicide is selfish or cowardly) to justify the choice not to suicide, whereas this was expressed quite often by Indian participants and, to a lesser extent, by Australian participants.

Others/loved ones was a main deterrent across countries, but the role of this was different. In Italy, where this was the second most frequent theme, a greater number of participants wrote that they would not want to hurt the people who loved them, and slightly fewer wrote that they would not kill themselves because they are loved and receive support. In India loved ones (particularly, "family" or "parents") were the main deterrent to suicide (e.g., "*It stops me from suiciding when I think of my parents*," IN121m) and the division into the two subthemes was equal. Some Indian participants mentioned the shame that suicide would bring to the family. In Australia, where loved ones also were the most important deterrent, many more participants referred to the effects of suicide on others and the pain this would give them.

"Life" was another major theme across cultures, but it was much more important in Italy than in the other two cultures. In Italy this was, in fact, the most important deterrent, expressed mainly as love for life/value of life and the concept that, whatever happens, life is always worth living (e.g., *"Because I believe life must be lived at its best and there are many things to try, to see, to love. I prefer the suffering at the naught of death,"* IT54f). Love for life was the second most important deterrent against suicide among Indians.

Similarly, hope (and curiosity) for the future and a belief in change were important deterrents across all three cultures, although they were more important for Italian and Australian participants. In particular, compared to the other countries, Italian participants expressed curiosity about the future, whereas this was mentioned only a few times by Australians. Conversely, the Australian participants mentioned hope and a belief that things would change as the second most important deterrent (e.g., *"Life is a journey and things can only get better,"* AU48m).

In all three cultures, participants quite often reported the will to face the problem but, in India, a positive attitude towards life and problems, expressed as the acceptance that life has its ups and downs and that pain and problems are a part of life, was more prevalent as compared to Italy and Australia (e.g., *"It would be like admitting to have lost the battle of life, which I could even lose, alright, but before I would like to shoot all the cartridges that I have available,"* IT182m). Indians revealed a more fatalistic view of life, as expressed by the concept that life is not solely for the individual (sometimes it was mentioned that life is God's) and that people have certain responsibilities and plans that they must fulfill before dying. Linked to the belief that problems can be faced is the opinion that suicide is not the only option (cited quite frequently in each country but more by Italians and Indians) and the importance of feelings of self-confidence, pride, and love for oneself (scarcely reported by Australians, but mentioned much more often by Indians, followed by Italians). Also the fear of death, pain, and the unknown, as well as the lack of courage to kill oneself, appeared more often as a deterrent for Italians and Australians, whereas this was very rarely mentioned by Indians. Future projects and activities, such as hobbies, which give a meaning to life, were mentioned in each country, but more by Italians and Australians than by Indians. Two other answers that showed differences between cultures were the hope that they would receive help and support (cited more often by Australians) and that, if life were really horrible, maybe nothing would stop them (occasionally mentioned by Italians, but almost absent among Indian and Australian participants).

What Should Be Done for Youth Suicide Prevention

When asked how much is being done to prevent youth suicide in their country, overall, participants stated that very little or not much is being done. This was followed by the participants criticizing that nothing or almost nothing is done and, on the other hand, an equal number of students who believed that a fair bit or a lot is being done. Italians were the ones who most often believed that little or not much is being done, followed by Indians and, least often, Australians. However, besides how much is being done, a number of students, particularly in Australia, suggested that what is being done is not enough and that more could be done. Both Indian and Australian students pointed out that services are not available for everyone (e.g., rural vs. urban areas; at-risk youth vs. those with unknown risk, etc.), and what is available may not be completely adequate and could be better, and that often people do not know what is available. In fact, a considerable proportion of students, particularly in Italy, answered that they had no idea about how much is being done in their country, and some of them interpreted this as an index that not much is being done and that, if something is being done, they had not been made aware of it. Often students, across cultures, but particularly in Australia, complained that suicide does not get adequate attention and is still treated as a taboo topic, something people avoid talking about. For instance:

> *Nowhere near enough. It is growing but it is still an issue that is kept in the dark. (. . .) It's like ignorance is bliss* (AU70m).
> *There is a lot, but not much that is spoken about often enough. It is more of a "hush-hush" topic* (AU27f).

Following participants' opinions about *how much* is being done, they were asked to suggest what *should* be done to prevent youth suicide in their country. Students across countries suggested quite similar youth suicide prevention strategies. Overall, the two main strategies were education and/or awareness about suicide, followed by providing (free, easily accessible, and confidential) counseling services. Other strategies were, in order, other more generic support and help services, showing an empathic attitude toward youth, promoting more general social change (also eliminating large-scale problems), and education about asking for help and where to get it. However, there were differences in the relative importance of these strategies in each country. In fact, while education/awareness about suicide was the leading theme across cultures, this was more often cited in Australia, followed by Italy and lastly India. The form of the education, when specified, was slightly different. For instance, in Australia, this was quite often about recognizing warning signs and, both in Italy and Australia, talking about and discussing the topic more, whereas in India this aspect of reducing the taboo about suicide was rarely mentioned.

School programs were the main strategy for education/awareness across cultures, but other means proposed were: group discussions, advertisements and TV in Italy; seminars, plays and advertisements in India; and campaigns in Australia (e.g., *"The attempted suicide victims should be given an opportunity to voice their experience through the media,"* IN202f).

Another difference centred around help-services which, although the second largest theme across cultures, were mentioned slightly more by Australians and Indians. The latter also more often specified the service as counselling (which they underlined should be confidential), whereas in Australia and Italy this was more often a generic support or help service. For instance:

Systems to identity + support at risk kids. They need to be approached as generally they won't approach help themselves (AU201m).

On the other hand, help-lines were mentioned only a few times by Indians, followed by Australians and, rarely, by Italians. It was also observed that Italian participants generally referred to services for youths and, sometimes for their parents, such as centers where they could go to receive support and help, whereas Indians and Australians more often restricted those services to suicidal youth. This might reflect the idea of creating more specialized services but also the association of suicide with mental illness and, therefore, seeing services as something for "those kinds" of youths and not for any youths who might need help. Furthermore, educating youths to seek help and informing them about where to go was more central among Australian students, followed by Italians, but was infrequent among Indians. Furthermore, the former more often suggested "encourage to talk" as a suicide prevention strategy.

Besides basing the responsibility of youth suicide prevention on government and institutions, that is, providing services and education programs, quite often participants saw suicide prevention as something that includes everyone. This point was suggested more strongly in Italy, followed by India, where students quite often recommended having an "empathic ear" toward youths (e.g., *"Each person in his/her little own way should do something: for instance, listen a bit more, and not just the words,"* IT109f). This was less frequently suggested by Australians. Italians also included more activities and initiatives that promote the value of life. Italians and Indians, slightly more than Australians, pointed out that some kind of moral education about life and values was needed. On the other hand, a small number of Indians, and fewer Australians, suggested moral education against suicide, and Indians were the only group, although infrequently, to recommend the use of laws to prevent youth suicide.

A final difference in the prevention strategies was a more general change in society and the reduction/elimination of social problems. This was suggested more often by Indians and less by Italians and Australians. Furthermore, the focus in India was more about actual problems (e.g., poverty and unemployment) than values and attitudes. A few students in Italy and Australia expressed a pessimistic view about youth suicide prevention.

It is interesting to note that one of the main strategies to prevent suicide, that is, control of means, widely recognized as contributing to a reduction of suicide, was mentioned by only one student in Australia.

When asked about the role of family and friends, all participants, with a few rare exceptions, thought that they could help in the prevention of youth suicide. Overall, their contribution was seen as a "loving and supporting role," that is, giving support, love, and attention to the person, listening and understanding, and helping to solve their problems. However, in Italy, compared to the other two countries, there was a greater focus on the social aspects of "loving and supportive role", the importance of being there and not making the person feel alone, as well as a relatively larger focus on valuing the positives in life. For instance:

By truly listening instead of waiting one's own turn to talk (. . .) (IT226m).
In my opinion, simply by not being deaf to the scream for help of a young person (IT229m).

In India, compared to the other countries, there was a bigger role for family and friends in helping with or solving the problem, in addition to giving emotional and moral support (e.g., *"By talking to them, making them feel wanted, letting them know that they are not fighting their battles alone, that no one is truly an island,"* IN26f). Indian participants also felt that educating youths against suicide was important. It is worth noting that Indians mentioned the important role of family and friends in youth suicide prevention more than participants in the other two countries.

Australians' answers were similar to those of Italians and Indians, but there was a greater focus on communication, that is, talking to the person and making the person talk. Furthermore, the "guardian role," that is, the role of being attentive to suicide warning signs and signs of malaise, and the "mediating role," that is, putting the person in contact with services or asking for help, were mentioned more often by Australians than Italians, but these were almost never mentioned by Indians. Examples of these roles are:

> *Provide someone the person can talk to, try to note if person is showing any changes, and talk to someone (e.g., counselor) about this. Encourage the person to see a counselor (AU52f).*
> *If they were more aware of the signs and acted on them without worrying about how the person would react* (AU198m).

Help-Seeking: With Whom Would They Talk About Their Suicidal Intention. . .If Anyone?

When asked whom they would talk to if they were considering killing themselves, most participants in all three countries answered "no one" or "friends," followed by "family" and, especially in Australia, some kind of professional (such as a psychologist, counselor, psychiatrist, or help-line). More specifically, Italian and Australian participants wrote "no one" as the most frequent answer, but this was more common for Italians (e.g., "*Maybe with a female friend, but if I had one I would not be thinking about suicide, so no one,*" IT180m). In India, this was the second most frequent answer (e.g., "*I don't or can't speak about suicide,*" IN151m), whereas the most frequent answer for Indians was friends, which was also the second most frequent answer for Italians and Australians. Family was the third most frequent category for both Italians and Indians (albeit this was much less frequent in Italians compared to the other two groups) and the fourth among Australians. Similarly, although professional help was the third most frequent answer both in Italy and Australia, this was mentioned more than twice as much by Australians and was, therefore, a much more important option for Australians than for Italians or Indians (e.g., "*A counselor – someone who I don't know personally, and who would listen without judgment,*" AU57f). Indians were least likely to ask for professional help.

Australians were more likely to talk about suicide to their partners than either of the other two groups. Also, while few Italians and Australians would talk to a priest or spiritual guide, more Indians would talk directly to God. Other possible helpers were a stranger (more frequent in Italy and Australia) or a nonspecified "someone," trusted or close to them (in Italy and India). Particularly in India, occasionally participants suggested teachers, neighbors, and elders. Participants in all three countries seldom stated that they would write a letter or a diary or would talk to their pets. The findings are shown in the table below.

Category	Italy			India			Australia			Total
	I option	II option	Total	I option	II option	Total	I option	II option	Total	Total
Family	25 (III)	25	50 (III)	66 (II)	39 (II)	105 (III)	61 (III)	36	97 (IV)	252 (III)
Friend(s)	83 (II)	31 (II)	114 (II)	113 (I)	33 (III)	146 (I)	88 (I)	46 (III)	134 (II)	394 (II)
Partner	24	1	25	11	6	17	33	13	46	88
Teacher	1	4	5	3	9	12	0	1	1	18
Professional	22	26 (III)	48 (IV)	7	16	23	61 (III)	61 (II)	122 (III)	193 (IV)
Priest	15	9	24	2	1	3	4	10	14	41
God	1	1	2	14	15	29	5	3	8	39
Someone...	17	7	24	17	9	26	2	2	4	54
Stranger	4	8	12	1	3	4	9	9	18	34
Other	2	7	9	3	13	16	4	6	10	35
No one	95 (I)	108 (I)	203 (I)	44 (III)	74 (I)	118 (II)	66 (II)	74 (I)	140 (I)	461 (I)

Female and male participants gave fairly similar answers, and differences were found mainly in the order of resources (e.g., as second option, family was the third category among Indian females and the second among males). However, Australians had greater gender differences in help-seeking. If feeling suicidal, females would rely more on professional help than would males, and males would talk more to their family.

Summary

The analyses of the open-ended survey questions showed several differences between cultures, as well as differences within cultures. For instance, the question on feelings towards death indicated more positive feelings in Indians compared to Italians and Australians. Participants from the three countries also gave different words when they thought about the word "suicide," such as pain, loneliness and despair in Italy; family, cowardice and other negative judgments in India; and pain, depression and sadness in Australia. In addition, the kinds of attributions used to describe youths who make suicide attempts and youths who complete suicide, as well as constructs linked to youth suicide preventions (deterrents, help-seeking and prevention strategies) showed the influence of cultural factors on the participants' answers. For instance, overall, participants across countries believed that family and friends can help in the prevention of youth suicide, but the role was different. Italian participants gave more importance to social support and making the person not feel alone, as well as a relatively bigger focus on valuing the positives in life. In India, compared to the other countries, there was a bigger role for family and friends in helping with or solving the problem. Indians also suggested relatively more often that family and friends should educate and give arguments against suicide. Australians put a greater emphasis on talking and making the person talk. Furthermore, the "guardian role" and the "mediating role" were more often mentioned by Australian than Italian participants, and were almost never mentioned by Indian participants.

The Focus Groups

Thirteen groups, formed by 96 students, met over 24 focus group sessions. This section summarizes and compares the results of the three cultures represented.

Beliefs about the Afterlife

When asked if they believed in life after death, the majority of Italian and some Australian participants had a nonstructured spiritual belief that there might be something (e.g., energy, general consciousness, or memories) after death, but they reported not knowing what this might be. Some Australian and a few Italian participants said that they did not believe in or did not have an opinion about any kind of existence after death. Only a few Italian and occasional Australian participants reported a religious concept of an afterlife (usually Catholic in the former and also non-Catholic Christian in the latter).

In contrast, approximately half of the Indian participants reported religious beliefs about an afterlife, usually Hindu (but this was not consistent among the participants) and, less often, Christian. In one of the groups, participants pointed out how religious beliefs were forced on them by parents, but that they, personally, did not believe in an afterlife. In fact, the other half of the group generally did not believe in an afterlife, except those few participants who believed that "something" remains after death (e.g., memories or energy). The following is an extract from the discussion among Indian participants (IN2):

> *M4: According to the Hindu culture, life after death is possible. In Hindu culture, if a man does not fulfil his worldly pleasures then his soul will not go to moksha[9]. If a man fulfils all his worldly pleasures, he'll go to the moksha.*
> *F3: Even I don't believe because after death we don't know.*

---

[9]   See Chapter 7.

*M4: I don't believe. After death the person doesn't know where he went,
that's what I believe. Our culture believes that after death there is a life,
but there's no proof.*
Mod: What about your beliefs?
*F5: It's forced on us. It's our parents who say something like that. We have to
do something for our parents.*

In regard to the second question (Is there any difference between what happens
in the afterlife for young people who kill themselves and those who die in other
ways?), the majority of Italian and Australian participants believed that there are
no differences and that what happens is the same for everyone. Some participants,
slightly more often amongst the Italians, believed that, if there is any difference, it
would be based on the way these people lived rather than the way they died. A
few others repeated their lack of belief in an afterlife or that they did not know
what might happen in the afterlife for anybody.

Indian participants were divided into two main groups also on this question:
those (slightly more) who thought that youths who kill themselves suffer some
sort of punishment (in accord with Hindu or Christian beliefs) and others who
believed that there is no difference. The latter usually thought that there is no soul
or afterlife, whereas a small number of participants believed that the souls of youth
who died by suicide would go to God anyway. Here is an extract that express a
range of views (IN5):

*M2: We have to be reborn. Until you purify your soul, you have to rebirth
again and again, until you finish that off [Mod: So what will happen if a
person commits suicide?] He will again be reborn . . . he has done a bad
thing so he will be reborn. If he had done good things, he will go to Heaven.*
M3: After suicide, he dies, that's it!
*M4: It is our culture, if a person commits suicide . . . he has to do what he has
left undone. In the next birth he has to complete that. This is not what I personally believe, it is my culture.[I think that] if a person dies by a normal death or
by suicide, he will be buried or burnt, he will change into another form.*
*M2: God will give some punishment for committing suicide . . . They will be
roaming around. . . .*
M6: Our life is from God. God has sent us on a mission . . . He will go to hell.

Some Indian participants also commented on the effects of religious beliefs on
suicide risk. Generally, belief in an afterlife was seen as a deterrent against suicide
(e.g., fear to go to Hell, and not receiving a funeral), but a few participants dismissed such protective beliefs.

In all three countries, a minority of participants made the point that people who kill themselves are not concerned about the afterlife but on ending "this" life and their troubles.

Attitudes toward Suicide

Ordering participants from the three cultures from the least to the most judgmental, Italians were first, followed by Australians and then Indians. Italian participants generally had a nonjudgmental and rather accepting attitude towards suicide. This should not be interpreted to mean that Italians had positive attitudes (apart from those few participants who believed that suicide is a courageous act), but rather that they rarely expressed negative opinions (e.g., selfish) and had an overall empathic attitude towards suicide. Suicide was seen as something that should not be judged but understood. On the other hand, some Australian participants expressed negative views stating, for instance, that suicide is selfish, bad, or stupid, whereas a few had a more accepting and empathic attitude. However, despite differences in their personal attitudes, participants from both countries believed that there is a negative attitude towards suicide among other people and that suicide is a topic that people (and, in Australia, the media and prevention programs as well) avoid talking about. Italian participants mentioned that they believed that people judge a suicidal person because they feel guilty and responsible for the event and because suicide is something that scares people. Furthermore, Australians indicated a general negative attitude towards people's expression of feelings (which was never mentioned by Italians), which might indicate a greater difficulty for Australian youth, particularly men, in expressing suicidal feelings compared to Italians. For instance:

> *that stigma that is attached to, stigma attached to men expressing themselves to other people, that they're not keeping it all inside ... unfortunately you grow up in a society where it's, you know, you don't...it's not really, you know, comfortable talking about it with people* (AU3f).

Many Indian participants reported negative attitudes toward suicide and youths who kill themselves. Some participants believed that suicide is a crime, at least partially as a consequence of the Indian law against suicide, a "bad thing," foolish, selfish, and wrong. In all groups, participants noted the negative attitudes that society has toward people who die by suicide. They also indicated that society's judgments affect the family in several ways (bringing shame to and a "black mark" on the family), and the members of the family who are not married (especially the daughters) will have difficulty finding a spouse. However, despite the fact that many participants reported negative personal or social attitudes towards suicide, some participants did not express any opinion, and a few expressed a more accepting attitude or believed that a person who kills him-/herself is courageous. Unlike participants from the other two countries, only a few Indian participants stated that suicide is a taboo topic. However, in the feedback forms on the focus groups sessions and in-person at the end of the session, many participants said that it was the first time they had ever spoken about this subject and that suicide is a taboo topic.

The Thoughts and Feelings of Suicidal Youths

For the exercise called *Stick figure*, I drew a stick figure and told participants that he/she represented a young person who was on the verge of attempting suicide (but did not die). Participants were asked to describe what they believed that individual would think, say, and feel before engaging in this act.

In all three cultures, participants believed that suicidal youths have similar thoughts before killing themselves, that is, they have thoughts that support their choice (e.g., finally I will end my suffering, life is not worth living, suicide is the only solution), negative thoughts about themselves (e.g., I'm a failure, I'm not worth living), thoughts about others (e.g., no one did or can help me, I will miss my family) and the method of suicide. However, there was a difference in the relative frequency and content of these thoughts. In fact, Italian participants rarely believed that people have negative thoughts about themselves whereas these kinds of thoughts were mentioned more often by Australians and Indians, in both cases reporting mainly thoughts of failure, lack of achievement, and the unworthiness or meaninglessness of their lives. Indians, more than anyone else, suggested that suicidal youths think that they cannot face the situation. Both Italians and Indians were more likely than Australians to believe that the suicidal person would think of others, but in different ways: Italians put more emphasis on thoughts about not having been helped and about the blame or guilt of others, whereas Indians put more emphasis on being a burden on others and on not being loved and cared for.

With regard to what suicidal youths say, this was generally the most neglected part across cultures and groups because the majority of participants thought that, if a suicidal person communicates something about the suicide intention, he/she is likely to do so indirectly (e.g., saying that "life is meaningless") or through non-verbal communication (e.g., body communication or recklessness). Across cultures, some participants believed that those who talk about suicide do not do it, but some others commented on the danger of this myth. Other participants believed that a suicidal youth might say goodbye, pretend to be happy, pray, or leave notes and letters.

The greatest variety of answers between groups and across cultures concerned feelings. In Italy, the most consistent answers across groups were that a young person, before trying to take his/her life, feels despair, loneliness, confusion, fear, pain and suffering, and sadness. In India, these feelings were loneliness, disappointment, irritation and anger, hopelessness, worthlessness and meaninglessness (of life and themselves), shame, sadness, and depression. Australian participants believed that suicidal youth might be sad and depressed, but that they might also feel happy, relieved (from their problems), and in peace (because everything will be over soon). Other feelings mentioned across groups were anger, fear and anxiety, feelings of control and power, pain, and emotional pain.

Basically, across cultures, participants thought that suicidal people feel sad and depressed (although some participants, especially in Australia, suggested opposite feelings such as happiness). Feelings of loneliness and hopelessness and despair were suggested more often by Italians and Indians. Fear and anxiety was suggested more often by Italians and Australians compared to Indians. Anger was mentioned more often by Australians and Indians, and the latter was the only group to believe that suicidal youth feel shame.

Figures 1–3 summarize the key themes emerged in the three countries.

Differences Between Attempted and Completed Suicide

In Italy and Australia, the question just analyzed stimulated discussions about possible differences between people who attempt suicide and people who die by suicide. In Italy some participants believed that a suicide attempt usually is a request for help or to seek attention whereas people who die are more often people who do not want any help or who think that they cannot be helped anymore. A few Australian participants pointed out differences among youths who self-harm or make a "cry for help" (an expression which was not used by the Italians) and those who attempt suicide. Self-harm and cries for help were seen as attention-seeking behavior or aimed at inflicting pain on oneself, whereas in the suicide attempt there is the intention to die. For instance:

> ... like there's a line down the middle between the kids that just want some attention and want someone to go "oh, you're really struggling right now," and someone that really is just at the end (AU2f).

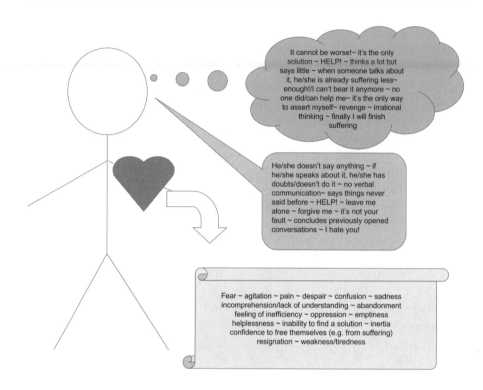

Figure 1. Italian participants.

Unlike Italians and Australians, Indian participants never mentioned differences between attempted suicides and completed suicides. This might reflect a mental representation that the main difference between the two acts is a difference in the outcomes (death) rather than in the intentions or aims of the act. Therefore, if this hypothesis is correct and the cultural representation of attempted and completed suicide is the same (or very similar), whatever the participants believed about completed suicide (e.g., reasons and negative attitudes) applies also to non-lethal suicidal behavior.

Reasons for Youth Suicide

The focal point of the explanatory model of youth suicide for Italian participants was on other people who were seen as contributing to or causing a person's suicide. In fact, Italian participants focused largely on interpersonal factors, in particular loneliness and having no one to talk with who listens or who is really close to

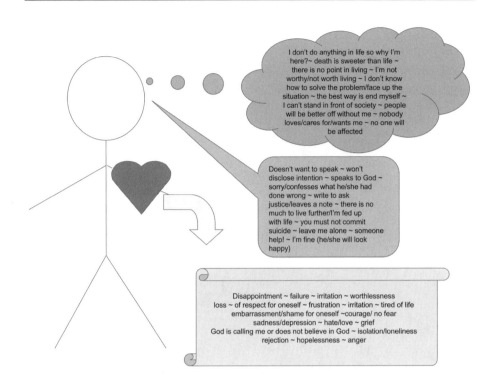

Figure 2. Indian participants.

the person. Other people were seen by participants as "involved" in the suicide because they did not understand or did not help the young person or, to a lesser extent, because they caused the difficult situation that lead to the suicide (e.g., abandonment). For instance:

I see it [reasons for youth suicide] as really centered on the person and his/ her relationship with society. I mean, the relationship ... the interaction with others, with peers, with relatives (IN1f).

Another important reason for suicide, for some participants, was that the person built a fake identity because of a lack of acceptance of who he/she really was or a desire to not disappoint others' expectations. Other reasons mentioned were: not feeling integrated in society, break-up of a love relationship, problems in the family, relational problems and bereavement, and the sense of guilt or the fear of people's judgments for something they have done. Other reasons proposed by Italian participants referred to intrapersonal factors, particularly feelings of

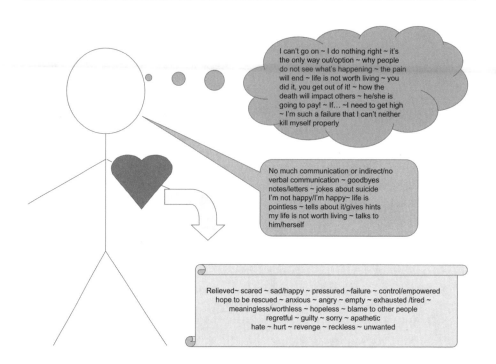

Figure 3. Australian participants.

worthlessness and lack of self-acceptance. Participants often indicated as reasons the lack of plans or projects for the future or reasons and purposes to live for, a lack of interests and hobbies, or the loss of something that had previously given meaning to life. Depression was mentioned during the sessions but not as commonly as it was in Australia and, similarly to India, not as a reason for the suicide but more as a feeling. In fact, some participants argued that people tend to describe suicidal persons as mentally ill or say that the person was not conscious of what they were doing in an attempt to "exorcize" suicide and make it look like something that happens only to "certain" people, to protect themselves from the idea of suicide (i.e., "It happens to abnormal people not to [people like] me"), and to protect society and family. For example, *"potentially everyone can suicide and this scares us"* (IN4m).

Events and problems (such as exam failure or illness) received less attention from Italian participants, and their relevance was generally based on the impact that this has on the specific person (e.g., the way people see and interpret the problem and the understanding and support that they receive from others) rather than on the event or problem *per se*. A concept that was central among Italian participants, which was mentioned also by some participants from the other two cultural groups, but in a less consistent way, was the representation of the suicidal youth as someone who is deeply suffering (i.e., suicide as a result of the pain, suffering, and the malaise of living).

Indian participants saw the lack of support and care and help from others (usually family) for coping with a problem, as well as being neglected, alone, or isolated, as important reasons for youth suicide. However, usually they gave more emphasis to the role of others as causes of suicide. The most frequently mentioned interpersonal issue among Indian participants was love failure, an issue largely attributed to the lack of freedom for many Indian youths to be in a relationship with the person they love and the Indian custom of arranged marriage (which takes the form of child marriage in some areas). Other than arranged and child marriages, other cases of love failure described by Indian participants were due to unreciprocated love. Cases of altruistic suicide were described frequently (e.g., "*Many people sacrifice their life,*" IN2f), and this kind of suicide included situations in which the young person (generally a woman) kills herself so as not to bring (or because she has brought) shame on the family (e.g., because of rape, unmarried sex or pregnancy) and, therefore, suicides as a means to preserve the family's name. Being a burden on the family was very often seen as a cause of youth suicide and usually focused on being a financial burden (e.g., as a result of disability, physical illness, or school fees).

Other reasons referred to intrapersonal factors and included the failure to achieve in life, an inability to cope and face problems, frustration of ambitions, and lack of freedom. Among external causes, failure at exams or at entrance tests was considered to be one of the main causes of youth suicide among Indian participants, particularly in poor families. In addition, poverty, financial problems (e.g., debt and bank loans, loss of a job and unemployment), and corruption were described as important causes of suicide. However, these events *per se* were not generally seen as leading to suicide but rather for the shame they brought on the person and the family.

Indian participants saw important reasons for youth suicide as gender-specific. They often referred to violence against women and a social view of women not only as inferior, but as "the one to blame" for whatever happens to them (e.g., being raped or pre-marital sex not followed by marriage) and to others (e.g., the death of a husband or misbehavior of children). Furthermore, women were generally presented as dependent on their family and without a life of their own, such as:

*Because most of the women don't think much of their own lives. It's only
their husband's, children, and father's lives. Most women in India, they don't
think anything of their own lives* (IN3f).

The dowry has been described as an important cause of suicide among young
Indian women because it makes women a financial burden on the family and also
because, if the woman's family does not have enough money to pay as much as
has been demanded as dowry from the husband's family, she becomes a victim of
physical, mental, and emotional harassment, and even torture by the in-laws and
the husband. Sexual abuse and corruption and bribery, which were seen as affecting particularly women, were also presented as a major cause of youth suicide.
Gender-related issues also emerged in regard to male suicide. A few participants
observed that men are exposed to social expectations related to job and status and
pressure to achieve, whereas generally there is no pressure on these aspects for the
majority of females. Linked to this was the expectation that men continue the family business, leading to a lack of freedom in the choice of professions.

In the Australian participants' explanatory model of youth suicide, interpersonal factors played an important role. Participants often referred to expectations
(usually by parents or friends) and the failure to meet those expectations as an
important reason for youth suicide. Pressure to do well at university was seen
as another important reason. A further reason mentioned was social isolation
and lack of social support, which were at times seen as a result of family conflicts
and problems and a lack of friends or close friends (i.e., meaningful relationships).
In particular, some participants noted that youths who killed themselves did not
get the help and the attention they asked for and needed. Another factor mentioned
by a few participants was the idea that youths who kill themselves might have
"played a part" (similar to what was reported by some Italians) or felt that they
do not fit in with or meet their peers' social stereotypes or expectations.

Intrapersonal factors were also central, especially depression (both as a mental
illness and as a state-of-mind), homosexuality (for men), and lack of aims, purpose, and direction in life. In particular, being depressed or homosexual was presented as a sort of Australian "script" for suicide. Another important factor
(especially for men) was being unable (or not knowing how) to show emotions.
Australian participants also believed that suicidal youths do not seek help and that
they internalize problems. A few participants attributed this attitude to sociocultural aspects (the "Australian culture"). Furthermore, the social isolation was
often expressed as being lonely and isolated (rather than "alone"), which perhaps
describes more intrapersonal characteristics. In fact, occasionally, participants stated that suicidal people retire to their homes during the period before killing
themselves.

Among external/situational factors, which were mentioned less often compared to the other two sets of causes, was failure at university (or, more rarely, at work), usually linked to the expectations about this (personal or from their family). In addition, financial problems (e.g., bankruptcy and debts, and alcohol and drug-related expenses) were seen as a reason by some participants. Alcohol and drugs were also mentioned as an element in the suicide path, preceding or aggravating it. Australian participants indicated some gender differences, particularly in problem-solving strategies. Australian men rely on themselves whereas women express their problems to others. This was thought to be based on a cultural stereotype which sees Australian men as macho, expected to be tough, strong, and without emotions and problems, or not worrying about them. As a consequence, men were represented as not expressing their emotions (suicidal feelings included) for the fear of judgment because of not meeting the social image of Australian men, which puts them at risk of suicide more than females who, at the opposite extreme, can cry. A few others referred to a cultural attitude of not taking things seriously, the lack of support when needed, or the tendency towards superficial conversations, such as:

> . . . everybody tries to put a light-hearted spin on everything and that makes things okay if, you know, maybe for half a day or something, you feel better, you know, for half an hour with your mates or something and then, and then when they're all gone, you're back in the dark again (AU4m).

A further difference was related to homosexuality, believed to be more accepted and acceptable in women and a more important cause of suicide for Australian men.

What Keeps Some Youths Alive in Spite of Difficulties

The two main reasons why both Italian and Australian participants claimed that they would not kill themselves were their loved or close ones and having a purpose in life (although the former received slightly more emphasis in Italy and the latter in Australia). The first reason was usually expressed as the love for or from someone, receiving support from others and having responsibilities towards someone, but also as not hurting loved and close ones and causing their suffering. In Australia, participants expressed this first main deterrent relatively more often with the concept of having "at least someone" who gives support, listens and shows that he or she cares. In Italy, there was also the deterrent effect of not being able to see their loved ones anymore after death.

Having something to look forward to, a goal, projects, life plans, and things that the person enjoys doing and that give meaning and purpose to life were also very relevant deterrents for Italian and Australian participants. A few Australians expressed this as having something positive in life. In both countries, some participants also pointed out that other people can make life worth living. The following conversation (AU3) illustrates this.

> *F1: ... having a goal to work toward so having a sense of purpose and, like, the important thing is that they're achievable goals I suppose, not huge massive ...*
> *M1: I think having a sense of purpose and a sense of belonging and goals in life is motivation to live and if you don't have that motivation to live you're more likely to commit suicide ...; if you're active, if you have a purpose then your life has meaning ...*
> *F2: ... you have to make sure what your doing is actually meaningful to you not you're just doing it for the sake of doing it ...*
> *Mod: Anything you want to add?*
> *F3: ... you want to be sort of achievable goals ... and suppose not putting all your eggs in one basket is another important thing like having lots of goals at the same time so if you fail at one you still got another two you know ...*

Appreciation and love for life, curiosity, hope for the future and a positive attitude towards life and problems were other main deterrents in Italy. Of these, only the hope for a change in the future and, less often, curiosity about the future were cited by some Australian participants. A few Australian participants discussed the consequence of suicide on one's personal or family image.

In India, the family was mentioned very often and was the principal deterrent compared to the other two cultural groups. Here the focus was more specifically on the family only but, similarly to Italians and Australians, Indians cited the love for and from their families, the desire to not hurt them and make them sad, and the consequences that suicide would have on them, as important deterrents. This latter aspect (putting a "bad name," stigma, on themselves and their family) appeared to be particularly relevant for Indians. Apart from the stigma for their family, a negative attitude towards suicide (as foolish or as a sin) was sometimes given as a reason why Indian participants would never kill themselves. For some participants, this was a result of their religious beliefs on suicide.

Duties and responsibilities towards family, society, and the country were also important deterrents for Indians, whereas Italians and Australians mentioned only the responsibilities for someone who is dependent on the person and, overall, this received less emphasis than, for instance, being loved and receiving support. Another main deterrent in India was the belief that people have to face problems and failures in life, that there is a solution for every problem and, as some of the Indian participants stated, suicide is not the solution. The value and love for life was a deterrent against suicide as well.

Youth Suicide Prevention

How much is done in Italy, India, and Australia?

Both Italian and Indian participants generally believed that nothing or very little is done in their home country for youth suicide prevention. Australian participants generally believed that something is done in Australia, but that it is not enough. Across cultures, participants agreed that more needs to be done. A common criticism was that there is much more focus on other issues (e.g., alcohol, smoking, drugs, and drunk-driving) than suicide, and initiatives are not usually specific to suicide prevention. Another criticism was that, if there are help-services available, these are not publicized, and so people are not aware of them. Furthermore, help-services are based on the concept that the person in distress will look for help, but some participants doubted that a suicidal person would do so. Italian and Australian participants attributed the lack of focus on suicide and suicide-specific initiatives to the taboo toward this topic, and it was also believed that, in Australia, suicide programs have been ineffective because they have been developed without listening to the young people's voices.

In India, some participants complained that services are available only in big cities and not where they are really needed (e.g., villages), and they criticized the lack of investigation into the causes of suicide (especially for suicide in women). Other Indian participants argued that, in addition to nothing being done for suicide prevention in India, the media (including movies) and people encourage suicide in some situations (e.g., in cases of rape). For example, "*I don't think very much is done to prevent youth suicide in India. In fact, as far as I'm concerned, I think it's pretty much encouraged in some cases. Through movies*" (IN3f).

Help-seeking: To whom would Italian, Indian and Australian participants talk if they were considering killing themselves?

The majority of Italian participants believed that, if they had made the decision to kill themselves, they would not talk to anyone mainly because, if they had reached that decision, it meant that people did not understand or help them or because they did not want to be stopped. Some Italian participants stated that they would not talk to anybody or would not talk directly about suicide. Those participants who would talk to someone usually chose to talk to a friend.

Indian participants were equally divided into three groups: those who would not talk to anyone, those who would talk to parents, and those who would talk to friends. Participants who would not talk to anybody reported that they would not do so mainly because of the consequences that the disclosure would have, that is, other people would know about their suicidal thoughts and the person's situation could become even worse. Although some participants affirmed that they would never talk to their family or parents, others believed that parents would be the best option. Nevertheless, participants generally agreed that the majority of youths in India cannot talk to their parents and, according to some participants, to anyone at all, because of the lack of freedom and fear of talking with parents, in particular with fathers. In this regard, it was also pointed out that women often cannot talk to their friends for fear of the situation that is creating the problem becoming known to others. For instance (IN5):

M1: If there is a particular person we can talk to about this? I don't think so. The main problem in India, when children are thinking to suicide, no one . . . there is no person to whom we can freely talk . . .
M2: . . . the majority of students can't go and speak to their parents; in many cases, especially girls, they cannot go and speak to their girlfriend also. Just in case they go and speak to other people and then it becomes a big, major issue. Boys at least can go and speak to the other persons.

Although generally Australian participants thought that youths who kill themselves do not talk to anyone, some Australian participants thought that, if they themselves were considering suicide, they would talk to friends or peers. Conversely, some participants excluded friends or close friends because these might judge them or change their opinion of them or might be unable to cope with the situation. A few participants said that they would talk to siblings. Some participants excluded the possibility of talking to parents, whereas others reported that they would talk to them.

Across cultures, participants defined the characteristics that the "someone" to whom they could talk to about their suicidal ideation must have in the same way. Above all, this person must not judge them but listen and understand, not interfere with the decision or say what to do, maintain confidentiality, and must not get worried or upset. In a few instances, it was suggested that this person should have been in a similar situation. The issue of confidentiality was particularly central for Indians, whereas not being judged was particularly important to Australians. Although this description could match with what are, at least, supposed to be the characteristics of counselors and other professionals, across countries, professional help was usually dismissed, especially in India, followed by Italy. Stigma towards professional help was the main reason why participants would not go to a counselor, in particular, the belief that people who see a counselor are crazy. However, this stigma was reported more by Indians and Italians than by Australians, where professional help was selected by more participants. Another important reason why Indian participants said that they would not seek professional help was the belief that counselors do not maintain confidentiality, and so they feared that their problems would be known by others. A further reason for Italians and, even more so, Australians was the lack of emotion and the coldness of professionals.

Social stigma toward professional help was mentioned less often by Australians who were a little more positive toward the idea of professional help, although they also had generally negative opinions of professionals. However, this should not be interpreted as a sign of a general acceptance of help-seeking considering that, in several instances, Australian participants reported the stereotype and expectations that "strong" people and men do not show emotions or have problems and, therefore, do not seek or need help.

Warning signs

In all three countries, participants believed that a friend would manifest suicide warning signs mainly through nonverbal communication, followed by indirect verbal communication. A change in behavior (usually from positive to negative but possibly also from negative to positive) was seen as the main sign across countries (e.g., "*I think that change is an important thing because some people are introverted and negative anyway*," AU2f). Italians were generally more vague about the content of the warning signs whereas behaviors identified by Indians and Australians were isolation/being alone (social withdrawal), withdrawal from activities/commitments, and use or abuse of substances. On this latter point, participants from both countries saw drinking or drinking more as a sign, whereas Indians thought that taking up smoking or smoking more was also a sign. This was never mentioned in Australia where, on the contrary, starting to use drugs or using more drugs was more often mentioned as a sign. In Italy, any substance use/abuse was a less central sign. It is relevant to note the disparities between ways of seeing substance use because, while in India there was more emphasis on beginning to drink and smoke, in Australia, and to some extent in Italy, using drugs or using them more were emphasized. This might suggest that drinking and smoking are seen as less "normal" and less socially acceptable in India than in Italy and Australia, as stated by a student who said "*drinking and smoking are considered signs of a [a person of] bad character*" (IN5m). Risk-taking behaviors (e.g., abusing drugs and drunk-driving) were seen as other main warning signs by both Italians and Australians, as was recklessness by Australians. Being angry and irritable was also considered a relevant sign in India and, to some extent, in

Australia. Some participants from these two countries saw body language as an important sign.

Those participants who believed that the person might show suicide intentions through indirect communication suggested that, for instance, the person might speak in a pessimistic or depressive way, talk about death and hatred for life, say goodbye, and not make plans for the future. Australians also suggested that making jokes about suicide was a possible sign. However, both Italians and Australians recognized the difficulty in seeing warning signs because the person may not show signs, the signs may not be obvious or they may be ambiguous, as well as people's general reticence to admit that a loved one wants to die. Especially in Australia, participants identified the issue that people do not expect "some" people, for example, strong or popular youths, to be thinking about killing themselves. In contrast, Indian participants rarely showed doubts about what warning signs were, and only a few stated that sometimes there are no signs. Italians and, to some extent Australians, underlined the role of others in paying attention and noticing possible signs and, as some Australians noted, to not ignore them when they are perceived. Some of these participants commented on the difficulty in acknowledging if a friend wants to kill him-/herself because they did not know what to do in such circumstances.

> *Just to elaborate on what everyone's just been saying, I think you all have to be open to the idea that someone might be thinking about suicide because if you don't, if you, if they've never thought that they'd be the sort of person to even consider that, the warning signs could be so blatant but you'd never really pick them up because you'd just sub-consciously be thinking they'd never do that (...). You think people are just walking around and you go "oh yeah, they'll be right," you know, but apparently a lot of people aren't all right and we've already sort of shut ourselves off to the possibility that they may not be alright. We just assume that they will be and then not care.*
> (Au2Mix: 1035/1045m)

Suggestions for youth suicide prevention strategies

A similarity across cultures was views on the possibility of preventing youth suicide. Mental health services (e.g., one-to-one counseling and help-lines) played only a relatively small role in this task. There was also a common criticism that much more attention (and money) is spent on the prevention of other youth problems, like drug or alcohol use and drunk and speed-driving, but governments and society do not pay the same attention to preventing people from killing themselves.

Overall, participants across countries proposed similar youth suicide prevention strategies, although there were differences in the details of the strategy and the relevance of one strategy compared to other strategies, and some strategies were culturally-specific. The three main strategies proposed across countries (to different degrees) were: awareness and education about suicide and help-services, prevention based on close friends and relatives, and social changes, but there were, as mentioned above, differences across countries.

Italian participants focused most on people close to the young person, in particular family and friends, when suggesting youth suicide prevention strategies. First of all, the participants recommended that close ones must be careful and be alert to the person's feelings and intentions and possible warning signs. Italian participants pointed out the active role of others in offering help and dialog (e.g., *"a form of 'nearness' (...), as she, I've the attitude, I mean, if there is something that makes me suspicious, I start asking one question after another!"*). Listening to suicidal youths, making them feel understood, showing love and care, and being close were seen as central to suicide prevention.

Indian and Australian participants also believed that, in order to prevent youth suicide, there should be more dialog between significant others and youths, and they should provide more support and understanding. Australians also suggested educating youths, parents, and the community to offer help and support (and about how to do so) and to care. As a way to achieve these aims, some participants across countries proposed educating parents on the parental role. While in Italy the preventive role of close ones was the main strategy, many of the strategies that Indian participants suggested for youth suicide prevention in India referred to more general changes at a society level (i.e., "social changes") in two ways: by reducing society's problems and by changing attitudes. In particular, participants highlighted the need to take action against bribery and corruption (especially among the police), violence and crime against women (e.g., dowry death, harassments, rape, and the "casting couch"), and actions for the fulfillment of people's basic needs (e.g., reducing poverty). Indians also suggested that society as a whole should be educated so as to change attitudes towards women and women's roles (e.g., *"Equality of the sexes, how a girl is not really a burden. That will be a good start,"* IN3f), to recognize the importance of women's education and independence, and to change society's expectations about men's duties. The participants felt that society puts too much pressure on and applies too many rules to youths. Hence, one way to prevent youth suicide would be to reduce the pressure on and the rules for them. Another attitude that some participants thought needs to be changed is aimed at developing an open mind toward mental problems and reducing the stigma towards help-seeking. This strategy was also mentioned by some Italians who suggested, for example, changing the image of adolescents (underlining the positive characteristics of youths) and eliminating the stigma about help-seeking.

A social change suggested by Australian participants was to increase the involvement of people in other people's lives, reducing Australians' individualism and social isolation, and also changing social attitudes toward showing emotions and asking for help (e.g., the Australian stereotype of macho men). Education and community activities were two of the means proposed for achieving these changes.

Education and awareness about suicide, warning signs, help-seeking, and help-services available were suggested across cultures but were seen as a major strategy particularly by Australians. Across countries, participants strongly supported education programs in schools and the media, although generally they expressed discontent with existing education programs and, particularly Australians (followed by Indians), on the current way in which the media (re)presents suicide. Both Indians and, even more so, Australians, suggested the use of the arts in education, and some Australian participants specified the advantage of using the arts and activities for suicide education and awareness. For example, the arts can facilitate the expression of feelings, attract people's attention and engage them, and make it less depressing and uncomfortable to talk and hear about suicide, as stated by these participants (AU1):

> *F1: I think theatre groups gain, um, young peoples' attention, just to be able to have something that's familiar and that they see all the time and just to be gaining their attention, so that they listen to the message. Because I think a lot of the time the problem is that the message is there, but people aren't engaging, like they're just not listening to it [sounds of accord by participants].*
>
> *F3: Also, just to make the whole thing less depressing as well, if you used music or something enjoyable or something. It's not an easy topic for some people [F2: Yeah] so just to engage them a bit at the beginning, to just try and make them feel comfortable and ... take the pressure off a bit.*

Other than education about suicide, warning signs, help-seeking, and help-services available, participants also suggested education about other topics. For example, both Italians and Indians suggested a sort of moral education about life and life values and, for the Indian participants, about youth's responsibilities and

---

against suicide. Australian participants more than the others believed that suicide prevention strategies should focus on educating people, particularly men, to ask for help and express their feelings.

With regard to professional help, participants across cultures recommended having more and better counseling services, in particular, having more counselors in schools so that this service is easily accessible and free (and also to reduce the stigma towards professional help, especially in India and Italy). Indian participants underlined the relevance of counseling services because generally youths cannot talk to parents about problems, nor to anybody about suicide. They highlighted the necessity that these services maintain confidentiality, which was seen by Indians as the main reason why participants tend not to go to counselors. There was also a call for a more pro-active role by counselors in general to organize scheduled appointments and be active in checking how participants (or workers in work places) are, rather than just waiting for people to approach them. Furthermore, participants suggested that counselors should give classes and educate participants about several issues (e.g., sharing feelings, what to do if a peer has problems, seeking help, and learning coping-skills), as well as organizing group discussions.

Both Italian and Australian participants recommended organizing groups similar to those for people with alcohol or drug addiction (e.g., Alcoholics Anonymous) or like the focus groups in which they were participating. These groups were described as having several benefits: (1) they are an occasion to socialize and meet new people, (2) participants can become aware of the helping services available, (3) the participants can encourage people to talk about suicide and reduce the taboo, (4) the participants can get to know a psychologist whom they can then personally approach, and (5) the groups offer a chance to open up and share their feelings and also find out about other people's experiences. For instance:

> *I think, um, as well as another strategy, everybody should be involved in something like this. I found it an easier way to talk about it because everybody is expecting to talk about it, so everybody's prepared to listen, and it's hearing everybody else's point of view as well. I think in high schools especially maybe everybody people should do forums like this – In the classrooms split everybody into groups about this size and have like a forum about suicide and strategies and warning signs and places to go for help and things like that (AU2f).*

The importance of having the opportunity to discuss the topic of suicide in a comfortable, free and supportive environment was also highlighted in the answers

participants gave in the feedback form they filled in at the end of the second
session. For instance:

> *I felt at ease because although the topic was very delicate, it has been hand-
> led with naturalness, with the awareness that anyone present could have
> thought about it and without making them feeling accused or different,
> uncomfortable* (IT21m).
> *It was very comfortable to say many things openly to everyone. Thank you
> for having given such an opportunity. Thank you again* (IN20m).

Participants particularly appreciated the opportunity to talk about a topic that
was present in the lives of many of them (i.e., their own or close ones' suicidal
ideation or behavior) but was often difficult to talk about.

Another strategy mentioned by Italian and Australian participants (and mentioned in one Indian focus group) was to involve youths in school and community
activities (e.g., sports, the arts, community events, meditation, and yoga). Activities
were seen as important because these activities help youths find reasons to live, discover their good qualities, and reduce social isolation, while increasing support,
amplifying the feeling of belonging, building relationships and a sense of community and, in the opinion of some Australians, promoting a healthier lifestyle. The
involvement of the community in several ways, including organizing activities
and "creating more community," was strongly supported by Australian participants.

Looking at more country-specific suggestions, the Italian participants believed
that teachers could have an important role in suicide prevention, but they discarded this possibility because of their very negative image of teachers. Some
other Italian participants suggested involving youths in volunteer work as a
way to feel useful and responsible for somebody and not feel worthless. Some
Indian participants discussed the use of laws against suicide and the arrest of
the suicidal person as a suicide prevention strategy. However, although a few participants supported this option, legislation was generally seen as an inefficient
means for suicide prevention. In an Australian group, having "good" websites
for education, counseling, and forums about suicide was suggested.

Summary

As in the results of the survey, participants from the three countries reported some
similarities and differences in the focus group sessions. For instance, the majority
of Italian and Australian participants believed that there are no differences
between what happens in the afterlife for young people who kill themselves
and those who die by other deaths. However, in India, a good proportion of the

participants also thought that youths who kill themselves suffer some sort of punishment. In considering the beliefs about the kinds of thoughts, communications and feelings a young person has before trying to kill him/herself, participants believed that suicidal youths have similar thoughts before killing themselves, but there were cultural differences in the proportion and content of these thoughts. The part about what suicidal youths might say was generally neglected by participants across cultures and groups because the majority of participants thought that, if a suicidal person communicated something about their suicide intention, they did so indirectly or through non-verbal communication.

The greatest variety of answers between groups and across cultures was in relation to feelings. In Italy, the most consistent answers across groups were that a young person, before trying to take his/her life, feels despair, loneliness, confusion, fear, pain and sadness. In India, these were loneliness, disappointment, irritation/anger, hopelessness, worthlessness and meaninglessness (of life and themselves), shame, sadness and depression. Australian participants believed that suicidal youths might be sad and depressed, but they might also feel happy, relieved and at peace.

Differences and similarities emerged also among the answers related to warning signs in suicidal peers. Across countries, participants believed that a friend would manifest suicide warning signs mainly through non-verbal communication, followed by indirect verbal communication. A change in behavior was seen as the main sign across countries. Italians were generally more vague about the content of the warning signs, whereas Indians and Australians indicated social withdrawal, withdrawal from activities/commitments and use or abuse of substances as possible warning signs. Both Italians and Australians recognized the difficulty in perceiving warning signs in a peer and, especially the former, the role of others in paying attention and catching possible signs. Participants in all three countries provided several suggestions for how to prevent youth suicide in their country and while some of them were similar, others were country-specific.

Discussion

There were many differences identified between students in the three cultures on rates and attitudes toward suicide and suicide prevention. There were also complex associations between social class, gender, religion, spirituality, and personal suicidal history and attitudes. A detailed presentation and discussion of these findings can be found in Colucci (2008b). This discussion will focus primarily on the implications of the study for the cultural meanings of suicide and suicide prevention.

Rates and Attitudes

There were clear cross-cultural differences in the prevalence of suicide ideation, plans, and attempts. More than half of the Italian and Australian participants reported suicidal thoughts compared to only a third of the Indian participants. There were also notable differences by gender. While in Australia there was a similar percentage of male and female participants who thought about suicide, in Italy more men had thought about suicide, and in India more women reported past suicide ideation.

The country with the lowest percentage of attempted suicide was Italy, followed by Australia, whereas India, which was the country with the lowest incidence of suicide ideation, reported the highest percentage of attempts. While in Italy and Australia there was a similar distribution by gender, in India more than twice as many females had attempted suicide as males. More Indian and Australian participants obtained higher scores on the suicide risk scale but, while scores were higher among Indian females compared to males, in Italy there was a tendency towards the opposite, and in Australia there was no difference by gender. These participants were not randomized or stratified and, therefore, no generalizations can be made on prevalence of suicidal behavior in these countries. Nevertheless this finding is important as it indicates that many of the participants involved in this study had a first-hand experience with suicide. It also suggests that suicidal ideation, plans, and attempts are quite frequent among the college student population, as indicated by previous studies (e.g., Westefeld et al., 2006) and that Indian young females might be particularly at risk of suicide. A previous study has shown that approximately 20% of the suicide attempters in the Padua catchment area (in Italy) were young people aged 15 to 24 years (Meneghel et al., 2004). However, youth suicide attempts are less common in Italy compared to other countries. In contrast, suicide attempts are a considerable problem in India (even if statistics are underestimated because suicide attempts are still considered a punishable offence) and, in Bangalore, the age range of most concern is 20–24 years (Gururaj & Isaac, 2003). In Queensland, 12.4% of high school students reported a lifetime history of deliberate self-harm (De Leo & Heller, 2004).

On the open-ended survey questions, the participants were asked if they believed there was any difference between males and females in youth suicide. A majority of Italians had the incorrect belief that there are no differences in youth suicide by gender. In India, participants reported no differences between males and females, for the most part in agreement with the actual statistics. A majority of Australian female participants were aware that suicide rates are higher among Australian males, whereas an equal proportion of males either agreed with this view or thought that there are no differences. These data indicate the presence of incorrect knowledge about youth suicide, in particular among Italian and Australian men. Italian and Australian women also identified differences in the method (more violent and lethal in men), but men rarely did so. In addition to the frequency and method of suicide, many participants across countries also specified the differences between genders in the causes of youth suicide, often attributing this to expectations for men in India and Australia (in the latter, these also included the expectation to be a "macho man"), and the lesser importance given by Indian society to violence and harassment directed toward Indian females.

The findings on spirituality and belief in the afterlife have been discussed in Colucci (in press). The protective effects of spirituality/religion argued in Colucci (2008c) and Colucci and Martin (2008) are partially confirmed in the finding that Indian participants who were not religious/spiritual reported more suicidal ideation and attempts and higher scores on the suicide risk scale than the religious/spiritual participants did. However, participants from Italy and Australia did not show any statistically significant difference on the basis of their religiosity/spirituality. These data can be interpreted in various ways. It could be attributed to a widespread growing atheism among young people. However, Whitla (2005) found that, although almost half of the Italian students in her study reported that they attend a place of worship six or less times annually, compared to Australian students, they placed a higher importance on religion. The finding from Whitla's study and the results of the current study also indicate that, because Catholicism is the most common religion amongst Italians (in fact roughly 80% of the religious/spiritual participants identified themselves as Catholic), those aspects of Catholicism that Durkheim (1897/1997) noted as being protective against suicide, could be part of the Italian culture as a whole, independently of what participants state their religious beliefs are. Without doubt, the link between religious beliefs and/or affiliation and suicide is complex. This is demonstrated by the observation that the same religious affiliation showed a different relationship with suicidal behavior in different countries (e.g., non-Catholic Christians had higher suicide risk scores in Italy and in Australia than in India) and that, although being religious/spiritual might protect people from suicidal ideation and behavior (e.g., among Indians in this sample), being affiliated with a minority religion might expose people to a greater risk of suicide, as was the case for Muslims in the Indian sample. The question is further complicated when trying to relate people's religious affiliation and spiritual beliefs to religious and spiritual beliefs towards suicide.

Both the mean scores on the 21 items and the four factors that compose the Attitudes Towards Youth Suicide (AtYS) scale indicated more negative attitudes in India, followed by Australia and then Italy. Australian participants also believed more that suicide is preventable compared to Italians and Indians. Italians and Australians showed more acceptance and more of a tendency to normalize suicide than did the Indians.

The finding that Italians endorsed a less negative attitude does not mean that Italians saw suicide more positively. Some Italian participants expressed more negative attitudes than others, and the mean scores on some questions were on the negative side of the scale. But the Italians generally showed a more compassionate and understanding attitude toward suicidal youths than participants in the other two countries (especially Indians) generally did. When attitudes toward suicide were examined in relation to the participants' own suicide risk scores, it was observed that, both overall and in each country, participants at higher suicide risk endorsed less negative attitudes towards suicide and considered suicide as more acceptable and normal than those participants who were at lower risk of suicide. How can the finding that people with more negative attitudes towards suicide might be at a lower risk of suicide, and overall Indians, followed by Australians, had the most negative attitudes, coexist with the knowledge that Indians' and Australians' youth suicide rates are higher compared to Italian rates?

Although the literature shows that negative attitudes might be a deterrent against suicidal behavior (e.g., Eshun, 2003), data on this topic are ambiguous. One reason for this might be the multifaceted consequences of negative attitudes. While, on the one hand, a person's negative attitude towards suicide may act as a deterrent against suicidal behavior in the individual, on the other hand, a widespread negative attitude may also act as a suicide risk factor for the population (possibly acting as a deterrent to help-seeking and thus preventing the person from communicating suicidal intentions to others and seeking help). Thus, the difficulty in sharing thoughts about suicide could then lead to higher rates of suicidal behavior among Indians whereas, in Italy, youths may feel more comfortable to talk about it because, although suicide was described as a taboo topic across countries, the attitudes of Italian participants was overall more accepting and understanding. A similar observation was made in a study on Australian youth, where the authors (Fullagar, Gilchrist & Sullivan, 2007) pointed out that, if participants see suicidal thoughts as taboo, youths may be reticent to seek help when feeling depressed or suicidal themselves and they may also be less likely to intervene if a friend is in distress.

Besides this hypothesis of a complex effect of negative attitudes, another issue that needs more investigation is that, although a culture might endorse a general negative attitude toward suicide, nevertheless, in some circumstances, suicide might be seen as an acceptable behavior and in others it might even been reinforced and become a socially expected reaction. This seems to be particularly so in regard to female suicide (see Tousignant, Seshadri, & Raj, 1998).

While analyzing the survey (and also in the focus groups), I often observed participants in all three cultures avoiding writing or saying the word "suicide" and writing (or saying) a pronoun instead (e.g., "it"), leaving dots (e.g., "...") or substituting the word "suicide" with "the fact" or "the event" (or something similar), which could be interpreted as an expression of a tendency to avoid talking about suicide and viewing it as a taboo topic that they felt uncomfortable writing or talking about. The need to talk more about suicide and eliminate the stigma and taboo was mentioned at various times, especially by Italians and Australians. Although Indian participants less often stated that suicide was a taboo topic, some Indian participants indicated that they had never spoken about this topic before participating in this research project. Furthermore, although suicide seems to be an unspoken topic in all three countries, this might be for different reasons: in Italy because of the blame and responsibility for the act placed on people close to the suicidal youth; and in India because suicide is judged very negatively and viewed as cowardly, stupid, foolish, irresponsible, and childish, bringing shame on their family. In Australia, besides the negative judgments specific to suicide expressed by some participants, part of the stigma about suicide might reflect a general negative stigma for mental illness that applies also to suicide because of the recurrent association of suicide and depression or mental illness made by Australian participants. The stigma could also be more generally related to the negative attitudes toward expressing feelings, particularly by Australian men, given that suicidal ideation and behavior can be seen as an extreme form of expression of feelings. It would be useful to further understand the dynamics underpinning the stigma and taboo for suicide, checking these and other hypotheses, and considering culturally-different and gender-specific reasons behind the taboo and the stigma (and, therefore, the different meanings of these) when developing programs aimed at their reduction.

Participants' Explanatory Models of Youth Suicide

The findings from this study, first of all, showed the limit of treating the reasons for youth suicide as an "accumulation" of single-factors. Participants' explanatory models were, in fact, based on an intersection of several factors and were not necessarily an event or a problem (e.g., exam failure) to be seen as leading to suicide but rather the "meaning" and the impact of that event for the person, the family, and society (e.g., shame and lack of fulfillment of social expectations) and the concurrent presence of other factors (e.g., lack of support, personal representation of the person as meaningless and worthless, cultural representation of a "macho" man without emotions, and of women as inferior, the one to blame, and a burden).

The Italian participants' explanatory model of youth suicide focused mainly on interpersonal issues, in particular on loneliness and not having a person to talk to, who listens, or who is really close to the person. A similar result was found in the ranking-order task, where loneliness/interpersonal problems was the most highly ranked reason for youth suicide. Furthermore, lonely/loneliness/alone was the second most frequent word in the word association task and the most often cited word in the open-ended question about the characteristics of youths who kill themselves. This latter task also showed that Italians often "blamed" others for not having helped, listened, or understood the suicidal person. In the same way, focus group participants saw other people "involved" in the suicide and blamed them (especially the family) because they did not understand, did not help, did something to the person that created a crisis, or could have prevented the suicide (by giving support, care, and love).

The greater involvement of others in the suicide indicated by Italian participants might be justified by the view that suicide, although it is an individual choice, is also a collective responsibility (see Whitla, 2005). Farber (1975) underlined the presence of "social accountability" in Italy where people may be held responsible for encouraging an antisocial act or for not intervening to prevent one from happening. One is expected to make efforts to prevent a potentially suicidal person from taking his or her life. Furthermore, Farber noted that Italians are extrapunitive rather than intropunitive, that is, they tend to blame others rather than themselves for difficulties. This observation creates a basis upon which to build an argument about the construct of "guilt." Quite often Italian participants indicated that those close to the people who killed themselves would feel "guilty." The concept of guilt is strongly embedded in the Catholic religion. There is even a prayer (with the Latin name *mea culpa,* which means "my guilt") as an official acknowledgment of faults and errors, based on the Catholic view that human beings are born to sin (e.g., Adam and Eve's original sin) and are sinners (therefore the sacrament of the confession to ask for forgiveness). Although the concept of guilt is not exclusively Catholic, it is central in that religion. Since Italian culture is largely monotheistic, infused by Catholicism (to which everyone is exposed, even the growing proportion of Italians who claim to be agnostic or atheist), the involvement of others in the explanatory model of suicide and their partial blame for the act can be explained by two main factors: the fact that Italy is a collectivistic society where people rely on and feel responsibility for each other, but also the propagation of the religious concept of "feeling guilty" into every aspect of life, including explanatory models for suicide. This conclusion is in opposition to the impression expressed by Farber (1975) that guilt is relatively unimportant in Italians, and this issue is worthy of further exploration.

Another concept that was central among Italian participants was the representation of a suicidal youth as someone who is suffering deeply and cannot see any solution other than suicide. This emerged both in the focus groups but also in the word associations (where pain/suffering was the most frequent word and despair/desperation was the fourth most frequent word) and in the open-ended question where the most frequent intrapersonal attributions were desperate/no hope, suffering, seeing suicide as the only option and lack of purpose/meaning in life. This latter was another of the most important factors reported by Italian participants in the focus groups as leading to youth suicide.

Family and society (and their judgments) were central in the explanatory model of youth suicide given by Indian participants. In fact, family/parents was the most frequent term in the word association task. The family was seen as triggering or contributing to the intention or decision to suicide (killing oneself because of being a burden on the family; bringing shame to the family or not fulfilling the family's expectations or one's duties toward the family and society; or because of the lack of freedom for young people regarding marriage and career). This means that, even though Indians usually attributed youth suicide to some situational factor or events, generally the problem by itself was not seen as a cause of suicide, but rather it was what the event meant from the perspective of judgments from and duties toward family and society. For instance, being raped might lead to suicide because the woman was now viewed negatively by society and had brought shame to her family, more so than because of the personal trauma. Similarly, for a woman who had pre-marital sex, became pregnant, and was then abandoned by the man (a typical case mentioned during the focus groups and in the case vignettes), the "real" problem appeared to be the fact that the woman was not a virgin anymore and would be seen as a "loose" woman, and so the parents would have difficulty finding a husband for her. The same process applied to exam failure, which was seen as a failure to meet family and society's expectations and might also show that the person is of "bad character," as was indicated in one focus group. The person who dies suicide by is often seen in a negative way (as indicated through several methods used in the study), usually as someone who is not able to face and cope with the problem, a selfish person (e.g., not caring for the consequences that suicide has on the family and society), and a coward.

For the Indian participants, then, the expectations of the family and society were depicted as the main cause of suicide but, simultaneously, when facing problems, many youths, particularly women, have no one to talk to about their suicidal thoughts. Furthermore, if they kill themselves, they are judged negatively, especially for the effects that this behavior has on their families (e.g., "putting a black mark"), unless they were a burden on the family (e.g., raped women or those with alcohol and drug addiction or with chronic diseases), in which case suicide appeared to be more socially acceptable or, as a few women suggested, even encouraged. A similar view of suicide as an immoral act because it socially affects others negatively was found also by Osafo, Hjelmeland, Akotia, and Knizek (2011a) in Ghana.

Australian participants showed both similarities and differences with the participants from the other two countries. For instance, Australians reported aspects that were found in both Italian and Indian samples with regard to the involvement of others in the suicide. In fact, Australians were close to Indians in seeing others as a main reason leading to suicide (e.g., because of family expectations and pressures such as school pressure). In their explanatory model of youth suicide, others were also viewed as "responsible" because they did not support or help the person or, more rarely, because they did not understand the person or neglected warning signs. On the other hand, Australians often saw suicidal youths as isolated and not talking to anyone, not expressing their feelings (especially men), not asking for help, and showing either no warning signs or only very subtle signs. Some Australians also reported that people do not know what to do when someone seems to be suicidal, people do not pay attention to signs and, more generally, people do not get involved in other people's lives (which might at least partially reflect the belief that Australia is an individualistic society). This presents a bind. On the one hand, the participants indicated that suicidal young people, especially men, do not express their emotions and ask for help but, on the other hand, when they do express (directly or indirectly) their emotions or suicidal thoughts, they might not be taken seriously or receive any support. In two focus groups, participants also mentioned that suicidal or depressed people might be avoided or laughed at by friends.

This is similar to the Indian participants except that, for the Australian participants, several factors were seen as influencing men more, whereas in India they influenced women more. Australian participants stated that youths feel pressure to perform well at school/work and meet people's stereotypes and expectations but, if they do not succeed, they find it difficult to express their feelings (especially men who are expected to be tough and "not cry"). There is also a fear of being seen as "wacko" or negatively judged if they express suicidal intentions. Furthermore, they lack support from family and friends or have superficial relationships (e.g., just a laugh together). In the survey's open-ended questions, only a few participants perceived other people as being "part" of the problem. They referred more often to intrapersonal factors, in particular to depression or mental illness. Depression/depressed was the second most frequent term also in the word association task (and sad/sadness was the fourth) and was often used during the focus group sessions. My impression was that some of the participants simply integrated a scientific term in their vocabulary as a substitute for "sad," whereas others referred to depression as a psychiatric disorder. However this is interpreted, the great majority of Australians mentally constructed a suicidal youth as sad or depressed, perhaps also because suicide prevention campaigns and education programs in Australia often present a strong link between depression and suicide. That suicide is talked about in reference to mental illness and depression was also found by Bourke (2003) in a sample of young Australians. For some Australian participants, drugs and alcohol use/abuse were an integral part of the "path" to suicide, a step that people take as a kind of "first remedy," which failed to help or actually aggravated the situation and was followed by suicide. In contrast, Italian students' use of substances is less a form of coping compared to Australians (Whitla, 2005). Lack of direction and purpose/meaning in life was also a central factor in Australian participants' explanatory model (and when suggesting suicide prevention strategies).

Australian participants also indicated the presence of individualism in their society and less opportunity to rely on other people, and they also referred to the lack of support from family and friends. Individualism has been found in research to have a relationship with suicide (Lenzi, Colucci, & Minas, 2012; Lester, 1997). Individualism among Australian youth and lower social support might explain in part the higher rates of suicide in Australia as compared to Italy, a collectivistic society where, as emphasized by Farber (1975), the availability of succor from family members and the loyalty to the family is deep-seated in the culture.

Gendered-Meanings and Explanatory Models of Suicide

As indicated above, especially during Indian and Australian focus groups, both male and female participants pointed out various aspects that differentiated suicide by young women and men, and the majority of these were related to social expectations and judgments. Australian participants underlined some factors that increase the risk of suicide in men but protect women, particularly in regard to problem-solving strategies: men rely on themselves whereas women externalize their problems. They thought this might be due to a cultural stereotype which sees Australian men as "macho," expected to be tough, strong, and without emotions and problems (or not worrying about them). This concept of the male image was also mentioned in the Italian questionnaire but did not receive much emphasis in the focus groups. Baume and Clinton (1997) also saw the male-sex role stereotype as a factor for Australian youth suicide. An Australian study on depression

(Brownhill, Wilhelm, Barclay, & Schmied, 2005) showed gender differences in the expression of depression. While Australian women were more prone to express emotions by crying or seeking out others for help and were less exposed to the pressure to not display emotional distress, men had an avoidance/aversion to showing signs of weakness or vulnerability. Thus men's experience may remain hidden and misunderstood. This may also be true specifically for the expression of suicidal thoughts, as was found in this project.

Indian participants saw important reasons for youth suicide as gender specific. In particular, suicide was linked to violence against women and to a social view of women not only as inferior, but as "the one to blame" for whatever happens to them (e.g., rape and pre-marital sex not followed by marriage) and to others (e.g., death of husband or misbehavior of children). Unlike men, who in a few instances were viewed as a kind of "investment" for the family, women were depicted as more likely to be a burden, especially in poorer families (because of the dowry the family has to pay to arrange a marriage for them) and in all situations where women bring shame to the family's name (e.g., loss of virginity through pre-marital sex or sexual abuse). Although already in the survey (particularly in the question about gender differences) where both females and males attributed female suicide to various forms of harassment and violence (including rape and dowry-related torture, "unmarried" pregnancy, and lack of freedom and independence), these factors were described more in-depth in the group sessions. In the survey, participants also pointed out that women have more rules and have to face more difficulties in life. It is worth noting that, exclusively in the Indian sample, and across methods, a few participants indicated that women cannot express their emotions and that, in some instances, females might be forced to kill themselves. A form of forced or expected suicide is *sati*[10] (i.e., widow burning, spelled also suttee or sati, in which the widow follows the dead husband onto the funeral pyre), a custom that also existed in other countries, such as China, Mesopotamia, and Iran but has characterized India and Hinduism (see Chapter 7 for Lester's exploration of this phenomenon). While worldwide overall fewer women kill themselves than males, suicide in women in India has an ancient root: episodes of *jauhar* (or *johar*), a mass suicide of women to avoid molestation by the invaders (Vijayakumar, 2004), have been recorded.

Another form of female suicide that has an old history is dowry suicide, in which brides are driven to kill themselves by harassment and violence inflicted by their in-laws because they are not satisfied with the dowry they received from

---

[10]   Because of the high level of regulation and oppression that characterizes the sociocultural setting of both sati and dowry suicides, these could be forms of *fatalistic* suicide, using Durkheim's (1897/1997) typology.

the bride's family. When the dowry demands are not met, husbands and in-laws render significant mental and physical harassment on the young brides in an effort to encourage her family to fulfill their dowry obligations (Kumar, 2003).

Several scholars have written about Indian women's low social and family status, and the violence and torture performed on them, and some of them have underlined the relationship between the condition of Indian women and suicide (e.g., Tousignant et al., 1998).

In summary, this study and existing literature suggest that suicide for Indian women might assume various meanings: an "exit point" (as escape) from harsh life conditions and harassment (e.g., dowry suicide), a form of protest and denouncement (e.g., after rape and "couch-jobs"), a residual of historical and religious forms of self-sacrifice (e.g., sati) and of other culturally-encouraged suicides (e.g., to not bring shame to or be a burden on the family), and as an act to gain control of their life (e.g., because of the numerous rules they must obey and duties they must fulfill, especially in regard to men in the family). In this last instance, suicide for some Indian women might represent an act of rebellion and revenge, or an act of power, as Meng (2002) argued is the case for some Chinese women.

Although gender issues were generally related to the situation of women in India, participants pointed out that men are exposed to social expectations related to job, status, and pressure to achieve, whereas generally there is no pressure in these aspects for the majority of females. Data collected on suicides by young and middle-aged Indian adults (Lalwani, Sharma, Rautji, & Millo, 2004) also documented the presence of educational and occupational problems among males.

These gender issues, particularly violence and torture of women in several forms, were very significant in the explanatory model of youth suicide. Nevertheless, some Indian participants suggested that the situation is changing. Women are starting to be more independent and socially respected. Male participants were aware of the situation of women and felt that this needed to change, beginning, as some of them suggested, with more control of crimes against women. This acknowledgment is certainly a positive sign, but these social changes will take time, and it is important that people involved in suicide prevention are aware that these gender issues do exist and consider the *gendered-meanings* of suicide in the development of prevention strategies.

Protective Factors and Deterrents

When participants were asked what would prevent them from killing themselves, even if their life was unbearable, participants from all three countries mentioned somewhat similar motivations but also demonstrated differences in relation to the kind of deterrents and the relevance of them, both in the survey and in the focus groups. In fact, while "others/loved ones" was one of the principal reasons why participants across cultures stated they would not suicide, at a deeper analysis, this answer partially assumed different meanings in each sample.

Participants across countries underlined the love for and/or from someone, receiving support and care from others, and having responsibilities towards someone, but also not hurting them, as reasons to not suicide. In the analysis of the survey question, many Australian participants referred to the effects of suicide on others and the pain this would give them more than because they felt loved and received support, whereas in Italy and India both these categories of reasons were given. On the other hand, in the focus groups, the consequences that suicide would have on the family (i.e., bringing a bad name or stigma on themselves and their family) was seen as a particularly relevant deterrent by Indian participants. Besides the negative judgments about suicide from the family, a negative judgment toward suicide was sometimes given more generally as a reason why Indians and, to a lesser degree Australians, would not kill themselves (although Australians mentioned this only in the survey, while Indians brought it up in the focus groups as well as the survey). Italians rarely expressed negative judgments towards suicide (e.g., that suicide is selfish or cowardly) to justify their choice not to suicide. Duties and responsibilities toward family, society, and the home country were also important deterrents for Indians, whereas Italians and Australians mentioned only the responsibilities for someone who is dependent on the person and, overall, this factor received less emphasis than the factors mentioned above about others/loved ones.

These could be seen as a kind of "fatalistic" view toward life evident among Indian participants, expressed in the concept that life is not the individual's alone (a few participants stated that life is God's) and that people have certain responsibilities and plans that they must fulfill before dying. Appreciation of and love for life, curiosity, and hope for the future and a positive attitude towards life and problems were other main deterrents but, while all of these were central for Italians, only the hope for change and in the future and, less often, curiosity about the future, were cited by some Australian participants, and the value of and love for life and a positive attitude by Indian participants. The latter also gave more importance to the belief that people "have to" face problems and failures in life. Linked to this was the opinion that suicide is not the only option, which was cited more by Italians and Indians.

One of the issues addressed by Whitla (2005) in her comparison between Italian and Australian students concerned coping strategies, and she found that Italian youths generally had more positive ways of coping with difficulties compared to Australians. This supports my finding that Italians (and Indians) showed a more positive attitude towards life and problems. This attitude among Italians was also noted by Farber (1975), when he observed the tendency of Italians, in the face of difficult conditions to use the expression *pazienza*, which is more than "patience" but, as he pointed out, also involves toleration and acceptance of hardships, which he saw as counter-suicidal.

Having something to look forward to, a goal, projects, life plans, and things that the person enjoys doing and that give meaning and purpose to life, was also a deterrent for Italian and Australian students, whereas this appeared to be a less important deterrent for Indians. On the other hand, responsibilities and duties towards others and society and life plans imposed by others were mentioned quite often by Indians. The way I interpret this is that the difference was not that Indians did not see life projects and goals as deterrents as much as the other two cultural groups did, but rather that the source of these projects and plans was different. This appeared to be based more on personal choices for Italians and Australians (even though in some instances Australians, and to a lesser extent, Italians, underlined the expectations and pressure from family and others). Furthermore, apart from life plans and projects, having hobbies and interests was often presented as being protective against suicide by Italians and Australians and also, although less so, for Indians. This was particularly evident in the case vignettes, where youths who are unlikely to kill themselves were often described as having hobbies and being involved in extra-curricula activities (such as the arts and sports).

These were the main reasons why participants said that they would not kill themselves, but there were some similarities and differences in other, less often mentioned, factors. For instance, the fear of death, pain or the unknown, and the lack of courage to kill oneself appeared to be a deterrent more for Italians and Australians, whereas these were very rarely mentioned by Indians. On the other hand, Indians indicated that God (e.g., belief in) was a deterrent from suicide more often than the other two samples.

Studies on protective factors are scarce compared to the number of studies on risk factors (although in my opinion, it is more productive to prevent suicidal behavior by focusing on increasing what keeps people alive than what leads some people to end their own life). This previous research partially support the findings that emerged in Italy (Whitla, 2005), India (Gururaj, Isaac, Subbakrishna, & Ranjani, 2004), and Australia (Donald, Dower, Correa-Velez, & Jones, 2006).

Help-Seeking Behaviors

Both in the survey and in the focus groups, participants were asked to whom they would talk if they were thinking about taking their own life. Overall the most frequent answer was "no one," followed by friends and family and, to a lesser extent, professional help (e.g., psychologist, counselor, psychiatrist, GP, and help-lines), but there were differences as well as similarities across cultures. The majority of Italian participants, both in the survey and in the focus groups, stated that they would not talk to anyone, but the focus groups offered the opportunity to understand the meaning of this answer in depth. Italian participants believed that, if they made the decision to kill themselves, they would not talk to anyone, mainly because, if they reached that decision, it would mean that people did not understand or help them, or it would be because they did not want to be stopped. Some other Italian participants stated that they would not talk to anybody or would not talk directly about it, but they would make other people understand or would expect other people to sense it. However, those participants who would talk to someone usually said they would choose to talk to a friend and, fewer, to a family member.

Indian participants were distributed mainly in three groups: those who would not talk to anyone, those who would talk to friends and others, and some (fewer) who would talk to parents. The focus groups revealed that the participants who would not talk to anybody would refrain mainly because of the consequences that the disclosure would have, that is, other people would know about the suicidal intention and thus the person's situation could become even worse. Another point made in the focus groups was that, although some participants said that they would never talk to their family or parents, while others believed that parents would be the best option, generally participants agreed that the majority of youths in India cannot talk to their parents (and, according to some participants, to anyone at all) because of the lack of freedom and a general fear of talking with parents. In this regard, it was also pointed out that women often cannot talk even to their friends for fear that the situation that is creating the difficulty will become known to others. Besides the fear of social judgments and family punishments, the fact that in India a suicide attempt (and suicide) is a criminal act could also lead to secrecy and a lack of willingness to seek help. Furthermore, in a study with young women from the Indian subcontinent, Ciarrochi and Deane (2001) observed that parents are positioned as upholding values that view sharing problems outside the family as inappropriate and that designates "outside help" as unacceptable.

Across methods, "no one" and "friends" were the two main answers also among Australians. However, some participants excluded friends or close friends because these might judge or change their opinion of them or be unable to cope with the situation. While a few participants affirmed that they would talk to siblings, some participants excluded the possibility of talking to parents, whereas others reported that they would talk to them. Similar results were shown in a sample of high school students (De Leo & Heller, 2004), where most of the youth who reported deliberate self-harm did not seek help before or after their most recent self-harm episode, and those who did seek help primarily consulted their friends, followed by a family member. Ciarrochi and Deane[11] (2001) found, in their sample of university students in Australia, that youths most likely in need of help are those least willing to seek help for emotional problems and suicide ideation and, if they did seek it, they were the least likely to benefit from it.

Across methods of help-seeking, however, the greatest difference between cultures was in relation to professional help, which appeared to be a much more important option for Australians than Italians or Indians, who generally excluded or seldom mentioned professional services. Focus groups revealed that stigma towards professional help (which was reported more by Indians and Italians compared to Australians) was the main reason why participants would not go to a counselor, in particular, the belief that people who go to counselors are mad/crazy. Another important reason why Indian participants stated that they would not ask for professional help was the belief that counselors do not maintain confidentiality, and this was a big concern. The impossibility of relying on external help, including but not restricted to counselors, was confirmed in a study by Marshall and Yazdani (1999). However, although Australians said relatively more often than Italians and Indians that they would talk to a professional (in particular a counselor or psychologist), they often expressed a rejection of this kind of help or did not mention this as the first, or most likely, choice. In particular, some Australian participants, even more than Italians did, complained about the lack of emotions and the coldness of professionals. The (relatively) greater reliance on professional help might be due to a greater association of suicidal behavior with mental problems/illness in Australia. This is partially confirmed by the greater role that depression (and, more rarely, other mental disorders) appeared to play in Australians' explanatory model of youth suicide.

Chiu and colleagues (2005) pointed out that belief systems and explanatory models of mental health (as well as stresses related to gender role) have an impact on one's treatment choices. Osafo, Knizek, Akotia, and Hjelmeland (2012) also observed that the view of suicide as a mental health issue results in an approach to suicide prevention from a health-service perspective. It is important to realize

---

[11] These authors found a help-negation effect for suicidal thoughts, believing that youths should solve their own problems, and a negative attitude toward professional help were potential barriers to seeking help. Ways suggested by the authors to encourage young people to seek help included: the establishment of relationships with young people before a need arises so that, when it does, the young person already has an established and trusted source of professional help to turn to, and creating easy to access help and increasing mental health literacy (e.g., awareness of services available and what to expect from these). All of these strategies were also recommended by participants in the current study.

that a suicide prevention strategy based mainly on professional help, which con-
forms to the "medicalization" or "psychiatrization" of suicide (underestimating
its sociocultural implications) and which may be discarded by many and not fit
into people's explanatory models, might compromise the efficacy of help offered
to suicidal people. These considerations should be taken into account more when
planning help-services for youth suicide.

How Much is Being Done and What Should be Done to Prevent Youth Suicide

The first of these questions asked participants how much they thought is being
done in their home country for youth suicide prevention. Italians participants were
the ones who believed most that youth suicide prevention is lacking, whereas both
in India and Australia, although the majority of participants had a similar opinion,
a few of them believed that a fair bit or a lot is being done.[12] However, across
countries, and across methods generally, participants were not satisfied with what
is actually being done, and they often suggested that more should be done and
done better, although a few of them, mainly in the survey, appreciated the fact that
the situation is better than it was in the past or is better compared to other countries. Both in the survey, but even more (and in more depth) in the focus groups,
participants indicated several limits for prevention. A common criticism, across
countries, was that there is a greater focus on other issues (e.g., alcohol, smoking,
drugs, and drunk-driving) than suicide, and initiatives are usually not specific for
suicide prevention. Another criticism was that, if there are help-services available,
these are not publicized, and so people are not aware of them and/or about how to
get to them. It is worth noting that, across methods of prevention, a considerable
number of participants answered that they had no idea about how much is being
done in their country, some of them suggesting that this might be an index that not
much is being done and that, if something is done, they were not made aware of it.
Furthermore, they believed that help-services are based on the concept that the
person in distress should look for help, but, across countries, some participants
doubted that a suicidal person would do so. Lastly, these services are not for
everyone. They are found more in urban areas than rural areas, are more for
the wealthy rather than poor strata of the population, and for youths at risk than
youths at unknown risk. Another point underlined across samples, but particularly
by Italians and Australians, was that suicide is not spoken about, is a taboo topic

---

[12]   The findings were similar across methods of prevention, although both Indians and Australians
       were more critical toward what and how much is done for youth suicide prevention in their
       country in the focus groups compared to the questionnaire.

that is kept hidden, and some of the participants in the focus groups attributed the lack of focus on suicide and suicide-specific initiatives to this taboo. This was strongly remarked by those participants who stated that my research was the first chance they had ever had to talk (or to talk openly) about suicide.

The second question was about what participants believed should be done for suicide prevention in their country. Overall, participants suggested similar youth suicide prevention strategies: education about suicide and about the help-services available and, less frequently, how to seek and get help; talking more and discussing suicide, thereby reducing the taboo; more and better counseling and support services and help-lines; help to find reasons to live for (mainly through the involvement of youths in activities); and reducing sociocultural problems and changing society/values (e.g., less pressure in Australia and less unemployment and abuse towards women).

However, although, overall, participants across countries proposed similar youth suicide prevention strategies, there were similarities and differences in the details of the strategy and the relevance of a strategy compared to the others, whereas some strategies were culturally-specific. In fact, while education/awareness about suicide was the principal theme across cultures, this seemed to be more central for Australians. Also the specific forms and topics of the education programs were slightly different. Across countries participants recommended education/awareness about suicide and, less often, about help-services available. In Australia, education was quite often about recognizing warning signs and, both in Italy and Australia, about talking and discussing the topic more. In India this aspect of reducing the taboo about suicide was rarely mentioned but a few participants recommended education *against* suicide (e.g., that suicide is a crime, a bad thing). The strategy of organizing occasions for discussion on the topic is supported by Fullagar and colleagues (2007) who found, in a sample of rural and urban Australian youths, that young people talk about suicide between themselves anyway. For this reason, the authors labeled as simplistic attempts to prevent discussions of suicide (for fear of imitation), citing Philo's observation (1996) that the absence of discussion merely serves to reinforce the stigma and the taboo, which in turn prevents young people talking about suicidal feelings. Some of the Australian participants in this study confirmed this impression, for instance, when they noted the very limited coverage of suicide in the media.

Australian participants, more than the others, believed that people, particularly men, should be educated to ask for help and express their feelings. With regard to the methods for carrying out this education/awareness, across countries, participants strongly supported education programs in schools and through the media, although they generally expressed discontent with other education programs and, particularly Australians and Indians, on the current way in which the media represents suicide. Both Indians and more so Australians suggested the use of the arts (e.g., theatre) and entertainment (e.g., music concerts) in education/awareness programs for youth.

Many of the strategies that Indian participants suggested for youth suicide prevention in India referred to social change. However, while in the survey participants focused more on the reduction/elimination of social problems (in particular violence and crimes against women, corruption, poverty, and unemployment), in the focus groups they also mentioned changes in attitudes (mainly changes in the attitudes towards women and women's role and changes in societal expectations toward men's duties). Some participants also suggested reducing the stigma toward professional help, which was also mentioned by some Italians. Italians and Australians also proposed social changes, but fewer of them did so or saw this as the most effective strategy in comparison with Indians. The focus for the change was also partially different. In Italy, this was also aimed at changing society's values and attitudes toward youths, and in Australia, towards reducing pressure, increasing the involvement of people in other people's lives, reducing "Australian individualism" and social isolation, and modifying social attitudes toward showing emotions and asking for help (e.g., the Australian stereotype of "macho men").

Besides placing the responsibility for youth suicide prevention on government and institutions (i.e., providing services and education programs), quite often participants saw suicide prevention as something that included everyone. This point was suggested more strongly in Italy, followed by India, where participants quite often encouraged compassion and understanding toward youth. This was less frequently suggested by Australians. Italians also included more activities and initiatives that promote the value of life.

Italian participants focused greatly on people close to the young person, in particular family and friends, when suggesting youth suicide prevention strategies, recommending that close ones must be careful and alert to understand the person's feelings and intentions and catch possible warning signs (an "empathic ear"), and pointed out the active role of others in offering help and listening. The role of close others was underlined also by Indians and Australians, but less frequently and in different ways. This was particularly evident in the survey question investigating participants' opinions about parents' and friends' roles in the prevention of youth suicide, where both Italians and Indians gave more emphasis compared to Australians to the "loving and supporting role." However, Italians, above all, underlined the social aspects (e.g., giving attention and support) and the importance of being a reliable presence and not making the person feel alone, whereas Indians focused more on the role of family/friends in helping with or solving the problems that the person was facing. Australians put a greater emphasis on the communication aspect of this role, that is, talking and making the person talk. Furthermore, the "guardian role" (i.e., the role of being attentive to suicide warning signs and signs of malaise) and the "mediating role" (i.e., putting the person in contact with services or asking for help) were more present in Australians than Italians and were almost never mentioned by Indians.

In regard to professional help, I have already noted that mental health services (e.g., one-to-one counseling and help-lines) were generally seen as less relevant compared to the other three main themes just indicated. However, Australians relied relatively more on professional help, followed by Indians. Nonetheless, across countries participants recommended having more and/or better counseling services, in particular an increase of counselors in schools, so that services are easily accessible (and also to relieve the stigma toward professional help, especially in India and Italy) and free, and having counselors with a more proactive and comprehensive role (e.g., who arrange scheduled appointments, give classes and organize group discussions). A similar call for more proactive management and support programs for people at risk of suicide (as well as education and support for close family and friends) was made by family and close friends of some young Australians who killed themselves and were interviewed after the suicide (Nirui & Chenoweth, 1999).

Indians pointed at the need for having counselors who assure confidentiality because the lack of this was seen as one of the main obstacles for the use of these services by youths. Therefore, programs for schools such as those suggested by Gururaj and Isaac (2003) should reconsider the utility of training teachers in counseling techniques because participants might feel threatened by having to say personal things to their teachers, and instead of just increasing school counselors, these programs should keep in mind critical issues such as confidentiality, which is particularly relevant for Indians.

In regard to the proposal of organizing groups, Italian and Australian participants, mainly in the focus groups, proposed organizing groups similar to those for alcohol or drug addiction or similar to the focus groups, highlighting several benefits of this strategy. The organization of self-help groups (where women can get together and talk, without being judged), similar to focus groups, was also suggested by the South-Asian women who took part in the study of Chew-Graham and collaborators study (2002).

Another relevant strategy for Italians and Australians, and mentioned less often by Indians, was to involve youths in school and community activities (e.g., sports and the arts). Furthermore, in the discussions, Australians strongly supported the involvement of the community in several ways, including organizing activities and "creating more community." The emphasis of Australian participants on creating and involving community has been also been suggested by Scott, Ciarrochi,

and Deane (2004) who recommended, after observing the link between individualism and hopelessness and suicide ideation, training programs (e.g., in schools)
emphasizing "citizenship" and community responsibility and eliminating dysfunctional individualistic beliefs.

There were also country-specific strategies. For instance, India was the only
sample in which a few participants suggested the use of laws to prevent youth suicide, but this was generally seen as an ineffective strategy. In fact, Latha and
Geetha (2004) were critical of this law, stating that it does not prevent people from
killing themselves or deter attempts, and that the decriminalization of the suicide
attempt will reduce the social stigma and put attempters in a better position to ask
for help.

In an Australian group, "good" websites for education, counseling, and forums about suicide were suggested. A youth web-based service (with forums open
to members for parts of the week), which began as part of the youth suicide prevention initiative but which, over time, became broader, has been supported by
the Australian government and other sponsors (http://au.reachout.com).

In this regard, a few participants across countries stated that they would talk
about their suicide ideation on the Internet (to an online counselor or a stranger
on the net, as was indicated in the help-seeking sections), and others in the survey
also suggested a website or Internet based-counseling. This highlights the need to
consider new and "modern" sources of help (such as websites with forums) and to
improve and check existing ones and make youths aware of these.[13]

As already criticized in earlier chapters, too often suicide prevention strategies
developed for one setting seem to be applied to another setting without considering that they might be inadequate or not socially acceptable. A general lacuna in
the development of prevention programs is the lack of consideration given to the
opinions of the direct users of services and strategies (Colucci, 2004). Furthermore, strategies for young people are generally designed by adult "experts,"
whereas the richness and elaborateness of the strategies proposed in the present
study are evidence of the fact that young people seem clear and confident about
what they think should be done and how, and why what is currently done does not
work. Thus, together with the considerations and observations made by local and
international experts (see, for instance, the indications by Chowdhury et al., 2005;
Colucci, Kelly, Minas, Jorm, & Chatterjee, 2010a; and Gururaj & Isaac, 2003;
Reddy & Arora, 2005; Vijayakumar, 2005, for India; WHO, 2001, for South-East
Asia, and Burns & Patton, 2000, for Australia), indicate that it is fundamental that
we listen and act upon young people's recommendations and not dismiss their
experience of their own life.

---

[13]   I found a terrible website in Italy where youth can leave suicidal letters before killing themselves!

Other "Meanings" that Need More Research

Before moving to the conclusions, it is important to note a few other constructs that emerged in this research and that, I believe, deserve a greater attention by the scientific, clinical, and policy-making communities: the meaning of death, the meaning and description of the words "suicide" and "suicide attempt," and the meaning of suicide methods.

Attitudes towards death are important aspects of the evaluation and subsequent treatment of at-risk adolescents, as indicated by Gutierrez, King, and Ghaziuddin (1996), and Gothelf and collaborators (1998). However, we cannot ignore cultural/traditional views on death. The present study showed that, although the negative feelings towards death were prevalent across cultures, this was much more so in Italy and Australia than in India, where this answer was almost as common as the feeling of acceptance and resignation to death. Furthermore, participants from all three cultures quite often reported mixed feelings (e.g., fear and peace, hope or curiosity), but this was much more so in Italian participants, followed by Australians, and, lastly, Indians. This already gives an indication that, if someone (e.g., a researcher or a clinician) decided to interview a person about death in order to have an understanding of the person's suicide risk, this person must remember that feelings towards death are partially culturally determined and, for instance, mixed feelings are more likely in Italy, whereas acceptance would be found more in India. A similar acceptance of death as part of life and, therefore not feared, has been noted also in the traditional Maori worldview (Langford & Richtie, 1998).

Another important observation is that the relatively few people (less than 20 for each country) who expressed only positive feelings towards death (e.g., peace, end of pain, etc.) were largely, proportionally to the prevalence of such at-risk participants in the sample, represented by participants at greater suicide risk (i.e., who had made a suicide plan and/or a suicide attempt). On the other hand, quite a few of those with positive feelings justified these feelings with religious beliefs. Although these data cannot be generalized, they could suggest that both people at risk of suicidal behavior and strongly religious people might see death as something positive. Therefore, the issue of the meaning of death and, linked to this, feelings toward it, must be considered in-depth both in suicide risk assessment and suicide research.

The reason why I inquired about the definition of the words "suicide" and "suicide attempt" was to investigate whether the definition of the terms, besides the actual meanings of these constructs (as suggested by Kidd, 2004), might also vary and, if so, what varies from a cultural point of view. The data collected certainly suggest that the definitions vary, not only between-groups but also within-groups, particularly for the phrase "attempted suicide," which is not even clearly defined among experts (O'Carroll, Berman, Maris, & Moscicki, 1996; Wagner, Wong & Jobes, 2002). Whilst the word suicide was generally defined in a nonambiguous way, only a small part of the sample clearly stated that it must be a voluntary or intentional act. Across cultures, but especially in India and, to a lesser degree, in Australia, participants very often used particularly vague descriptions for suicide attempt and quite often included cases where there was either low or no intention to die. The vagueness of the definitions provided, and the inclusion in their descriptions of behaviors/acts not aimed at death, suicidal thoughts or plans, or even death by suicide in the category "attempted suicide," highlights that, in any research, these terms need at least an operational definition, otherwise we risk measuring something different each time we use the word "suicide attempt" in suicide research. Therefore, I recommend that participants in suicide projects are provided with some sort of definition or, at least, a more delimited and precise concept like "try to kill yourself" or "made a suicide attempt with the intention to die." Words such as suicide attempt, attempted suicide, and parasuicide can be interpreted in various ways, and this fact threatens the validity of research findings (and comparisons between studies, which can become more complicated in cross-cultural research). This might also be true about "suicide ideation," a term that we, familiar with the topic, take for granted, but might not be so obvious for laypersons. Evidence of this is the fact that this word was rarely used by participants (both in the questionnaires and focus groups), even though they were all educated youths and some were psychology students. There is also evidence that people at low or high risk of suicide assign different meanings to the concept "suicide" (e.g., Ketelaar & O'Hara, 1989). Thus the considerations made above are relevant also for clinical assessment, and additional care must be taken when applying an instrument developed in one sociocultural setting to a different setting.

Moving on to the third "meaning," some scholars have indicated that the method of choice for suicide, besides being dependent upon the availability, might have a specific meaning (see Colucci & Martin, 2007a). Lester (1993) indicated that, for some methods, there were shared cultural attitudes whereas, for others, individual conceptions appeared to be more important. Focusing on the cultural meaning, Bourne (1973) observed in China that suicide by hanging carried the implication of great anger and resentment. The Hindu *Saiva Puranas* advocate suicide by fire or by falling from a mountain cliff in order to obtain a post-death existence of unalloyed sensual pleasure (Thakur, 1963). Venkoba Rao (1975) described another use of suicide in India – *sallekhana* or suicide by starvation. This suicide was sanctioned by the Jain religion and prescribed for ascetics, but Gandhi began using starvation as a political weapon and, subsequently, this has been undertaken by several other political leaders, and some of these have ended fatally. A form of suicide associated with young Indian women, dowry suicide, occurs by burning (Tousignant et al., 1998), and burning is also the method used in sati. More generally, burning seems to have some kind of meaning that associates this method of death particularly with women.[14] In this regard, Raleigh, Bulusu, and Balarajan (1990) observed among Indian immigrants residing in England and Wales that burning was a culturally acceptable method and common among women but not amongst men.

Looking back to my own work, while collecting the data for a research project on suicides in Padua (Dello Buono, Daru', Colucci, & Pavan, 2004), I noticed that a few people who appeared to have identity-related issues (for instance, a young woman who had been separated from her family at a young age and was adopted by a new family, but indicated not feeling integrated) chose methods that implied the decomposition of the body, such as collision with a train (as was the case for this woman), which might represent the "breaking" also of the physical identity.

The choice of a suicide method may be influenced or determined by the social acceptability of a particular method as well (Cantor & Baume, 1998; Canetto & Lester, 1995). As Mishara (2006) pointed out, the "preferred" suicide methods vary, and availability of means is not the only determinant of suicide method. Mishara noted that while firearms are a leading cause of suicide deaths in the US (often attributed to their easy access), among Inuit people in Northern Canada, where almost every family owns a firearm, firearms are much less frequently used for suicides than is hanging. There is a commonality here with Australian Aboriginals, who often kill themselves using hanging.[15] That the method is not only dependent upon its availability was also pointed out more than 30 years ago[16] by Burke (1979, p. 200), who noted that Indian migrants in the UK tended to use psychotropic tablets less than domestic agents, arguing that "when household or garden chemicals are widely used in rural communities or among traditional groups, these may be preferred to the analgesics of big industrial cities and more passive personalities there."

This suggests that it is not just the "physical" availability of a method that determines its use, but the "mental" availability and representation of the method also plays an important role. The social context and cultural belief system of the

---

[14]   Here I cannot avoid thinking about witch-burning during the crusades!

[15]   I want to highlight that, to date, I have not been able to understand from indigenous health experts what the meaning of this method might be among indigenous populations. I have been told that often they hang from a tree. I believe this is not due just to the availability or the degree of lethality but has a cultural meaning that we ought to understand.

[16]   In this regard, it is important to observe that the majority of writing that attempts to "contextualize" the method beyond its availability are generally dated indicating, possibly, a desire by today's scholars to dismiss the cultural meanings and social acceptability of suicide methods in favor of the more "controllable" availability.

individual will also have an influence here. Furthermore, a method may also be chosen for its ability for hiding the suicidal nature of the act (e.g., car accidents or drugs overdose). In this regard, M. V. D. (1957) suggested that some Indian women kill themselves by setting a fire to their kerosene-soaked clothes, and this method helps the family to obtain a verdict of accidental death in case there is a police inquiry. Monk (1987) also demonstrated that the popularity of different methods, like fashions, also change over time.

Exploring issues concerned with these meanings of methods was not an aim of the present project. However, some participants across groups linked some suicide methods to certain aims for the act. For instance, across groups, the use of pills or cutting were often associated with attention-seeking. Although this reflects the fact that these are methods of low-lethality and, therefore, their choice might be mainly due to a low intent to die, there is the possibility that this method might be chosen by some youths specifically to communicate the need for attention and help, based on the meanings that these methods have.

The most evident association of a method with a meaning was found in Indian culture. As already indicated before, suicide by self-burning has historically been linked to Indian society (Kumar, 2003). For instance, this has been part of the Indian history of suicide as a means used by widows to show love and fidelity to their dead husband in the ritual of sati, and was also used to avoid shame and escape sexual dishonor after the defeat of their men, in the mass suicide known as Jauhar (Vijayakumar, 2004). In a few instances, Indian participants also cited cases where some women who do not get along with their in-laws or are harassed by them, burn themselves. In some participants' stories, self-burning was suggested as a method (generally used by women) of protest, denouncement, or demand for revenge.

A small number of participants also referred to the use of seeds and pesticides for farmers' suicide. Certainly this might also be due to availability, but farmers also have ropes available, which would give a more secure, faster, and less painful death (farms in low income countries usually also have wells). Given that participants attributed farmers' suicide to loans and financial problems, I do not exclude the hypothesis that, in this case, the method used might also be partially symbolic – seeds and pesticides bought through loaned money (a cause of the suicide) to kill oneself.

Lastly, in Australia one participant noted that the feelings a young person had before killing him/herself are expressed in the method. For instance, a violent method shows anger.

Besides the method chosen, the specific form of the method might also be culturally determined. For instance, in Micronesia, hanging usually takes the form of leaning into a noose from a standing or sitting position (Hezel, 1989). Also the place where the suicide is acted out might have, besides a personal meaning, a sociocultural justification. For instance, Kumar (2003) commented that, in the dowry suicides, because the young wife is expected to perform the majority of the cooking duties for the family, it is not unexpected that the kitchen and living areas are the most common sites for the self-immolation act. In India, suicide by drowning at holy places like Varanasi and Prayag was supposed to relieve the soul from the never-ending cycle of birth and death (Vijayakumar, 2004).

While there is a huge amount of research on the aspect of the availability of methods, the stories told in this research, and the hypotheses I developed through them, call for research also on the meaning of suicide methods, that is, the message that these methods might communicate and who are the recipients of this message.

Conclusions

The Italian, Indian, and Australian participants involved in this project believed that the sociocultural environment (including the people around the suicidal person) plays an important role in youth suicide. However, the focus on the social context was slightly different. In Italy and Australia, it was more about the immediate surroundings (e.g., family and friends and, in Italy, also teachers), whereas in India the larger social context (i.e., society) was central as well.

Italian participants had less negative attitudes towards suicide and viewed suicide in an interpersonal context, seeing the suicidal person as having few deep relationships, or none, and people around the person as not having helped, given support or understood the person. Therefore, although in Italy suicide is a taboo topic, this seems to be a result of admitting one's own responsibility for the act. Italian participants also had a more empathic outlook (e.g., a focus on the suffering of the suicidal person) rather than judgmental. Italians listed a series of reasons for suicide but usually they saw close ones as being a "part" of this act. This "involvement" of close ones could imply a greater potential for support for people who show some of the warning signs or a general malaise.

India, similarly to Italy, is generally seen as a collectivistic society but, in this case, the role of others appeared to be different. With some exceptions, Indian participants often had a very negative attitude toward suicidal people. The young person who kills him/herself was often seen as having failed to face life's problems and as being weak and responsible for the act (and, therefore, blamed for it), as having brought shame to the family and created bad consequences for the survivors' lives. In this context, it might be quite difficult for youths who are considering suicide to open up and talk about their feelings. In addition, people were seen as having responsibilities towards society and their families. Therefore, any situation that could lead the person to being a burden on the family (e.g., rape for an unmarried woman or being harassed by in-laws for a young wife and being unwilling to live with them; a man without a job or with financial problems; having a disability, etc) might lead them to be at risk for altruistic suicide, a type of suicide more acceptable in Indian society. Gender issues were particularly central in the explanatory model of suicide of Indian participants, in particular abuses against women and a social view of them not only as inferior but as "responsible" for whatever happens to them (e.g., rape or premarital sex not followed by marriage) and to others (e.g., the death of husband or the misbehavior of their children).

Besides noting the role that the social context plays in suicide, Australian participants attributed suicide relatively more often to personal factors and depression. Compared to the other two groups, suicide was seen more often as a matter to be dealt with by professionals rather than by friends and relatives. Australians also showed some negative attitudes toward suicide, but less so than Indians. This, together with the difficulty, particularly for men, of expressing feelings and asking for help, might create a barrier not only for help-seeking but also for "help-getting."

Some important suggestions for suicide prevention and research emerged in this study. First of all, there is the need to understand more in depth the complex relationship between attitudes and suicide highlighted in this study. Certainly reducing the stigma and the negative attitudes towards suicidal behavior is a primary and fundamental area of prevention, and it might be even more so for Indians, followed by Australians.

A few participants across countries believed that youths who kill themselves do not exhibit warning signs (although the majority believed that they might show them indirectly or nonverbally). However, research has pointed out that often, especially retrospectively, close ones could identify what were possible signs. For instance, in our study (Dello Buono et al., 2004) of 511 people who died by suicide in the Padua province (in Italy) during 1990–1999 (of which 117 were aged 18-34), we found that only 29% of the total sample did not previously communicate the intention to kill themselves as expressed, for instance, by suicide threats, previous attempts and written messages.

Education programs should help to change myths expressed by some participants, such as "people who say it do not do it" and "suicidal people do not show any signs," because both these attitudes are dangerous. With the first, there is the risk of not taking people who might really kill themselves seriously, as well as neglecting people who (even if they might not kill themselves) are expressing pain. The second, in my opinion, legitimizes people not "looking for" signs. On the other hand, people should be educated about what are the more frequent and the more unusual warning signs (bearing in mind cultural differences such as those showed in this study and in Colucci et al., 2010a, 2010b, 2011), to pay attention to these and not neglect any sign, and about what to do in case they perceive that a peer or a close one is at risk of suicide. This latter point is essential because, as some of the participants stated, it can be frightening knowing or wondering if a close one is suicidal because they would not know what to do in such circumstances. The lack of tools to deal with this disclosure (direct or indirect) and the reluctance to imagine that anyone (even a close one) might be considering killing themselves, may increase the chance that people will neglect signs. Hence, education and awareness in this regard are crucial, even more so in Italy (where participants were more uncertain about signs). Education should address the beliefs reported by some participants that people do not expect "some" people (e.g., strong or popular youths) to be at risk of killing themselves. Colucci, Kelly, Minas and Jorm recently developed, using a Delphi consensus method, "Suicide First Aid" guidelines for community members with local experts in India (Colucci, et. al., 2010a), the Philippines (Colucci, et. al., 2010b) and Japan (Colucci, et. al., 2011), which provide indications on how to recognize a person at risk for suicide and how to help the suicidal person before professional help is sought or the crisis is overcome. "Train the trainers" modules were also carried out in Japan and the Philippines based on the respective guidelines (see http://www.foundationawit.com/project3.1.html).

As observed in this series of studies, as well as this project, research should also address cultural variations in warning signs (e.g., starting to drink/smoke in India vs. an increase in the use of alcohol and drugs in Australia) and beliefs on what suicide warning signs are.

Although there were some similar answers, participants reported variations on suicide deterrents, ideas on youth suicide prevention and people they would talk to (if any!) if they were suicidal. Similarities and differences must be considered when developing universal (e.g., implementation of the knowledge that, across countries, friends and "no one" would be the first option if participants were feeling suicidal) and local (e.g., besides teachers, also neighbors and community elders might be worthwhile to educate in gatekeeper programs for young Indians) suicide prevention and intervention strategies for young people. There is also the need to reconsider the current prevention programs for suicidal youths in light of the culturally-different explanatory models of suicide (in particular, considering the role of mental illness and depression in these models) and the generalized stigma (more so in India and Italy) toward professionals. Both these aspects can make clinically-based suicide prevention strategies (and, more generally, the "psychiatrization" of suicide) unappealing and inadequate for most youths, thus compromising the possibility of offering them any help. New forms of prevention should also be considered (for instance, group discussions moderated by a psychologist in schools and on websites) and old ones should be re-considered. In regard to the latter suggestion, in Indian and Australian participants' opinions, the use of creative forms such as theater, music and poems would make education and awareness campaigns more appealing and effective for youth (see http://toofew ladders.webs.com for an example of arts-based suicide research and prevention projects). Italians also pointed out that current education programs do not attract youth's attention. Suicide prevention strategies should take into consideration the fact that, across cultures, participants would more likely talk to a friend/peer if they decided to talk to anyone about their suicidal intention. Furthermore, in Australia there is a greater need for "creating communities" and occasions for socialization while, in India, it is urgent to restructure counseling services so that youths will feel that their confidentiality is absolutely protected.

Prevention programs should also consider gender issues and gendered-meanings of suicide, an important but overlooked area of research. Canetto and Lester (1995) noted the gendered cultures of suicide as an important avenue for primary prevention, that is, suicide prevention programs ought to assess and focus on the meanings and acceptability of suicide for both women and men within a cultural group. Reddy and Arora (2005) recommended the development of gender-related legislation and action as part of the Indian National Strategy for suicide prevention, in particular policies for gender justice with a specific focus on young women. In the current study, Indian and Australian participants, both males and females, pointed out various aspects that differentiate suicide in young women and men, and the majority of these were related to social expectations and judgments. Therefore, it is important that people involved in suicide prevention are made aware that these gender issues do exist and are encouraged to consider the gender-related meanings of risk and protective factors in the development of prevention strategies and in clinical treatments for suicidal youths. In many countries and in several circumstances, female suicides are the result of violation of basic human rights such as freedom, respect and dignity. Thus, if we aim to prevent suicide, we must make our duty to contribute to the protection of women's rights and reduce violence against women (Colucci & Pryor, in press).

The research findings highlighted the fact that cultural determinants, systems of meanings and beliefs, and exploratory models cannot be neglected in suicide research and prevention because they are powerful influences on people's way of approaching suicide, both in regard to their own life and other people's lives (see also Colucci, 2006, 2009). Cultural factors also affect people's beliefs about the causes of suicide and ways to prevent suicide, which might determine help-seeking strategies, including the belief that help might be possible. In particular, the importance of people's spiritual and religious beliefs in their life cannot continue being neglected because these, as key phenomena in society influencing a person's identity, influence the nature and extent of expressions of suicidal intentions (see Mishara, 2006).

Kirmayer and collaborators (2007) observed that suicide may also be understood as a spiritual problem, having to do with a person's sense that life lacks meaning or the lack of connection with larger values that give purpose and direction to life. Although spirituality was not a specific focus of the present research, spiritual/religious beliefs are a part of the cultural milieu and, particularly in India, participants often referred to these when expressing their attitudes toward suicide, suicide deterrents and sources of help. Similar findings emerged also in a study with Ghanaians students (Osafo, Hjelmeland, Akotia & Knizek, 2011b). In this regard, the WHO South-East Asia report (2001) stated that spiritual leaders and faith healers occupy an important and unique position in South-East Asian societies owing to their stature, position, wisdom and their ability to influence people's beliefs and values. Therefore, in the WHO delegates' opinion, faith healers should be involved in suicide prevention activities at the community level as they are the first level of contact for many health problems. In addition, they argued, several nonpharmacological methods of management (such as yoga, meditation, acupuncture and reiki) are gaining popularity in South-East Asian countries, as well as everywhere in the world. Thus, the report concluded, it is vital to develop a better understanding of the role of these systems to incorporate positive, harmless and culturally-accepted methods. These considerations, supported by the results from this study, point to the necessity of understanding the impact that cultural (including spiritual) beliefs have on people's decision to take their own life and to develop culturally-appropriate suicide prevention strategies (see also Colucci, 2008c; Colucci & Martin, 2008; Colucci, in press).

In summary, I recommend that suicide prevention strategies consider cultural (and sub-cultural) issues, that such strategies should be based on the voices of the people for whom these services are developed, and that clinically-based approaches should be one option rather "the" main strategy (particularly because they might not meet the person's explanatory model, and professionals might not be included in the person's "list" of helpers). Suicide prevention also needs to be oriented towards increasing people's reasons for being alive (e.g., organization of creative activities and increasing their sense of community are few examples of what some participants requested) rather than just reducing reasons to die. Furthermore, spirituality should play a greater role in suicide prevention and needs to be more fully researched and understood. Activities aimed at the defense of human rights, particularly women's rights and the elimination of violence against women, would also contribute to preventing suicide.

A much richer discussion of this study can be found in Colucci (2008b) as well as in Colucci (2009) and Colucci (in press), but it is clear that the concept of suicide has different connotations and meaning in these three cultures. It is also clear that a combination of quantitative and qualitative methods enabled these differences to be explored and described in much greater detail than either methodology used alone.

In conclusion, while participants from the three cultures had partially similar and partially different ideas and beliefs on numerous aspects of suicide, there was no difference in the acknowledgment that suicide (fatal and nonfatal) is a source of concern, pain and struggle for suicidal youths and their close ones, and it is a problem for which not enough is being done. More and better needs to be done before it is too late, as this Australian male participant strongly stated while suggesting youth suicide prevention strategies:

"Basic, grass-roots education programs e.g., in schools, to raise awareness of the topic. They have stuff like that for safe driving, drug and alcohol use etc. but nothing for suicide. You don't hear about it unless it happens and by then it's too late. Someone's taken their own life before it's even really begun because they thought there was no other option for f. ... sake!!! It's a really tragic situation that no one seems to want to address or even talk about!!! Apologies for the rambling, but it's something I feel strongly about" (AU176m).

My hope is that more will be done in the future for youth suicide and that that "more" will be based on the voices, in different languages and from different cultures, of the young people.

Acknowledgments

I would like to express my deepest gratitude to Assoc. Prof. Harry Minas, Prof. Anthony Marsella, Prof. Graham Martin, and Assoc. Prof. Robert Schweitzer for sharing their knowledge and supervising my doctoral studies. I would also like to thank Prof. Guido Petter for having been a loving and exemplary mentor from my undergraduate studies up till his recent passing.

I am indebted to numerous people for the fulfilment of this research project. First of all, thanks to the participants and staff members from the University of Padua (Italy), Garden City College, Dr. Ambedkar College and Bangalore University (India); The University of Queensland and Queensland University of Technology (Australia). I am also thankful to Ms Lata Jacob (Medico-Pastoral Association, Bangalore), Prof. Shekar, and Prof. Gururaj (NIMHANS, Bangalore).

My thanks also go to my friends Silvia Filiberti and Christina Bachmann, and my Honours students and trainees (Alessandro Buffoli, Antonella Cagnoli, Barbara Sanna, Christian Turchi, Lara Pelagotti, Tomaso Scherini, Chiara Presciani, and Andrea Volpato) for their contributions to data collection or implementation. I am also grateful to Bridget Noronah, Shawn and David Askhanasy, Rebecca Haddow, and Zina Deamer for focus group transcriptions. I would like to thank Prof. Arthur Kleinman (Harvard Medical School), Prof. Robert Barrett (University of Adelaide), Prof. Michel Tousignant (Université du Québec à Montréal), and Greg Turner (Mental Health in Multicultural Australia) for their feedback during the research project development. This study resulted in me receiving the Emerging Research LIFE Award in 2009, and I would like to take this opportunity to acknowledge the contributions from the collaborators listed above. More generally, I want to express my gratitude to those scholars who have supported the cause for more culturally-sensitive and respectful suicide research and prevention.

This research project was supported by IPRS and UQIPRS competitive scholarships, the University of Queensland Travel Award, and Dr Helen Row–Zonta Memorial Prize 2005.

References

Ambert, A. M., Adler, P. A., Adler, P., & Detzner, D. F. (1995). Understanding and evaluating qualitative research. *Journal of Marriage & the Family, 57*, 879–893.
Barrett, R. J. (2001). An introduction to sociocultural psychiatry (CD-ROM). In D. Burke & L. Newman (Ed.), *Postgraduate course in psychiatry*. Sydney, Australia: NSW Institute of Psychiatry.
Baume, P. J., & Clinton, M. E. (1997). Social and cultural patterns of suicide in young people in rural Australia. *Australian Journal of Rural Health, 5*(3), 115–120.
Bernard, H. R. (1995). *Research methods in anthropology: Qualitative and quantitative approaches*. Walnut Creek, CA: Altamira Press.
Berry, J. W. Poortinga, Y. H., Marshall, S., & Dasen, P. R. (2002). *Cross-cultural psychology: Research and applications* (2nd ed.). Cambridge, UK: Cambridge University Press
Bloor, M., Frankland, J., Thomas, M., & Robson, K. (2001). *Focus groups in social research*. Thousand Oaks, CA: Sage.

Blumer, H. (1969). *Symbolic interactionism: Perspective and method*. Englewood Cliffs, NJ: Prentice Hall.

Boldt, M. (1988). The meaning of suicide: Implications for research. *Crisis, 9*, 93–108.

Bourne, P. G. (1973) Suicide among Chinese in San Francisco. *American Journal of Public Health, 63*, 744–750.

Borowsky, I. W., Ireland, M., & Resnick, M. D. (2001). Adolescent suicide attempts: Risks and protectors. *Pediatrics, 107*, 485–493.

Braun, K. L., & Nichols, R. (1997). Death and dying in four Asian American cultures: A descriptive study. *Death Studies, 21*, 327–359.

Brownhill, S., Wilhelm, K., Barclay, L., & Schmied, V. (2005). "Big build": Hidden depression in men. *Australian and New Zealand Journal of Psychiatry, 39*, 921–931.

Burr, J. (2002). Cultural stereotypes of women from South Asian communities: Mental health care professionals' explanations for patterns of suicide and depression. *Social Science & Medicine, 55*, 835–845.

Burns, J. M., & Patton, G. C. (2000). Preventive interventions for youth suicide: A risk factor-based approach. *Australian & New Zealand Journal of Psychiatry, 34*, 388–407.

Burke, A. W. (1979). Social attempted suicide: Young women in two contrasting areas. *International Journal of Social Psychiatry, 25*, 198–202.

Cantor, C. H., & Baume, P. J. M. (1998). Access to methods of suicide: What impact? *Australian & New Zealand Journal of Psychiatry, 32*, 8–14.

Canetto, S. S., & Lester, D. (1995). Gender and the primary prevention of suicide mortality. *Suicide & Life-Threatening Behavior, 25*, 58–69.

Carr, S. C., Marsella, A. J., & Purcell, I. P. (2002). Researching intercultural relations: Toward a middle way. *Asian Psychologist, 3*, 58–64.

Chew-Graham, C., Bashir, C., Chantler, K., Burman, E., & Batsleer, J. (2002). South Asian women, psychological distress and self-harm: Lessons for primary care trusts. *Health & Social Care in the Community, 10*, 339–347.

Chiu, L., Ganesan, S., Clark, N., & Morrow, M. (2005). Spirituality and treatment choices by South and East Asian women with serious mental illness. *Transcultural Psychiatry, 42*(4), 630–656.

Chowdhury, A. N., Banerjee, S., Das, S., Sarkar, P., Chatterjee, D., Mondal, A., & Biswas, M. K. (2005). Household survey of suicidal behaviour in a coastal village of Sundarban region, India. *International Medical Journal, 12*(4), 275–282.

Ciarrochi, J. V., & Deane, F. P. (2001). Emotional competence and willingness to seek help from professional and nonprofessional sources. *British Journal of Guidance & Counselling, 29*, 233–246.

Coggan, C., & Patterson, P. (1998). Focus groups with youth to enhance knowledge of ways to address youth suicide. In R. J. E. Kosky, H. S., Goldney, R. D., & Hassan, R. (Ed.), *Suicide prevention: The global context*. New York: Plenum.

Coggan, C., Patterson, P., & Fill, J. (1997). Suicide: Qualitative data from focus group interviews with youth. *Social Science & Medicine, 45*, 1563–1570.

Colucci, E., (in press), Spirituality, religion and suicide. In Pompili, M. (Ed.), *Suicide: A comprehensive perspective*. Qatar: Bentham EBooks.

Colucci, E. (2009). Cultural issues in suicide risk assessment. In U. Kumar & M. K. Mandal (Eds.), *Suicidal Behavior: Assessment of People-at-risk*, pp. 107–135. New Delhi, India: Sage.

Colucci, E. (2008a). On the use of focus groups in cross-cultural research. In P. Liamputtong (Ed.), *Doing cross-cultural research: Ethical and methodological considerations*, p. 233–252. Dordrecht, The Netherlands: Springer.

Colucci, E. (2008b). The cultural meaning of suicide: A comparison between Italian, Indian and Australian students. Unpublished doctoral dissertation, University of Queensland, Australia.

Colucci, E. (2008c). Recognizing spirituality in the assessment and prevention of suicidal behaviour. *World Cultural Psychiatry Research Review (WCPRR), Special issue: Suicide and Culture, 3*(2), 77–95.

Colucci, E. (2007). "Focus groups can be fun": the use of activity-oriented questions in focus group discussions, *Qualitative Health Journal, 17,* 1422–1433,

Colucci, E. (2006). The cultural facet of suicidal behaviour. *Australian e-Journal for the Advancement of Mental health, 5*(3), 1–13.

Colucci, E. (2004). Il suicidio adolescenziale [Youth suicide]. *Psicologia dell'Eta' Evolutiva, June*, 119–128.

Colucci, E., Kelly, C. M., Minas, H., Jorm, A. F., & Chatterjee (2010a), Mental Health First Aid guidelines for helping a suicidal person: A Delphi consensus study in India, *International Journal of Mental Health Systems,* 4, 4. Available online at http://www.ijmhs.com/content/4/1/4

Colucci, E., Kelly, C. M., Minas, H., Jorm, A. F., & Nadera, D. (2010b), Mental health first aid guidelines for helping a suicidal person: A Delphi consensus study in the Philippines, *International Journal of Mental Health Systems, 4,* 32. Available online at http://www.ijmhs.com/content/4/1/32

Colucci, E., Kelly, C. M., Minas, H., Jorm, A. F., & Suzuki, Y. (2011). Mental health first aid guidelines for helping a suicidal person: A Delphi consensus study in Japan. *International Journal of Mental Health Systems, 5,* 12. Avilable online at http://www.ijmhs.com/content/5/1/12

Colucci, E., & Martin, G. (2008). Spirituality and religion along the suicidal path. *Suicide and Life-Threatening Behavior, 38*(2), 229–244.

Colucci, E., & Martin, G. (2007a). Ethnocultural aspects of suicide in young people: A systematic literature review. Part 1: Rates and methods of youth suicide. *Suicide & Life-Threatening Behavior, 37,* 197–221.

Colucci, E., & Martin, G. (2007b). Ethnocultural aspects of suicide in young people: A systematic literature review. Part 2: Risk factors, precipitating agents, and attitudes toward suicide. *Suicide & Life-Threatening Behavior, 37,* 222–237.

Colucci, E., & Pryor, R. (in press). Violence against women. In Okpaku, S. (Ed.), *Global Mental Health.* Cambridge, UK: Cambridge University Press.

De Leo, D., & Heller, T. S. (2004). *Suicide in Queensland 1999–2001: Mortality rates and related data* Brisbane, Qld: AISRAP.

De Leo, D., & Meneghel, G. (2001). The impact of culture and religion on suicide in Italian society. *Listening: Journal of Religion & Culture, 36,* 160–173.

Dello Buono, M., Daru', E., Colucci, E., & Pavan, L. (2004). Predictors of suicide risk across the life cycle: A study of 511 suicides. *Rivista di Psichiatria, 29,* 340–348.

Diekstra, R. F. W., & Kerkhof, A. J. F. M. (1989). Attitudes towards suicide: The development of a suicide-attitude questionnaire (SUIATT). In R. F. W. Diekstra, R. Maris, S. Platt, A. Schmidtke, & G. Sonneck (Eds.), *Suicide and its prevention: The role of attitude and imitation*, pp. 91–107. Leiden, The Netherlands: E J Brill.

Domino, G., Moore, D., Westlake, L., & Gibson, L. (1982). Attitudes toward suicide: A factor analytic approach. *Journal of Clinical Psychology, 38*, 257–262.

Douglas, J. D. (1967). *The social meaning of suicide*. Princeton, NJ: Princeton University Press.

Donald, M., Dower, J., Correa-Velez, I., & Jones, M. (2006). Risk and protective factors for medically serious suicide attempts: A comparison of hospital-based with population-based samples of young adults. *Australian & New Zealand Journal of Psychiatry, 40*, 87–96.

Durkheim, E. (1897/1997). *Il suicidio: Studio Italiano di Suicidologia* [Suicide: Italian Study of Suicidology] (R. Scramaglia, Trans.). Milano: BUR.

Eckersley, R., & Dear, K. (2002). Cultural correlates of youth suicide. *Social Science & Medicine, 55*, 1891–1904.

Eshun, S. (2003). Sociocultural determinants of suicide ideation: A comparison between American and Ghanaian college samples. *Suicide and Life-Threatening Behavior, 33*, 165–171.

Eskin, M. (1999). Gender and cultural differences in the 12-month prevalence of suicidal thoughts and attempts in Swedish and Turkish adolescents. *Journal of Gender, Culture, & Health, 4*, 187–200.

Farber, M. L. (1975). Psychocultural variables in Italian culture. In N. L. Farberow (Ed.), *Suicide in different cultures*, pp. 179–184. Baltimore, MD: University Park Press.

Fullagar, S., Gilchrist, H., & Sullivan, G. (2007). The construction of youth suicide as a community issue within urban and regional Australia. *Australien e-Journal for the Advancement of Mental Health, 6*(2). Available online at http://www98.griffith.edu.au/dspace/bitstream/handle/10072/16202/47106.pdf?sequence=1

Garrison, C. Z., Jackson, K. L., Addy, C. L., McKeown, R. E., & Waller, J. L. (1991). Suicidal behaviors in young adolescents. *American Journal of Epidemiology, 133*, 1005–1014.

Gothelf, D., Apter, A., Brand-Gothelf, A., Offer, N. M., Ofek, H., Tyano, S., & Pfeffer, C. R. (1998). Death concepts in suicidal adolescents. *Journal of American Academy of Child & Adolescent Psychiatry, 37*, 1279–1286.

Gururaj, G., Isaac, M. K., Subbakrishna, D. K., & Ranjani, R. (2004). Risk factors for completed suicides: A case-control study from Bangalore, India. *Injury Control & Safety Promotion, 11*, 183–191,

Gururaj, G., & Isaac, M. K. (2003). *Suicide prevention: Information for educational institutions*. Bangalore, India: NIMHANS.

Gutierrez, P., King, C. A., & Ghaziuddin, N. (1996). Adolescent attitudes about death in relation to suicidality. *Suicide and Life-Threatening Behavior, 26*, 8–18.

Hein, S. F., & Austin, W. J. (2001). Empirical and hermeneutic approaches to phenomenological research in psychology: A comparison. *Psychological Methods, 6*, 3–17.

Hezel, F. X. (1989). Suicide and the Micronesian family. *The Contemporary Pacific 1*, 43–74.

Hughes, D., & DuMont, K. (1993). Using focus groups to facilitate culturally anchored research. *American Journal of Community Psychology, 21*, 775–806.

Joseph, A., Abraham, S., Muliyil, J. P., George, K., Prasad, J., Minz, S., . . . Jacob, K. S. (2003). Evaluation of suicide rates in rural India using verbal autopsies, 1994–9. *British Medical Journal, 326*, 1121–1122.

Kelly, G. A. (1955). *A theory of personality*. New York: Norton.

Ketelaar, T., & O'Hara, M. W. (1989). Meaning of the concept "suicide" and risk for attempted suicide. *Journal of Social & Clinical Psychology, 8*, 393–399.

Kidd, S. A. (2004). "The walls were closing in, and we were trapped": A qualitative analysis of street youth suicide. *Youth & Society, 36*, 30–55.

Kirmayer, L., Brass, G. M., Holton, T., Paul, K., Simpson, C., & Tait, C. (2007). *Suicide among Aboriginal people in Canada*. Ontario, Canada: The Aboriginal Healing Foundation. Available online at http://www.douglas.qc.ca/uploads/File/2007-AHF-suicide.pdf

Koch, T. (1999). An interpretative research process: Revisiting phenomenological and hermeneutical approaches. *Nurse Research, 6*(3), 20–34.

Kumar, V. (2003). Burnt wives: A study of suicides. *Burns, 29*, 31–35.

Lalwani, S., Sharma, G., Rautji, R., & Millo, T. (2004). Study of suicide among young and middle aged adults in South Delhi. *Indian Journal of Preventive & Social Medicine, 35*(3–4), 173–178.

Langford, R. A., & Ritchie, J. (1998). Suicidal behavior in a bicultural society: A review of gender and cultural differences in adolescents and young persons of Aotearoa/New Zealand. *Suicide and Life-Threatening Behavior, 28*, 94–106.

Latha, K. S., & Geetha, N. (2004). Criminalizing suicide attempts: Can it be a deterrent? *Medicine Science and the Law, 44*(4), 343–347.

Laungani, P. (2001). The influence of culture on stress: India and England. In L. L. G. Adler & Uwe P. (Ed.), *Cross-cultural topics in psychology*, pp. 149–169. Westport, CT: Praeger.

Lenzi, M., Colucci, E., & Minas, H. (2012). Suicide, culture and society from a cross-national perspective. *Cross-Cultural Research, 46*, 50–71.

Lester, D. (1993). How do people perceive the different methods for suicide? *Death Studies, 17*, 179–184.

Lester, D. (1997). Note on a Mohave theory of suicide. *Cross-Cultural Research, 31*, 268–272.

Marsella, A. J. (2000). *Socio-cultural considerations in the assessment of suicidal behavior: In pursuit of cultural and community indices, dimensions, and perceptions*. Unpublished technical report. Geneva, Switzerland: WHO/ Mental Health.

Marshall, A. P., Fisher, M. J., Brammer, J., Eustace, P., Grech, C., Jones, B., & Kelly, M. (2007). Assessing psychometric properties of scales: A case study. *Journal of Advanced Nursing, 59*, 398–406.

Marshall, H., & Yazdani, A. (1999). Locating culture in accounting for self-harm amongst Asian young women. *Journal of Community & Applied Social Psychology, 9*, 413–433.

Martin, G. (1996). Reported family dynamics, sexual abuse, and suicidal behaviors in community adolescents. *Archives of Suicide Research, 2*, 183–195.

McGrath, J. E., & Johnson, B. A. (2003). Methodology makes meaning: How both qualitative and quantitative paradigms shape evidence and its interpretation. In P. M. Camic, J. E. Rhodes, & L. Yardley (Eds.), *Qualitative research in psychology: Expanding perspectives in methodology and design*, pp. 31–48. Washington, DC: American Psychological Association.

Meneghel, M., Scocco, P., Colucci, E., Marini, M., Marietta, P., Padoani, W.,...De Leo, D. (2004). Suicidal behaviour in Italy. In A. Schmidtke, U. Bille-Brahe, D. De Leo, D., & A. Kerkhof (Eds.), *Suicidal behaviour in Europe*, pp. 211–217. Göttingen, Germany: Hogrefe & Huber.

Meng, L. (2002). Rebellion and revenge: The meaning of suicide of women in rural China. *International Journal of Social Welfare, 11*, 300–309.

Mishara, B. L. (2006). Cultural specificity and universality of suicide: Challenges for the International Association for Suicide Prevention. *Crisis, 27, 1*–3.

Monk, M. (1987). Epidemiology of suicide. *Epidemiologic Reviews, 9*, 51–69.

Morgan, D. L. (1997). *Focus groups as qualitative research*. Thousand Oaks, CA: SAGE.

Morgan, D. L. (1996). Focus groups. *Annual Review of Sociology, 22*, 129–152.

Morgan, D. L., & Scannell, A. U. (1998). *Planning focus groups* (Vol. II). Thousands Oaks, CA: Sage.

M. V. D. (1957). Homebound women of Saurashtra. *Economic Weekly, 9*(49), 1563–1566.

Nirui, M., & Chenoweth, L. (1999). The response of healthcare services to people at risk of suicide: A qualitative study. *Australian & New Zealand Journal of Psychiatry, 33*, 361–371.

Perkins, D. F., & Hartless, G. (2002). An ecological risk-factor examination of suicide ideation and behavior of adolescents. *Journal of Adolescent Research, 17*, 3–26.

Phan, T. T., & Fitzgerald, M. H. (1996). *Guide for the use of focus groups in health research (Volume 1)*. Sidney, Australia: TMH.

Pinzon-Perez, H., & Perez, M. A. (2001). A study of suicide-related behaviors among Colombian youth: Reflections on prevention and implications for health education. *American Journal of Health Education, 32*, 288–292.

Reddy, K. S., & Arora, M. (2005). Towards a national strategy to reduce suicide in India. *National Medical Journal of India, 18*(3), 118–122.

O'Carroll, P. W., Berman, A., Maris, R. W., & Moscicki, E. K. (1996). Beyond the tower of Babel: A nomenclature for suicidology. *Suicide and Life-Threatening Behavior, 26*, 237–252.

Osafo, J., Knizek, B., Akotia, C., & Hjelmeland, H. (2012). Attitudes of psychologists and nurses toward suicide and suicide prevention in Ghana: A qualitative study. *International Journal of Nursing Studies, 49*(6), 691–700.

Osafo, J., Hjelmeland, H., Akotia, C. S., & Knizek, B. L. (2011a). Social injury: An interpretative phenomenological analysis of the attitudes towards suicide of lay persons in Ghana. *International Journal of Qualitative Studies on Health & Well-being, 6*(4), 8708.

Osafo, J., Hjelmeland, H., Akotia, C., & Knizek, B. (2011b). The meanings of suicidal behaviour to psychology students in Ghana: A qualitative approach. *Transcultural Psychiatry, 48*, 1–17.

Raleigh, V. S., Bulusu, L., & Balarajan, R. (1990). Suicides among immigrants from the Indian subcontinent. *British Journal of Psychiatry, 156*, 46–50.

Roberts, R. E. (2000). Depression and suicidal behaviors among adolescents: The role of ethnicity. In I. P. Cuellar & A. Freddy (Eds.), *Handbook of multicultural mental health*, pp. 359–388. San Diego, CA: Academic Press.

Salander Renberg, E., & Jacobsson, L. (2003). Development of a questionnaire on attitudes towards suicide (ATTS) and its application in a Swedish population. *Suicide and Life-Threatening Behavior, 33*, 52–64.

Schilder, K., Tomov, T., Mladenova, M., Mayeya, J., Jenkins, R., Gulbinat, W., . . . Sakura, T. (2004). The appropriateness and use of focus group methodology across international mental health communities. *International Review of Psychiatry, 16*, 24–30.

Schwandt, T. A. (2000). Three epistemological stances for qualitative inquiry. In N. K. L. Denzin, Y. S (Ed.), *Handbook of qualitative research*. Thousand Oaks, CA: Sage.

Scott, G., Ciarrochi, J., & Deane, F. P. (2004). Disadvantages of being an individualist in an individualistic culture: Idiocentrism, emotional competence, stress, and mental health. *Australian Psychologist, 39*, 143–153.

Shweder, R. A., & Bourne, E. J. (1982). Does the concept of the person vary cross-culturally? In A. J. W. Marsella & G. M. White (Ed.), *Cultural conceptions of mental health and therapy*, pp. 130–204. Dordrecht, The Netherlands: D. Reidel.

Smith, J. A., & Osborn, M. (2003). Interpretative phenomenological analysis. In J. A. Smith (Ed.), *Qualitative psychology: A practical guide to research methods*, pp. 51–80. London, UK: Sage.

Smith, J. A., Jarman M., & Osborn, M. (1999). Doing interpretative phenomenological analysis. In M. C. Murray, K. (Ed.), *Qualitative health psychology*, pp. 218–240. London, UK: Sage.

Taylor, S. J., & Bogdan, R. (1984). *Introduction to qualitative research methods: The search for meaning*. New York: Wiley.

Thakker, J., Ward, T., & Strongman, K. T. (1999). Mental disorder and cross-cultural psychology: A constructivist perspective. *Clinical Psychology Review, 19*, 843–874.

Thakur, U. (1963). *The history of suicide in India: An introduction*. Delhi: Munshi Ram Manohar Lal.

Tomori, M., Kienhorst, C. W. M., de Wilde, E. J., & van den Bout, J. (2001). Suicidal behaviour and family factors among Dutch and Slovenian high school students: A comparison. *Acta Psychiatrica Scandinavica, 103*, 1–6.

Tortolero, S. R., & Roberts, R. E. (2001). Differences in nonfatal suicide behaviors among Mexican and European American middle school children. *Suicide & Life Threatening Behavior, 31*, 214–223.

Tousignant, M., Seshadri, S., & Raj, A. (1998). Gender and suicide in India: A multiperspective approach. *Suicide & Life-Threatening Behavior, 28*, 50–61.

Venkoba Rao, A. (1975). Suicide in India. In N. L. Farberow (Ed.), *Suicide in different cultures*, pp. 231–238. Baltimore, MD: University Park Press.

Vrale, G. B., & Steen, E. (2005). The dynamics between structure and flexibility in constant observation of psychiatric inpatients with suicidal ideation. *Journal of Psychiatric & Mental Health Nursing, 12*, 513–518.

Vijayakumar, L. (2004). Altruistic suicide in India. *Archives of Suicide Research, 8*, 73–80.

Vijayakumar, L. (2005). Suicide and mental disorders in Asia. *International Review of Psychiatry, 17*, 109–114.

Voracek, M., & Loibl, L. M. (2008). Consistency of immigrant and country-of-birth suicide rates. *Acta Psychiatrica Scandinavica, 118*, 259–271.

Wagner, B. M., Wong, S. A., & Jobes, D. A. (2002). Mental health professionals' determinations of adolescent suicide attempts. *Suicide & Life-Threatening Behavior, 32*, 284–300.

Wellings, K., Branigan, P., & Mitchell, K. (2000). Discomfort, discord and discontinuity as data: Using focus groups to research sensitive topics. *Culture, Health & Sexuality, 2*, 255–267.

Westefeld, J. S., Button, C., Haley, J. T. J., Kettmann, J. J., Macconnell, J., Sandil, R. & Tallman, B. (2006). College student suicide: A call to action. *Death Studies, 30, 931– 956.*

Whitla, M. M. E. (2005). Brief candles: Youth suicide in Australia and Italy. Unpublished PhD Thesis, The University of Melbourne, Melbourne, Australia.

WHO. (2001). *Suicide prevention: Emerging from darkness*. New Delhi, India: Regional Office for South-East Asia.

WHO. (2012). Country reports and charts available. Accessed 10 April, 2012 at www.who.int/mental_health/prevention/suicide/country_reports/en/index.html

Yamada, A. M., Marsella, A. J., Atuel, H. R. (2002). Development of a Cultural Identification Battery for Asian and Pacific Islander Americans in Hawai'i. *Asian Psychologist, 3*, 11–20.

Selection of lyrics from songs written by an Italian suicidal participant (donated as a gift, permission of anonymous publication granted)

He doesn't believe in himself although he is sincere, but no one appreciates his sincerity. No, he will not stand his useless life.

But by now he doesn't care anymore, he is even tired to complain: there is nothing left to do but let the time elapse, keeping on getting drunk/meditating to suicide."

...I would like to wake up and find out that the reality was the dream, that all this time wasted to invent my own world, which will disappear with me, has not passed.

Now really no, I can't bear it anymore and I will not be able to raise myself from down here. I won't even try, I already know I will lose, I won't rebel, a nothing I will remain.

Since I was born there hasn't been a day that, I could say, it was worth living. Since I was born everything has been going wrong and I already know it will always be like this.
The world goes in pieces, people always more silly, my inexistent past ... you that never dream of me.
But at home I have my father's gun...
But at home I have my father's gun...

I want myself to decide at least once,
I don't want to die before the day I will kill myself.
I will kill myself.
I hope so.

Cross-Cultural Research on Suicidality

An Example and a Critique

David Lester

The study of culture and suicide requires more than discussion of the role of culture in suicidal behavior. It requires empirical research. There are many methodological issues that arise in cross-cultural research. What is interesting in most discussions of these issues is that there is frequent criticism and very little guidance as to how the research should be conducted. This essay will review a few of the theoretical and methodological issues and then examine research conducted by the author on suicidality in the US and in Kuwait.

Theoretical Issues

Integrating Cultural Factors with Biological and Psychological Factors

Ratner and Hui (2003) noted that studies of cultural factors often fail, not only to take into account biological (and we might add psychological and social factors), but also to provide a coherent, integrated, systematic model of the role that each factor plays. Ratner and Hui noted that researchers typically favor one set of factors over the others. Although criticizing some authors for this bias, they fail to provide an example of what should be done.

There are some simple examples possible here. For example, culture may influence diet which may influence physiological processes such as neurotransmitter levels in the central nervous system. Mawson and Jacobs (1978) noted that the synthesis of serotonin requires the precursor amino acid L-tryptophan. Corn has low levels of L-tryptophan, and so individuals in cultures with high levels of corn consumption may have lower levels of serotonin, thereby making them more prone to behaviors such as depression and aggression toward others. Child-rearing practices may differ between cultures (Whiting & Child, 1953) and, thereby, affect the behavior of adults raised with these different socialization experiences.

Relating Psychological Differences to Cultural Differences

Related to the issue mentioned above, Ratner and Hui (2003) noted that researchers often report psychological differences between respondents into two or more cultures, but fail to explain the *cultural basis* for these differences. How do the cultures involved in the study generate these differences?

There are two approaches here. Sometimes researchers take a purely empirical approach. For example, Lynn (1971) used social indicators to measure the personality traits of extraversion and neuroticism in 18 industrialized nations. Social indicators such as the divorce rate and cigarette consumption were used to measure extraversion, while social indicators such as the suicide rate and caffeine consumption were used to measure neuroticism. The sample chosen was not based on any theoretical consideration, but merely those nations that collect reliable data for the required social indicators. Furthermore, there was little or no attempt to explain the differences identified, such as that the US appeared to be the most extraverted nation while Austria was the most neurotic.

An alternative approach is to find a theoretical basis for the study and choose an appropriate sample of cultures. Although using only a European sample of nations (thirty in all), Kondrichin and Lester (1997) argued that the Finno-Ugrian gene (found primarily in Finnish and Hungarian populations) was a risk factor for suicide. They found a strong association between the percentages of the population with this gene and the suicide rates of the nations. Since this gene is found primarily in Finnish and Hungarian individuals, it made sense to restrict the study to European nations and not to include nations in other regions of the world.

Ratner and Hui (2003) argued also that a study of a cultural influence on a behavior is often merely a study of national differences in the behavior. They gave a hypothetical example of a study, based on a hypothesis that individualism-collectivism is related to a behavior, carried out in China (a collectivist nation) and the US (an individualistic nation). Ratner and Hui noted that China and the US differ on a multitude of cultural factors, and one cannot assume that one of these cultural factors, rather than any other, is responsible for the difference in behavior identified.

Defining a Cultural Value

Ratner and Hui (2003) noted that researchers often use a term such as collectivism and assume that it means the same in all cultures. This is known as *construct bias.* Triandis (2001), for example, pointed out that collectivism in Korea is not the same as collectivism in Israeli kibbutzim, and Triandis identified sixty attributes on which collectivist cultures can differ, such as whether arguing within the in-group is acceptable or not.

Methodological Issues in Cross-Cultural Research

Measurement Problems

There are many measurement problems that arise in cross-cultural research:

(1) The problem of devising a measuring instrument in one language and then translating it into another has been widely discussed. Simply translating a scale from one language to another has been supplemented by back-translation, that is, translating the scale back into the original language in which it was first written to check on the adequacy of the translation (Merenda, 2006), as in Colucci's study (see above) where the instrument was pilot tested in the three cultures studied in order to check for ambiguities. The use of fluent bilingual translators has been suggested as a useful tactic here.[1]

(2) The items on the two versions of the test might not be equivalent. For example, a reference to "God" in a religiosity questionnaire might have different meanings for Christians, Muslims, Buddhists, and Hindus, let alone for different denominations within a religion (such as Methodists versus Roman Catholics or Shi'ite versus Sunni Muslims).

(3) The issue of item equivalence may also arise in the quantitative reliability analysis. For example, are the item-total correlations similar in the two cultures? Is the structure identified by factor-analysis similar? This and other related issues are known as *item bias*.

(4) There is a major bias in that most psychological measures are derived in the West (Europe and North America) or by psychologists in other cultures who have received their graduate education in the West. It would be of interest to develop psychological measures in other cultures by researchers immersed in those cultures.

(5) Are the psychological tests used adequate and meaningful (as well as reliable and valid)? The research by Hofstede (1980) on measures of collectivism-individualism, power distance and avoidance of uncertainty

---

[1] There are problems even in using English-language tests in the various English-speaking countries. For example, one test devised by Hans Eysenck in England uses the word *cheeky*, the meaning of which American respondents typically do not understand.

in 40 nations looks impressive on the surface. Ratner and Hui (2003) noted that Hofstede sometimes used only three items to measure these traits, and perusal of the items suggests that they were not very good operational measures. For example, one of the three items to assess avoidance of uncertainty was "How often do you feel nervous or tense at work?" Ratner and Hui felt that this item, which constitutes 33% of the score, had no ostensible relation to the construct of avoidance of uncertainty.

(6) Respondents in different cultures may respond differently to self-report questionnaires versus interviews and to researchers with different personal characteristics (sex, age, social class or caste, and accent or dialect). For example, research on respondents in Muslim cultures may require that the researcher be of the same sex as the respondents, while this is not the case in Europe or the US. Respondents in some subcultures may be made uncomfortable or anxious by direct questions about some issues, such as suicidal ideation, and, therefore, deny its existence. Respondents in different cultures also differ in the role of social desirability in responding to questions and the degree of familiarity with psychological tests. These issues are known as *method bias*.

(7) Related to this, respondents to questions from different cultures may differ in their response styles (Duh & Chen, 2007), for example, extreme response styles, midpoint tendencies, acquiescence response styles (saying "yes"), and pleasing response styles (trying to please the interviewer).

Sampling Problems

A major criticism of many cross-cultural studies centers around whether the samples are equivalent. Hofstede (1980) used employees of IBM in forty nations but, of course, the employees in the different nations might have differed in characteristics such as education and social class. Most research around the world is conducted on college and university students but, again, these student samples might not be equivalent. Indeed, within one nation, such as the US, the students tested at a rural state college (where I conduct my research) might differ considerably from students at a major research-oriented university.

It has been suggested that some large universities have sufficiently large subpopulations from individual cultures and nations so that a cross-cultural study could be conducted within the students at a single university (Karahanna, Evaristo, & Srite, 2002). This would eliminate some, but not all, of these problems. For example, foreign students attending major American universities tend to come from the wealthier, more educated and privileged classes of their home nations.

A Case Study: Research Comparing Respondents in Kuwait and the US

Ahmed Abdel-Khalek and David Lester have conducted several studies comparing the responses of undergraduate students at Kuwait University and at the Richard Stockton College of New Jersey. They have used psychological tests developed by European psychologists (including Lester, educated in England and the US) and by Abdel-Khalek (educated in Egypt).

In teaching an undergraduate course on statistical methods, we always point out that the logic and analyses depend on the fact that the samples in the study must be random samples. We also note that this is rarely the case. Most studies are conducted on convenience samples, such as all the students in the researcher's classes during one semester. We break the random-sampling rule all the time, and we break it in a way that is acceptable in our scholarly field.

In a similar fashion, ideally researchers choose a topic and then seek cultures or nations that would be most suitable for testing their cross-cultural hypothesis. In reality, convenience plays a role. There are a small number of active researchers in psychology who have developed collegial relationships with other active researchers around the world. These relationships play a large role in the choice of samples and determined the collaborative research reviewed in this chapter.

Abdel-Khalek and Lester have conducted four major cross-cultural studies, and the next sections will examine the results of their research.

Kuwaiti Students Versus American Students

Reliability Studies

Abdel-Khalek (1998a) developed the Arabic Obsessive-Compulsive Scale, and Abdel-Khalek and Lester (1998) found acceptable Spearman-Brown and Cronbach alpha reliabilities in responses from students in both Kuwait and the US (> 0.76). Abdel-Khalek, Lester, and Barrett (2002) reported factor analyses of this scale and identified three factors in each group. The first two factors had some similarities, but the third factor was different in the two groups.[2]

---

[2] The results of this and other reliability studies are shown in Table 1.

Table 1. The results of reliability studies

	Kuwait	USA	
Arabic Scales: Cronbach alphas			
Arabic Obsess-Comp Scale	0.76	0.82	Abdel-Khalek & Lester (1998)
Death obsession	0.96	0.91	Abdel-Khalek & Lester (2003a)
Kuwait Anxiety Scale	0.93	0.95	Abdel-Khalek & Lester (2003c)
Kuwait Anxiety Scale:			
men	0.94	0.95	Abdel-Khalek & Lester (2006d)
women	0.92	0.95	Abdel-Khalek & Lester (2006d)
Optimism	0.95	0.93	Abdel-Khalek & Lester (2006a)
Pessimism	0.93	0.88	Abdel-Khalek & Lester (2006a)
American Scales: Cronbach alphas			
Taoist orientation	0.69	0.80	Lester & Abdel-Khalek (2002)
Maudsley Obsess-Comp Inventory			
Checking	0.66	0.68	Abdel-Khalek & Lester (2002d)
Cleaning	0.63	0.71	Abdel-Khalek & Lester (2002d)
Slowness	0.47	0.35	Abdel-Khalek & Lester (2002d)
Doubting	0.56	0.55	Abdel-Khalek & Lester (2002d)
Collett-Lester Fear of Death Scale			
Death of self	0.80	0.91	Lester & Abdel-Khalek (2003b)
Dying of self	0.88	0.92	
Death of others	0.75	0.88	
Dying of others	0.85	0.92	
Reynolds Suicidal Ideation	0.95	0.96	Abdel-Khalek & Lester (2007a)
Brief scale	0.85	0.88	Abdel-Khalek & Lester (2007a)
Arabic Scales: Spearman-Brown			
Arabic Obsess-Comp Scale	0.77	0.82	Abdel-Khalek & Lester (1998)

Abdel-Khalek and Lester (2003a) found good Cronbach alpha reliabilities for a death obsession scale developed by Abdel-Khalek (1998b). Item-total correlations were high in both samples, but the factor patterns differed, with one factor identified for the Kuwaiti sample and two for the American sample.

Abdel-Khalek and Lester (2003c) reported high Cronbach alpha reliabilities for the Kuwait University Anxiety Scale (Abdel-Khalek, 2000) and good item-total correlations. The factor patterns differed, with three factors identified in the Kuwaiti sample and two in the American sample (see Table 2). It appears that the American students have a much more global experience of anxiety (with 51% of the variance accounted for by the first factor), whereas the Kuwaiti students make finer distinctions between the various symptoms of anxiety.

Table 2. Results of a factor analysis of the items of the Kuwait University Anxiety Scale (from Abdel-Khalek & Lester, 2003c; decimal points omitted)

	Kuwait factors*			US factors*	
	I	II	III	I	II
My nerves are strained	40	00	43	70#	06
I feel frightened	62#	17	−18	67#	06
I have difficulty breathing	01	67#	10	11	68#
I think of things that worry me	62#	17	00	87#	22
My heart races	02	79#	00	44	52#
I get dizzy	18	53#	−13	28	48
I expect bad things to happen	79#	00	−12	71#	13
I am a nervous person	00	00	93#	63#	14
My heartbeats are irregular	−16	89#	12	06	76#
I feel nervous	01	01	89#	80#	02
I am afraid of losing self-control	20	12	56#	69#	05
I am tense	50#	11	37	81#	09
I feel anxious	70#	02	11	75#	17
I am not at ease	72#	01	10	74#	21
I worry over the future	74#	00	00	85#	30
I feel unstable	69#	−12	19	76#	02
My muscles feel tense	47	16	25	60#	16
I feel jittery	39	00	57#	58#	32
I feel worried	62#	00	25	85#	00
I am restless	77#	−10	00	62#	21
% variance	27	20	13	51	7

#loading > 0.50.
*After a principal components extraction and an oblimin rotation.

Abdel-Khalek and Lester (2006a) found good Cronbach alpha reliabilities for an Arabic optimism-pessimism scale in both samples (Abdel-Khalek, 1996). The factor analyses indicated differences between the two samples, although the labels for two of the factors, based on the items with high loadings, were similar.

For a scale to assess a Taoist orientation to life developed in the US (Knoblauch & Falconer, 1986), Lester and Abdel-Khalek (2002) found reasonable Cronbach alpha reliabilities in both groups, although the alpha was lower for the Kuwaiti students (0.69 versus 0.80). The results of the factor analyses for the two groups were, however, quite different.

On the other hand, Abdel-Khalek and Lester (2002d) found only moderate Cronbach reliabilities for short scales to measure obsessive-compulsive traits using the Maudsley Obsessional-Compulsive Inventory, but these moderate reliabilities were similar in both the Kuwaiti and American students.

These studies consistently indicate good reliabilities in both countries for the scales used in the research, and Table 1 summarizes the results of various reliability studies that Abdel-Khalek and Lester have conducted. The factor-analytic patterns usually differ. (Table 2 presents one such example.) However, this latter problem is also found when several factor-analyses are conducted on a scale *within* one country. Factor-analytic patterns are not easily replicated.

Validity Studies

Abdel-Khalek and Lester (1999b) found that the Arabic Obsessive-Compulsive Scale had good criterion (convergent) validity with the Maudsley Obsessional-Compulsive Scale (Hodgson & Rachman, 1977) (correlations > 0.64) in both countries. Abdel-Khalek and Lester (2002b) found that scores on the Arabic Obsessive-Compulsive Scale were more strongly correlated in both countries with scores on the Maudsley Obsessional-Compulsive Scale than with depression scores. Abdel-Khalek and Lester (2002c) found that scores on the Arabic Obsessive-Compulsive Scale correlated in a similar fashion in both countries with the four subscales scores of the Maudsley Obsessional-Compulsive Scale (checking, cleaning, slowness, and doubting). The concurrent validity of the Arabic Obsessive-Compulsive Scale, therefore, seems to be good.

Correlates of scores in Kuwait and American students are shown in Tables 3 and a typical factor analysis of scale scores is shown in Table 4.

Differences In Mean Scores

Lester and Abdel-Khalek (1997, 1998a) compared responses of Kuwaiti and American students on the Beck Depression Inventory (Beck, Ward, Mendelson, Mock, & Erbaugh, 1961). They found two sex differences on the 21 items for the American students and one for the Kuwaiti students, albeit an item different from the two for the American students. The Kuwait students obtained higher depression scores than the American students overall and on almost every item. The two groups did not differ, however, on the item assessing current suicidality.

Abdel-Khalek and Lester (1999a) found that Kuwaiti students obtained higher scores than American students on the Arabic Obsessive-Compulsive Scale. Abdel-Khalek and Lester (2000) found that Kuwaiti students scored higher on the Beck Depression Inventory and the Beck Hopelessness Scale (Beck, Weissman, Lester, & Trexler, 1974), but not on Rotter's (1966) belief in an external locus of control scale.

Table 3. Correlational studies

	Kuwait	USA	
Arabic Obsess-Comp Scale &			
Age	−0.03	−0.21*	Abdel-Khalek & Lester (2000)
Age	−0.20*	−0.10	Abdel-Khalek & Lester (2003b)
Sex	0.11	−0.04	Abdel-Khalek & Lester (2000)
Sex	−0.18*	−0.08	Abdel-Khalek & Lester (2003b)
Obsess-Comp Inv.	0.68	0.64	Abdel-Khalek & Lester (1999b)
Obsess-Comp Inv.	0.71*	0.63*	Abdel-Khalek & Lester (2002b)
External locus of control	0.25*	0.26*	Abdel-Khalek & Lester (2000)
Depression	0.55*	0.31*	Abdel-Khalek & Lester (2000)
Depression	0.49*	0.19	Abdel-Khalek & Lester (2002b)
Hopelessness	0.43*	0.27*	Abdel-Khalek & Lester (2000)
Ego-grasping &			
Optimism	−0.30*	−0.42*	Lester & Abdel-Khalek (2003a)
Pessimism	0.37*	0.48*	
Suicidal ideation	0.29*	0.40*	
Death obsession	0.28*	0.34*	
Anxiety	0.44*	0.57*	
Obsess-comp	0.37*	0.52*	
Att toward Physician-Assisted Suicide &			
Age	−0.05	0.19*	Schaller, et al. (2003) & Abdel-Khalek et al. (2005)
Sex	−0.05	0.01	
Death anxiety	0.04	−0.10	
Fear of:			
Death of self	0.07	−0.01	
Dying of self	−0.02	0.05	
Death of others	−0.03	−0.01	
Dying of others	0.05	0.02	
Reynolds Suicidal Ideation &			
Age	−0.15*	−0.11	Abdel-Khalek & Lester (2007a)
Sex	0.14*	0.05	
Optimism	−0.41*	−0.33*	
Pessimism	0.61*	0.46*	
Ego-grasping	0.29*	0.40*	
Death obsession	0.53*	0.33*	
Anxiety	0.56*	0.49*	
Obsession-compulsion	0.35*	0.35*	

(Continued)

Table 3. Continued.

	Kuwait	USA	
Religiosity			
Optimism	0.25*	0.22*	Abdel-Khalek & Lester (2007c)
Pessimism	−0.18*	−0.12*	
Anxiety	−0.18*	−0.07	
Obsession-compulsion	−0.07	−0.02	
Death obsession	−0.05	−0.08	
Suicidal ideation	−0.15*	−0.23*	
Ego-grasping	−0.20*	−0.01	
Optimism			
Suicidal ideation	−0.41*	−0.33*	Abdel-Khalek & Lester (2006a)
Ego-grasping	−0.30*	−0.42*	
Death obsession	−0.29*	−0.03	
Anxiety	−0.46*	0.38*	
Obsession-compulsion	−0.32*	−0.27*	
Sex	−0.11	0.04	
Ego-grasping	−0.30*	−0.42*	
Death obsession	−0.29*	−0.03	
Anxiety	−0.46*	−0.38*	
Obsession-compulsion	−0.32*	−0.27*	
Sex	−0.11	0.04	
Pessimism			
Suicidal ideation	0.61*	0.46*	Abdel-Khalek & Lester (2006a)
Ego-grasping	0.37*	0.48*	
Death obsession	0.47*	0.34	
Anxiety	0.65*	0.44*	
Obsession-compulsion	0.49*	0.31*	
Sex	0.13*	0.05	

*significant at two-tailed $p < .05$ or better.

Abdel-Khalek and Lester (2002e, 2003a, 2003b, 2006b) found that Kuwaiti students obtained higher pessimism, suicidal ideation, death obsession, anxiety, and obsessive-compulsion scores than did American students and lower optimism and Taoist orientation scores. For scores on the death obsession scale, there was no sex difference for the American sample, but female Kuwaiti students obtained higher scores than male Kuwaiti students. Abdel-Khalek and Lester (2003c) found that Kuwaiti students obtained higher scores than American students on the Kuwait Anxiety Scale. Abdel-Khalek and Lester (2006a) found that Kuwaiti

Table 4. Results of a factor analysis of scale scores (Abdel-Khalek & Lester, 2002e)

	Kuwait	USA	
	Factor I unrotated	Factor I rotated	Factor II rotated
Optimism	−0.66#	0.09	−0.89#
Pessimism	0.84#	0.40	0.59#
Suicidal ideation	0.75#	0.46	0.52#
Ego-grasping	0.57#	0.50#	0.61#
Death obsession	0.71#	0.87#	−0.07
Anxiety	0.85#	0.63#	0.52#
Obsessive-compulsive	0.70#	0.65#	0.34
% of variance	53.4%	48.1%	14.3%

#loading > 0.50.

students obtained higher pessimism scores and lower optimism scores than American students on an optimism-pessimism scale. Abdel-Khalek and Lester (2007c) found that Kuwaiti students obtained higher scores on several measures of psychopathology than did American students.

The studies are consistent in finding that Kuwaiti students obtained higher scores on measures of psychopathology than do American students, and the results are summarized in Table 5.

Suicidality in Kuwaiti and American Students

Correlates of Suicidality

Obsessive-Compulsive Tendencies

Abdel-Khalek and Lester (2000) found that scores on Beck et al.'s (1974) Hopelessness Scale (as well as scores on a depression scale) were moderately associated with scores on the Arabic Obsessive-Compulsive Scale in samples of 144 American and 209 Kuwaiti college students.[3] The correlations for hopelessness were stronger for the Kuwaiti students than the American students (0.43 and 0.27, respectively). Scores on the Hopelessness Scale have been found to be strong predictors of future suicidal behavior (Beck, Brown, Berchick, Stewart, & Steer, 1990), and so this suggests a stronger association of suicidality with obsessive-compulsive tendencies in Kuwaiti students than in American students.

---

[3] There was also a positive association between scores on the Arabic Obsessive-Compulsive Scale and scores on a belief in an external locus of control scale in both Kuwait and American students.

Table 5. Differences in mean scores. Means and standard deviations are shown.[3]

	Kuwait	USA	
Depression	15.9 (8.6)	9.9 (13.4)	Lester & Abdel-Khalek (1998a)
Hopelessness	7.6 (5.0)	3.9 (4.0)	Lester & Abdel-Khalek (1998b)
External control	11.5 (4.0)	12.5 (3.7)	Lester & Abdel-Khalek (1998b)
Obsess-Comp	15.7 (5.5)	14.0 (5.7)	Lester & Abdel-Khalek (1998b)
Obsess-Comp	13.5 (6.6)	11.6 (5.5)	Abdel-Khalek & Lester (2002c)
Obsess-Comp	15.3 (5.7)	12.5 (5.5)	Abdel-Khalek & Lester (2002e)
Optimism	52.0 (11.3)	56.5 (9.4)	Abdel-Khalek & Lester (2002e)
Pessimism	28.4 (12.2)	22.0 (7.0)	Abdel-Khalek & Lester (2002e)
Suicidal ideation	20.4 (27.4)	17.5 (18.2)	Abdel-Khalek & Lester (2002e)
Ego-grasping	13.7 (2.5)	8.0 (4.2)	Abdel-Khalek & Lester (2002e)
Death obsession	32.0 (14.9)	22.0 (8.0)	Abdel-Khalek & Lester (2002e)
Anxiety	40.6 (11.5)	36.9 (11.5)	Abdel-Khalek & Lester (2002e)
Death anxiety			
Templer scale	9.1 (3.6)	8.1 (3.2)	Abdel-Khalek & Lester (2009) & Lester (2007)
Abdel-Khalek scale	66.6 (18.5)	45.2 (14.4)	
Collett-Lester scale			
Death self	22.5 (6.5)	21.6 (7.3)	
Dying self	24.0 (6.9)	24.3 (6.0)	
Death others	27.0 (6.2)	25.7 (4.9)	
Dying others	26.8 (6.6)	24.8 (5.1)	

	Sex Differences				
	Kuwait		USA		
	Men	Women	Men	Women	
Death obsession	29.4	32.7[1]	22.3	20.9	Abdel-Khalek & Lester (2003a)
Anxiety	36.0	42.2[2]	34.2	37.9	Abdel-Khalek & Lester (2006d)
Death anxiety	57.3	65.5[1]	35.8	45.2[1]	Abdel-Khalek et al. (2009)

[1]a significant sex difference between men and women.
[2]a significant difference between women in Kuwait and America.
[3]Differences on individual items of the psychological tests are not reported in this table.

Lester and Abdel-Khalek (1999) found that obsessive-compulsive scores were associated in 73 American students with depression scores ($r = 0.25$), mania scores ($r = 0.14$), and a history of attempted suicide ($r = 0.29$), but not a history of suicidal ideation ($r = 0.06$). In 87 Kuwaiti students, Abdel-Khalek and Lester (2002a) found similar results. Obsessive-compulsive scores were associated with depression scores ($r = 0.49$), mania scores ($r = 0.36$), and suicidal ideation

($r = 0.31$) but not a history of attempted suicide. In this sample of Kuwaiti students, a history of suicidal threats and attempts were both associated with depression ($r = 0.25$ and 0.26, respectively).

Taoist Orientation
Lester and Abdel-Khalek (2003a, 2007b) found that scores on a scale to measure having a Taoist orientation toward life were negatively associated with current suicidal ideation in both Kuwaiti students ($n = 460$; $r = -0.29$) and American students ($n = 273$; $r = -0.40$).[4]

Optimism-Pessimism
Abdel-Khalek and Lester (2006a) found that optimism and pessimism scores were associated with current suicidal ideation in both Kuwaiti students ($r = -0.41$ and 0.61, respectively) and American students ($r = -0.33$ and 0.46, respectively).

Religiosity
Abdel-Khalek and Lester (2007c) found that a simple measure of religiosity was associated with current suicidal ideation in both Kuwaiti students ($r = -0.15$) and American students ($r = -0.23$). Incidentally, in this study, the Kuwaiti students had higher scores on the measure of current suicidal ideation, but not significantly so. Some of these correlations are shown in Table 3.

Predicting Suicide

Lester and Abdel-Khalek (1998b) asked 222 Kuwaiti students and 183 American students whether they had thought about suicide, made threats about suicide or attempted suicide in the past and also whether they currently had suicidal ideation. They examined whether age, sex, belief in an external locus of control, depression, hopelessness, and obsessive-compulsive tendencies predicted these four measures of suicidality (see Study 1 in Table 6).

For current suicidal ideation, depression was the strongest predictor in a full multiple regression for both the Kuwaiti and American students (betas = 0.33 and 0.66, respectively). Age and sex had smaller contributions for the Kuwaiti students and hopelessness scores for the American students. For past suicide attempts, depression was the strongest predictor for both samples (beta = 0.39 and 0.34, respectively), with age making a small contribution in addition for the Kuwaiti students. For past suicidal ideation, depression again was the strongest predictor for both samples (beta = 0.31 and 0.43, respectively), with sex making a

---

[4]   Taoist scores were also associated with measures of optimism, pessimism, death obsession, anxiety, and obsessive-compulsive tendencies in both samples.

Table 6. Predicting suicidality

Variable	Kuwait	USA
Study 1: Predicting the response to item 9 of the Beck Depression Inventory (Lester & Abdel-Khalek, 1998b)		
Age	−0.12*	0.09
Gender	−0.15*	0.07
External control	0.02	0.01
Hopelessness	0.09	−0.21*
Obsessive-comp	0.06	0.07
Depression	0.33*	0.66*
R^2	0.49	0.61
Study 2: Predicting the Reynolds' suicidal ideation scale score (Abdel-Khalek & Lester, 2002e)		
Age	−0.05	−0.06
Sex	0.01	0.09
Optimism	−0.04	−0.11
Pessimism	0.35*	0.19*
Ego-grasping	0.01	0.01
Death obsession	0.28*	0.13*
Anxiety	0.19*	0.31*
Obsessive-comp	−0.08	0.06
R^2	0.47	0.35

small contribution in addition for the Kuwaiti students. Only age predicted past threats of suicide for the American students, while depression and sex predicted past threats of suicide for the Kuwaiti students. These results indicate a high degree of similarity in both Kuwaiti and American students, with depression the strongest predictor of past and current suicidality in both samples.

In a second major study to predict current suicidality (see Study 2 in Table 6), using samples of 460 Kuwaiti students and 273 American students, Abdel-Khalek and Lester (2002e) found that anxiety, death obsession, and pessimism were significant predictors of current suicidality for the Kuwaiti students (betas = 0.19, 0.28, and 0.35, respectively) and for the American students (betas = 0.31, 0.13, and 0.19 respectively) in full multiple regressions. The results were, clearly, highly consistent in the two samples.

Incidentally, in this second study, Abdel-Khalek and Lester used Reynolds (1987) Suicidal Ideation Questionaire and Abdel-Khalek and Lester (2007a) found that the scale had good internal consistency and concurrent validity in both Kuwaiti and American students. The factor analytic pattern was similar for the eight critical items of the scale in the two samples but differed for the factor-analysis of the full set of 30 items.

Discussion

This brief review of a series of cross-cultural studies by Abdel-Khalek and Lester has identified several consistent results. First, scales written in Arabic and translated into English have good reliability and validity in both Kuwait and the US. Second, correlates of measures of personality and psychopathology are similar in both cultures. Third, Kuwaiti students consistently obtain higher scores on measures of psychopathology than do American students.

In addition to the research reviewed above, Abdel-Khalek and Lester have conducted several small studies investigating the reliability and validity of Western scales in Kuwait, including the Collett-Lester Fear of Death Scale (Abdel-Khalek & Lester, 2003b, 2004), Thalbourne, Delin and Bassett's (1994) manic-depression scale (Abdel-Khalek & Lester, 2005a), and Schaller's scale to measure attitudes toward physician-assisted suicide (Abdel-Khalek, Lester, & Schaller, 2005; Abdel-Khalek & Lester, 2006c). Therefore, a fourth conclusion is that psychological measures devised in the West have good reliability and validity in Kuwait.

Incidentally, Abdel-Khalek and Lester have also studied the role of other variables in both countries including birth order and sibship size (Abdel-Khalek & Lester, 2005b, 2007b), subjective life expectancy (Lester & Abdel-Khalek, 2007a), and astrological sun sign (Abdel-Khalek & Lester, 2006b) in predicting suicidality and personality.

Are the Student Samples Equivalent?

The first issue is whether the students tested in both countries are equivalent. Abdel-Khalek and Lester have never compared the students in their studies to see if they are similar. Of course, the question should be, similar in what respects? Intelligence, academic ability, social class, or parental background? The students from both countries were undergraduates. However, social class and parental background may not be comparable variables in these two countries, but the students could have been compared for intelligence and academic ability. Kuwait University is the major university in Kuwait, whereas Richard Stockton College is a low-prestige state university, located in a rural area of New Jersey, serving mainly those students who live nearby. A more appropriate comparison sample might have been students from a major university in the US.

Interestingly, Abdel-Khalek and Lester have never reported the ethnic background or religious affiliation of the students in their samples.

Is a Comparison of Kuwait Versus the US Meaningful?

Kuwait and the US were chosen for this set of studies because that is where the researchers work. Kuwait is a Muslim culture, whereas the US, although multicultural, is primarily a Christian culture, especially in southern New Jersey where Richard Stockton College is located.

It is of interest to compare Muslim and Christian cultures, although it is debatable whether the psychological measures used by Abdel-Khalek and Lester in their research are the most relevant variables for a comparison of these two cultures. Again, just as the two countries were chosen for convenience, the variables chosen for study were those of interest to the researchers as psychologists studying suicidality. They were not necessarily the most salient for a comparison of Muslim and Christian cultures.

Abdel-Khalek and Lester (2003a) noted that their study on death obsession was conducted after the Iraqi invasion of Kuwait. The Kuwaiti students would have been about ten years old at the time of the invasion and may have witnessed or heard about the atrocities committed, resulting in posttraumatic stress disorder symptoms. Therefore, measures of psychopathology may be of special interest for studies of Kuwaiti students, but Abdel-Khalek and Lester did not build pre- and post-measures into their research.

Is this Set of Studies Valuable?

The research conducted by Abdel-Khalek and Lester is valuable since psychological tests developed in the West and in the Middle East were found to be reliable and valid in the other culture. The fact that the researchers engaged in a large series of studies also provides evidence that associations between these variables found in one culture are generalizable to the other culture, and this is an important finding for psychological research. There is nothing in the results of the research in this set of studies that suggests that different psychological theories are needed to explain behavior in these two particular cultures, an important conclusion.

What Next?

So far, Abdel-Khalek and Lester have not investigated the causes of the higher scores on measures of psychopathology of the Kuwaiti students compared to the American students. One area for future research may be the child-rearing experiences of the two groups of students. Might these experiences differ in a way that would predict the differences in psychological test scores?

Second, Abdel-Khalek and Lester have not moved beyond comparing students in different nations to comparing students from different cultures. To do this requires obtaining detailed information on the ethnic background and religious values of the students. For example, the samples in both countries might be restricted to second-generation individuals. The religious affiliations of the individuals might also be restricted, perhaps to Christians in America and Muslims in Kuwait, and comparisons made also between the different sects of each religion (such as Baptists versus Roman Catholics and Shi'ites versus Sunni Muslims).

Clearly much more research needs to be carried out!

References

Abdel-Khalek, A. M. (1996). *Manual for the Arabic Scale of Optimism and Pessimism.* Alexandria, Egypt: Dar Al-Maarifa Al-Jamiiyah. (in Arabic).

Abdel-Khalek, A. M. (1998a). The development and validation of the Arabic Obsessive-Compulsive Scale. *European Journal of Psychological Assessment, 14*, 146–158.

Abdel-Khalek, A. M. (1998b). The structure and measurement of death obsession. *Personality & Individual Differences, 24*, 159–165.

Abdel-Khalek, A. M. (2000). The Kuwait University Anxiety Scale. *Psychological Reports, 87*, 478–492.

Abdel-Khalek, A. M., & Lester, D. (1998). Reliability of the Arabic Obsessive-Compulsive Scale in Kuwaiti and American students. *Psychological Reports, 83*, 1470.

Abdel-Khalek, A., & Lester, D. (1999a). Obsession compulsion in college students in the United States and Kuwait. *Psychological Reports, 85*, 799–800.

Abdel-Khalek, A. M., & Lester, D. (1999b). Criterion-related validity of the Arabic Obsessive-Compulsive Scale in Kuwaiti and American students. *Psychological Reports, 85*, 1111–1112.

Abdel-Khalek, A. M., & Lester, D. (2000). Obsession-compulsion, locus of control, depression, and hopelessness. *Psychological Reports, 86*, 1187–1188.

Abdel-Khalek, A., & Lester, D. (2002a). Manic-depressiveness, obsessive-compulsive tendencies, and suicidality in Kuwaiti college students. *Psychological Reports, 90*, 1007–1008.

Abdel-Khalek, A., & Lester, D. (2002b). Convergent and discriminant validity of the Arabic Obsessive-Compulsive Scale for Kuwaiti and American college students. *Psychological Reports, 90*, 1261–1262.

Abdel-Khalek, A., & Lester, D. (2002c). Factorial validity of the Arabic Obsessive-Compulsive Scale in two cultures. *Psychological Reports, 90*, 869–870.

Abdel-Khalek, A., & Lester, D. (2002d). Using the short subscales of a questionnaire to assess subcomponents with low reliabilities. *Psychological Reports, 90*, 1255–1256.

Abdel-Khalek, A., & Lester, D. (2002e). Can personality predict suicidality? *International Journal of Social Psychiatry, 48*, 231–239.

Abdel-Khalek, A., & Lester, D. (2003a). Death obsession in Kuwaiti and American college students. *Death Studies, 27*, 541–553.

Abdel-Khalek, A., & Lester, D. (2003b). Obsession-compulsion and its relation to age and sex in Kuwaiti and American students. *Psychological Reports, 93*, 803–804.

Abdel-Khalek, A., & Lester, D. (2003c). The Kuwait University Anxiety Scale: A cross-cultural evaluation in Kuwait and the US. *Psychological Reports, 93*, 1109–1114.

Abdel-Khalek, A., & Lester, D. (2004). The factorial structure of the Arabic version of the revised Collett-Lester Fear of Death Scale. *Death Studies, 28*, 787–793.

Abdel-Khalek, A., & Lester, D. (2005a). Factorial structure of short scales measuring manic-depression in Kuwaiti undergraduates. *Psychological Reports, 97*, 128.

Abdel-Khalek, A., & Lester, D. (2005b). Sibship size, birth order, and personality. *Psychological Reports, 97*, 387–388.

Abdel-Khalek, A., & Lester, D. (2006a). Optimism and pessimism in Kuwaiti and American college students. *International Journal of Social Psychiatry, 52*, 110–126.

Abdel-Khalek, A., & Lester, D. (2006b). Astrological signs and personality in Kuwaitis and Americans. *Psychological Reports, 98*, 602–607.

Abdel-Khalek, A., & Lester, D. (2006c). Correlations of attitudes toward physician-assisted suicide, death depression, death obsession, and trait anxiety. *Psychological Reports, 98*, 734.

Abdel-Khalek, A. M., & Lester, D. (2006d). Anxiety in Kuwaiti and American college students. *Psychological Reports, 99*, 512–514.

Abdel-Khalek, A., & Lester, D. (2007a). The psychometric properties and correlates of the Reynolds' Suicide Ideation Questionnaire with Kuwaiti and American students. *Archives of Suicide Research, 11*, 309–319.

Abdel-Khalek, A. M., & Lester, D. (2007b). Sibship size, birth order, and personality among Kuwaiti college students. *Psychological Reports, 101*, 53–54.

Abdel-Khalek, A. M., & Lester, D. (2007c). Religiosity, health, and psychopathology in two cultures. *Mental Health, Religion & Culture, 10*, 537–550.

Abdel-Khalek, A., & Lester, D. (2009). Religiosity and death anxiety. *Psychological Reports, 104*, 770–772.

Abdel-Khalek, A. M., Lester, D., & Barrett, P. (2002). The factorial structure of the Arabic Obsessive-Compulsive Scale in Kuwaiti and American college students. *Personality & Individual Differences, 33*, 3–9.

Abdel-Khalek, A. M., Lester, D., Maltby, J., & Tomas-Sabado, J. (2009). The Arabic Scale of Death Anxiety. *Omega, 59*, 39–50.

Abdel-Khalek, A., Lester, D., & Schaller, S. (2005). Attitudes toward physician-assisted suicide and death anxiety in Kuwaiti students. *Psychological Reports, 96*, 625–626.

Beck, A. T., Brown, G., Berchick, R. J., Stewart, B. L., & Steer, R. A. (1990). Relationship between hopelessness and ultimate suicide. *American Journal of Psychiatry, 147*, 190–195.

Beck, A. T., Ward, C. H., Mendelson, M., Mock, J., & Erbaugh, J. (1961). An inventory for measuring depression. *Archives of General Psychiatry, 4*, 561–571.

Beck, A. T., Weissman, A., Lester, D., & Trexler, L. (1974). The measurement of pessimism: The Hopelessness Scale. *Journal of Consulting & Clinical Psychology, 42*, 861–865.

Duh, H. B., & Chen, V. H. (2007). Emerging issues in doing cross-cultural research in multicultural and multilingual societies. In N. Aykin (Ed.), *Usability and internationalization, Part 1*, pp. 65–73. Heidelberg, Germany: Springer-Verlag.

Hodgson, R. J., & Rachman, S. (1977). Obsessional-compulsive complaints. *Behavior Research & Therapy, 15*, 389–395.

Hofstede, G. (1980). *Culture's consequences.* Beverly Hills, CA: Sage.

Karahanna, E., Evaristo, R., & Srite, M. (2002). Methodological issues in MIS cross-cultural research. *Journal of Global Information Management, 10*(1), 48–55.

Knoblauch, D. L., & Falconer, J. A. (1986). The relationship of a measured Taoist orientation to Western personality dimensions. *Journal of Transpersonal Psychology, 18*, 73–83.

Kondrichin, S. V., & Lester, D. (1997). Finno-Ugrians and suicide. *Perceptual & Motor Skills, 85*, 514.

Lester, D. (2007). What do death anxiety scales measure? *Psychological Reports, 101*, 754.

Lester, D., & Abdel-Khalek, A. (1997). Gender and depression in undergraduate populations. *Psychological Reports, 81*, 1210.

Lester, D., & Abdel-Khalek, A. M. (1998a). Depression in college students in the United States and Kuwait. *Psychological Reports, 83*, 410.

Lester, D., & Abdel-Khalek, A. (1998b). Suicidality and personality in American and Kuwaiti students. *International Journal of Social Psychiatry, 44*, 280–283.

Lester, D., & Abdel-Khalek, A. M. (1999). Manic-depression, suicidality, and obsessive-compulsive tendencies. *Psychological Reports, 85*, 1100.

Lester, D., & Abdel-Khalek, A. (2002). Reliability and factorial structure of the Taoist Orientation Scale for samples of Kuwait and American students. *Psychological Reports, 91*, 114.

Lester, D., & Abdel-Khalek, A. (2003a). Correlates of an ego-grasping attitude in Kuwaiti and American students. *Psychological Reports, 92*, 488.

Lester, D., & Abdel-Khalek, A. (2003b). The Collett-Lester fear of death scale. *Death Studies, 27*, 81–85.

Lester, D., & Abdel-Khalek, A. (2007a). Some correlates of subjective life expectancy. *Psychological Reports, 100*, 57–58.

Lester, D., & Abdel-Khalek, A. (2007b). A Taoist orientation and mental health in Kuwaiti and American students. *Perceptual & Motor Skills, 105*, 921–922.

Lynn, R. (1971). *Personality and national character.* Oxford, UK: Pergamon.

Mawson, A., & Jacobs, K. (1978). Corn consumption, tryptophan and cross-national homicide rates. *Journal of Orthomolecular Psychiatry, 7*, 227–230.

Merenda, P. F. (2006). An overview of adapting educational and psychological assessment instruments. *Psychological Reports, 99*, 307–314.

Ratner, C., & Hui, L. (2003). Theoretical and methodological problems in cross-cultural psychology. *Journal for the Theory of Social Behavior, 33*, 67–94.

Reynolds, W. M. (1987). *The Suicidal Ideation Questionnaire: SIQ Form HS.* Odessa, FL: Psychological Assessment Resources.

Rotter, J. B. (1966). Generalized expectancies for internal versus external control of reinforcement. *Psychological Monographs, 80*, No. 1 (Whole No. 609).

Schaller, S., Lester, D., & Abdel-Khalek, A. (2003). Attitudes toward physician-assisted suicide and death anxiety. *Psychological Reports, 93*, 641–642.

Thalbourne, M. A., Delin, P. S., & Bassett, D. L. (1994). An attempt to construct short scales measuring manic-depressive-like experience and behavior. *British Journal of Clinical Psychology, 33*, 205–207.

Triandis, H. (2001). Individualism and collectivism. In D. Matsumoto (Ed.), *Handbook of culture and psychology*, pp. 35–50. New York: Oxford University Press.

Whiting, J. M., & Child, I. L. (1953). *Child training and personality.* New Haven, CT: Yale University Press.

Sati

David Lester

The aim of this chapter is to review what has been written about sati, the custom in India of widows dying on the funeral pyre of their husbands. It is written from the point of view of a psychologist (rather than an anthropologist) and will propose a research agenda for the psychological study of sati.

Suicide in the Hindu Religion

Sheth (1994) and Vijayakumar (2009) have both noted that suicide committed as a personal act motivated by emotions such as pride, frustration, and anger is censured in Hinduism. In contrast, other forms of voluntary self-termination of life are not considered to be suicide and are, therefore, not condemned. Self-sacrifice for the general good is admired, as is self-sacrifice to expiate sins such as incest. Ascetics are allowed to choose death by voluntary starvation, committed deliberately and without passion. For example, *mahaprasthana* (great journey) involves the individual going on a continuous walk after giving up all attachments and possessions and subsisting only on air and water. *Sati* is also a form of suicide that is permitted. As Weinberger-Thomas (1999) pointed out, sati refers to the woman who carries out this act and signifies "a chaste and faithful virtuous wife (p. 20), but the term is typically used, erroneously, to refer to the act itself.

It should be noted that the sacrifice (voluntarily or otherwise) of survivors of a deceased individual was not uncommon in India and other countries in historical times. It was thought in many cultures that a deceased emperor or warrior would need to have the same kinds of possessions and services in the after-life, and so possessions were buried along with the deceased and, sometimes, servants were also sacrificed. Sati is one of the few cultural customs where a survivor of a low-ranking individual was expected to sacrifice herself.

Sati

Sati[1], which means *virtuous woman* in Sanskrit, has a long history. Although best documented in India, it occurred in China, Mesopotamia, and Iran. It was

---

[1] Sati is also spelled as satee, suttee, and sutty

practiced by kings, whose queens were expected to die with them. Rajput queens in India sometimes committed suicide by self-immolation even when their husbands were killed in battle far away. The first memorial to sati was found in Madhya Pradesh in India in 510 AD (Baig, 1988), but the earliest historical instance is of the wife of General Keteus who died in 316 BC (Vijayakumar, 2004). Sati is named after Sati, the consort of the god Shiva. Shiva and Sati's father (Daksha) had an argument, and Sati was so angry at her father that the fire of her anger destroyed her. Shiva retaliated by sending a monster to destroy Daksha's head but later relented and allowed Daksha to be fitted with a goat's head. The higher castes (Brahmans, Kshatriyas, and Vaishyas) have interpreted this myth as indicating the way a widow should join her dead husband on his death – by immolating herself (Freed & Freed, 1989).

The *Vedas*, the most important of the Hindu texts, does not demand that women commit sati, although there is disagreement over one word. Some argue that it is the word for "go forth" while others argue that it is the word for "to the fire" (Yang, 1989). Most now think the *Vedas* encourages widows to get on with their lives and even remarry.[2] The British banned sati in 1829 (Cassels, 1965; Mehta, 1966), but about forty cases have occurred since independence in 1947, the majority in Rajasthan.

There are two types of sati. *Sahamarana* (or sahagamana) is where the widow ascends the funeral pyre and is burnt along with the body of her dead husband. In *Anumarana* the widow kills herself (usually on a funeral pyre, after the cremation of her husband (Yang, 1989), typically with his ashes or some memento of him, such as a piece of his clothing. Stein (1978) noted cases in the 18th and 19th Centuries in which women died on the funeral pyre of an important person, mothers died on a son's funeral pyre, and sisters died on their brother's funeral pyre. Weinberger-Thomas (1999) noted that pregnant women, women with infants, adulterous wives, pre-pubertal girls, women who were menstruating, women who had amenorrhea, and "disobedient" wives were not allowed to commit sati since they were considered to be impure in this state.

A debate has raged over whether widows went voluntarily or were forced (at knife point, sometimes bound and gagged) or drugged. To prevent widows changing their minds and trying to escape from the fire, exits from the fire were sometimes blocked, and roofs of wood were designed to collapse on the widow's head (Stein, 1978). This debate continues today in discussions of modern cases of sati. Daly (1978) observed that Indian men sometimes married children under the age of ten, and Narasimhan (1994) noted that eyewitnesses in the 19th Century

---

[2]   Lower castes see marriage with the deceased husband's younger brother as quite acceptable (Weinberger-Thomas, 1999).

reported that child widows aged eight and ten were sometimes forced onto the funeral pyre and bound hand and foot if they tried to escape. Some widows were drugged with opium. On the other hand, some widows asked to be bound and thrown on the pyre to prevent them fleeing and escaping their duty (Vijayakumar, 2004).

Sati in Modern Times

It has been estimated that about thirty women have committed sati in Rajasthan between 1943 and 1987 (Weinberger-Thomas, 1999), although the official count is 28. Weinberger-Thomas estimates that perhaps forty satis occurred in India as a whole in that time period. There was diversity in social class (one was even a street singer), but Rajputs accounted for 19 of the 30 satis in Rajasthan.

Baig (1988) documented cases in Rajasthan where the police did not dare to stop sati. One case has become extraordinarily famous, the sati of Roop Kanwar who committed sati in Deorala, Rajasthan, on September 4, 1987 (Ali, 1987).[3] Thousands watched her sati, yet the "facts" of the case are far from clear (Hawley, 1994). Roop Kanwar was a well-educated 18 year-old woman from the Rajput caste who was married for only eight months. Her 24 year-old husband died from gastro-enteritis, appendicitis, or a suicidal overdose. He had recently failed an exam required for entry into medical school. Dressed in bridal finery, she was watched by a crowd of about 4,000 as she died (Narasimhan, 1994). Although the government tried to prevent a celebration of this, some 25,000 people came to the village for a glorification ceremony. Money (estimates were as high as $250,000 within two weeks) was donated to build a temple in her memory. Roop Kanwar's brother-in-law and father-in-law were arrested but released without charges being filed. Roop Kanwar became a *sati-mata*, a deified woman with miraculous powers to grant favors (Narasimhan, 1994). There are rumors that she was forced into sati and may have been drugged (Kumar, 1995). She was escorted to the pyre by young men carrying swords who might well have stabbed her had she tried to flee (Narasimhan, 1994). She may have fallen from the pyre and needed assistance in mounting it (Hawley, 1994). Observers saw her flail her hands in the air as the flames touched her (Narasimhan, 1994), but one official claimed that she was blessing the crowd by this action. Others claimed that she cried out to her father for help (Hawley, 1994). There were rumors that she had

---

[3] All satis mentioned in this essay are listed, along with all others that could be traced, in Table 1.

Table 1. Modern cases of sati

Name[1]	Age	Relationship	Date	Place
From Weinberger-Thomas (1999)				
Died				
Hem Kanvar		husband	1943	Devpuri, Ajmer
Dayal Kanvar		husband	1948	Khud, Sikar
Jaet Kanvar			1951	Khandela, Sikar
Tara Kanvar			1953	Madho-Ka-Bas, Sikar
Sugan Kanvar		husband	1954	Jodhpur
Son Kanvar			1956	Khundraut
Sugan Kanvar	28	step-son	1959	Ujoli, Jodhpur
Jugal Kanvar	35		1966	Narsinghpuri, Sikar
Savitri		husband	4/1/1973	Kothri
Saviiti			10/3/1973	Golyana
Son Kanvar			1975	Maunda Kala
Sarasvati	35	husband	1/12/1978	Hathideh, Sikar
Javitri	18	husband	7/11/1979	Jari, Uttar Pradesh
Sohan Kanvar			2/29/1980	Neemri Kothariya, Nagaur
Om Kanvar	16	husband	8/30/1980	Jharli, Sikar
Dasiya		husband	1981	Kusuma, Banda, Uttar Pradesh
Roop Kanvar		husband	9/4/1987	Deorala, Sikar
Sartaj Kanvar				
Prevented				
Rup Kanvar (Bala)		adopted son	2/15/1943	Pipar, Jodhpur
Rasal Kanvar		husband	2/15/1943	Pipar, Jodhpur
Jasvant Kanvar	40	husband	3/12/1985	Devipura, Jaipur[2]
Other				
Desu		husband	10/26/1977	Osian, Jodhpur

She died upon hearing of her husband's death and was burned on his funeral pyre. A shrine was built to honor her to which worshippers come.

From Narasimhan (1990)[3]
Died

2 with no name			1960–1961	
no name			1980	Barnala
Dasiya		husband	1983	Kusuma, Banda
Gayatri		husband	1983	Pagnara, Bundelkhand
No name			1984	
No name			1986	Jabalpur

(Continued)

Table 1. Continued.

Name[1]	Age	Relationship	Date	Place
No name	25	husband	1986	Umaria, Madhya Pradesh
Prevented				
No name			1950s	Jaipur[4]
No name			1958–1960	Ajmer (Mukerji, 1979)
No name			1983	Madhya Pradesh (prevented)
From Thakur (1963)				
Died				
No name			1952	Rajasthan
No name	18	husband	1954 (6/11)	Jhansi
Thakurani		husband	1954 (10/18)	Jodhpur[5]
From this Chapter				
Died				
No name		husband	1943	(from Altekar, 1978)
Kuttu Bai	65	husband	2002 (8/2)	Madhya Pradesh
No name			1950	same village as the above case
Kanakani		husband	2006	Tulsipur, Madhya Pradesh
Karua Devi	90s		2006	Madhya Pradesh
Prevented				
Charan Shah	55	husband	1999	Bundelkhand, Uttar Pradesh
No name			2006	Madhya Pradesh

[1]Kanvar is a standard name for married women in these regions of India.
[2]Narasimhan (1990) reported that, in this case, the police deputy superintendent convinced the onlookers that, if the woman was a real sati, the pyre should burst into flames of its own accord. He forbade the relatives to light the fire, and they went along with this.
[3]Unfortunately, Narasimhan gives very little information on the cases that she reports.
[4]This woman ran from the pyre, but died two days later from her burns.
[5]Narasimhan (1990) notes that this case was in 1957, but both agree that she was the wife of Brigadier Zabbar Singh.

had been unfaithful (Hawley, 1994). As a result of this sati, Parilla (1999) noted that both women and men in Rajashan rallied to support the right to commit sati, while other groups fought to ban it (Kumar, 1995).[4,5]

---

[4] The role of pressure is illustrated by the case of Gayatri in 1983 where the village elders refused to cremate her husband unless she agreed to become a sati. The police watched her death along with thousands on onlookers (Narasimhan, 1990).

[5] The "facts" pertaining to this sati are presented later in a postscript to this essay.

Although there are other modern cases of sati, the case of Roop Kanwar has become the focus of most recent discussion. Hawley (1994) edited a book in which the only modern case discussed at length is that of Roop Kanwar. In a rare modern discussion of sati by a mental health professional, Bhugra (2005) discusses only her sati, concluding that cultural factors rather than psychiatric factors explain her sati and that of other widows. Indeed, Bhugra labels sati as "a type of nonpsychiatric suicide" (p. 73).

This focus on a case for which no unambiguous information exists is surprising, to say the least. Abraham (1997) noted that there has been an average of one sati a year in the state of Rajasthan in the last 40 years, with 28 widow immolations taking place within 200 miles of a sati temple in Jhunjunu since Independence in 1947. There are, therefore, many cases to explore.

Altekar (1978) reported the sati of his sister in 1946 within 24 hours of the death of her husband. Inamdar, Oberfield, and Darrell (1983) reported the case of a 16-year-old girl (Om Kanvar) who died on the funeral pyre of her 22-year-old husband, a van driver who had died of tuberculosis. They noted that she was the 7th reported case in the state of Rajasthan in recent years and the second that year. As in the case of Roop Kanwar, the site of her sati became a shrine for pilgrims, with reports of miracle cures of deaf and mute individuals.

Another case is that of Kuttu Bai, a 65-year-old widow whose husband died after a prolonged illness in Panna in the province of Madhya Pradesh.[6] The sati took place the day after his death, on August 2, 2002. Accounts differ, as with the case of Roop Kanwar, as to whether she went voluntarily and calmly or whether she was forced on to the pyre.[7] The crowd of 2,000 who watched the sati is reported to have prevented police officers from stopping the ceremony. In the same village, another woman committed sati in 1950, and the site of this sati has become a shrine. This raises the possibility of modeling and imitation impacting the decision of a widow to commit sati.

On August 23, 2006, the BBC news website reported another case of sati – Janakrani, who immolated herself on her husband's (Prem Narayan) funeral pyre in the village of Tulsipur in Madhya Pradesh. Her sons reported that there was no ceremony and that she "slipped away" to commit the act by herself. On September 21, 2006, the BBS news website reported another case – Karua Devi, again in Madhya Pradesh. She was in her 90s and dressed in full bridal gear. One of her sons lit the funeral pyre. She is reported to have desired to commit sati and was

---

[6]   (news.bbc.co.uk/2/hi/south_asia/2176885.stm and 2180380.stm; www.indianexpress.com/oldStory/29260/)

[7]   One group most clear in its view that this sati was involuntary is the Communist Party of India (Anon, 2002) (pd.cpim.org/2002/sept22/09152002_mp_sati.htm).

encouraged by her sons and some villagers. She was a member of the upper-caste Hindu Rajput community. The report also noted that one widow in the state in the previous month had been prevented from committing sati by members of her family. Sen (2002) mentions a sati on November 11, 1999, in the Bundelkhand region of Uttar Pradesh, a widow (Charan Shah) aged 55, who had nursed her husband through tuberculosis for over twenty years. He died four years after one of her three sons had died, and the grief was too much for her, according to press cuttings.

There are, therefore, many cases that could be investigated by means of psychological autopsies. Furthermore, there is a huge control group available for study – namely all those widows that do not commit sati and, as is apparent from some cases, widows who desired to commit sati but were prevented from doing so. It is remarkable that three cases were reported from the same state by BBC news in one month, two successful and one prevented. This suggests that cases are more common than hitherto thought. Vijayakumar (2004) noted that the police sometimes intervene and prevent the act, providing an opportunity for conducting a psychological autopsy study of those who die by sati compared to those who are prevented.

Attitudes toward Sati

There have been no studies of attitudes toward sati. While many women in this region support the occurrence of sati, support is not unanimous (Hawley, 1994). How do men and women in Rajasthan view sati? How do the views in this region compare with those in other regions? What personal characteristics affect these attitudes, characteristics such as age, caste, religion, education, family ties, and family structure?

Explanations for Sati

Sharma (1978) noted that Durkheim (1897) classified sati as *altruistic suicide*, and Vijayakumar (2004) followed this. Of the three types of altruistic suicide (obligatory, optional, and acute), Durkheim viewed sati as obligatory. Altruistic suicide occurs in societies where social integration is too strong, and obligatory altruistic suicide occurs when the sense of duty is a ruling factor. However, sati may fit better into Durkheim's category of *fatalistic suicide* since the newly widowed woman seems in some cases to be too strongly regulated. This might be the case if the woman is psychologically persuaded or forced into the act. (Physical force would change the act into murder rather than fatalistic suicide.) In order to accurately classify a sati into a Durkheimian typology, therefore, some knowledge of the sati's motives is essential, and this is rarely available. It may also be that any particular sati may have more than one of these motives and so fit into two or even three categories. It does seem that the one category that does *not* seem to be appropriate for any sati is *anomic* suicide.

Those in India favoring sati see the benefits as accruing not just to the husband, but also to the wife and to her descendants. Therefore, Sharma (1978) viewed sati as a *sacrifice* rather than a *suicide*, and Sharma suggested a new term for the behavior – *suifice* (suicide + sacrifice).

In contrast to this view, Weinberger-Thomas (1999) saw sati as having *egotistical*[8] elements. After exploring the history and mythology associated with sati, Weinberger-Thomas viewed the sacrifice as unrelated to duties toward the husband. The sati becomes a heroine, with temples established in her name, openly in the past and surreptitiously today. Cults develop centered around her. The sati represents the powers of femininity. Weinberger-Thomas quotes a Rajasthani saying: What matter that the husband dies if his wife's dream comes true? (p. 167).

Baig (1988) suggested that the psychodynamics underlying support for sati among the *men* in the society involve blame for the wife for not keeping her husband alive and a fear that wives will not be faithful to their husbands, a fear that constrains widows after their husbands' deaths. Parrilla (1999) noted that sati is believed by some to facilitate spiritual salvation for the husband, while the wife is subsequently revered as a goddess (Harlan, 1994). Sati is thought to ensure that the sati's descendants will be admitted to heaven for seven generations and that family members will be spared reincarnation.

Weinberger-Thomas (1999) has documented how satis from earlier times are venerated in many regions of India, and recent satis are similarly venerated even though any celebration of their lives and deaths is forbidden by the government. There are daily services at their shrines (often the home in which they lived), sometime surreptitiously and sometimes under the pretense of celebrating a sati from historical times.

There is also an economic rationale for sati. Under the law of inheritance in Bengal (*dayabhaga*), widows inherit their husband's estate, over-ruling the claims of his relatives. Sati, therefore, keeps the man's assets in his family. Vijayakumar (2004) noted that sati is rare in Kerala where matriarchy prevails, unlike Bengal where wives are entitled to half of their husbands' property, leaving his relatives eager to be rid of them. Abraham (2005) noted that the women in Rajasthan

---

[8]   This is not the same as Durkheim's concept of egoistical suicide, which involves a very low level of social integration.

(where sati has been common) are extremely subjugated. Their illiteracy rate is among the highest in India, and the treatment of widows is particularly cruel there.

Modeling

Weinberger-Thomas (1999) cited examples from historical times of ten or twelve satis occurring in a single family line. She also noted a case from 1822 where the sati chose as a venue the place where a sati had burned herself five months earlier. Weinberger-Thomas noted similar *modeling* in modern satis. Sometimes the villages where satis take place are only a few miles from one another, and these regions have many sites (marked by sati stones and temples) where satis took place in historical times. The case of Bala (see below) is interesting since Bala claimed that she had been a sati in a previous life but, since she had cursed her in-laws in that previous life, she had to be reborn in order to die again, but this time in an appropriate manner. Roop Kanvar's sati in 1987 took place in a village where two historical satis are commemorated, both of whom were wives in her husband's family line.

Psychiatric Speculations

After discussing the case of Roop Kanwar, Bhugra (2005) felt that it was unlikely that women who committed sati were suffering from "formal mental illness." However, none of these women had been given a psychiatric evaluation prior to the sati, and so there are no data with which to test Bhugra's opinion. Bhugra does note the possibility of the widows being in a possession trance or in a state of depersonalization as a result of severe bereavement, but he dismisses these possibilities as unimportant compared to cultural influences.

In contrast to Bhugra's opinion, Inamdar et al. (1983) noted that women committing sati were often young and childless or old women, and they faced miserable lives, but nonetheless:

At a moment of great loss and stress and exposed to the multiple pressures of family and society, within a strong and ancient mythological tradition, a vulnerable individual may assent to and commit a self-destructive act that is ultimately immortalized. (p. 133)

It is this element of *vulnerability* that has been neglected in previous discussions of sati.

Weinberger-Thomas (1999) also suggested viewing sati as a form of possession. In her description of sati occurring in Bali (Indonesia), she describes the sati as "breaking out" in the way a fever or passion breaks out. The sati herself is overcome by a frenzy, and the possessed woman becomes a vehicle of a god or spirit. Weinberger-Thomas noted also that this frenzy also overcomes the spectators sometimes. Weinberger-Thomas also noted that two satis in 1943 in India (see the case of Bala below) both began to shake and speak in a gravelly voice, and this was taken to indicate possession.

It is critical that, in the future, methodologically sound psychological autopsies be conducted on widows who commit sati, as well as locating widows who have committed sati who have had contact with medical, mental health, and social services in the months and years prior to their suicide so that some sense of their psychological and psychiatric state can be ascertained.

Historical Data

Although there are few data on sati in modern times, some data can be found on sati in the 19th Century. Inamdar et al. (1983) noted that 2,366 cases of sati occurred in India in 1821. Yang (1989) reported data from cases of sati from Bengal from 1815 to 1828, during which time period there were an average of 581 cases each year. There were also satis in other regions (Bombay and Madras), but 90% occurred in Bengal. There were cases in both the upper castes and the lower castes, although the relative percentages varied from district to district.[9] In the whole of Bengal in 1825, 2.7% of the cases were aged 0–19, and 4.7% were over the age of 80, of whom one widow was over the age of 100. The modal age group was 40–49 (19.1%).

Yang noted that some widows committed sati many years after their husband's death. Sixty-year-old Jhunia committed sati 15 years after her husband's death, while 70-year-old Karanja committed sati 40 years after her husband's death. 70-year-old Hulasi committed sati on the funeral pyre of her son, 16 years after her husband's death. For these women, Yang suggested that sati may have been a form of ritual suicide motivated at least in part by personal considerations. Yang noted that, after 1822, more of the widows came from impoverished families, and

[9] However, Yang presented no data on the relative proportions of each caste in the population.

most left little property. In one sample of 79 satis, 25 husbands had died wealthy, 13 in middling circumstances, and 41 in poor circumstances.

Sati in Other Cultures

Counts (1980), who has studied the suicidal behavior of women in the Kaliai district of Papua New Guinea, noted that, in the past, elderly widows sometimes immolated themselves on their husband's funeral pyre. The German and Australian colonial governors considered this behavior to be a form of ritual murder rather than suicide, and they outlawed it. Counts saw neither term (suicide or murder) as appropriate for this custom since it differed so much from what North Americans and Europeans regard as either suicide or murder. Neither term describes the behavior, the interpersonal relationships involved, or the attitudes toward the widow and those assisting in her death, nor do they predict how the community will respond to her death.

Sati in America

MacLeod (1931) documented sati in North American Indian tribes, including the Shoshone and Comanche, where widows were often immolated at the funeral of their husbands, and the Natchez where both widows and widowers were put to death on the death of their spouse (although MacLeod noted that this was carried only for royalty).

Is it always women who commit sati? Devereux (1961) documented a similar behavior in the Mohave, a Native American tribe living in the southwest of the US. The Mohave belief system claimed that the best way to be with your loved one in the after-death is to die soon after them. As a result, attempted sati became so common that precautions were taken at funerals to prevent it. According to Devereux, the Mohave believed that women were more prone to this than were men but, based on the data that he was able to collect, the behavior was equally common in men and women.

In one case from around 1906, a 40-year-old man, Utu:ra, tried to jump on the funeral pyre of his 30-year-old wife who had died, probably from pneumonia. He ran toward the funeral pyre, but tripped and fell, so that his hair burned. He was saved. In another case, a son took his father's horse out of state to race, and his father scolded him for this, whereupon the son shot himself. At the funeral, the father tried to jump on the pyre, but his relatives, although they were angry at him for the way he had treated his son, restrained him.

Although sati has not been documented in Hindus in modern America, cases have been reported of Indian husbands murdering their wives by setting them alight (Singh & Unnithan, 1999), reminiscent of the dowry burning that is common in India.

The Status of Women

Women are oppressed throughout the world. As Johnson and Johnson (2001) have noted, "Today, in every corner of the globe, some women are denied basic human rights, beaten, raped, and killed by men" (p. 1051).

It has been noted that women have particularly low status in India where female feticide (i.e., the selective abortion of female fetuses), female infanticide, murder, dowry murder, and suicide are forces that decrease the female population relative to the male population (Freed & Freed, 1989).[10] Freed and Freed quoted a man in the village in which they stayed in 1958, "You have been here long enough to know that it is a small thing to kill a woman in an Indian village" (pp. 144–145).

In some countries, abandoned women are social outcasts. In India, widows are treated very harshly. An article in *The Economist* (Anon, 2007) described 1,300 widows at an ashram in Vrindavan in Uttar Pradesh, who pray for three hours each day in return for a token that they can exchange for three rupees (seven cents) and a handful of uncooked lentils and rice. They are entitled to a state pension of $3.70 a month and the food ration that is given to poor Indians, but only about one quarter of the widows receive these. The article noted that widows are "unwanted baggage." In the past they were encouraged to die on their husband's funeral pyre, and those who did not were forbidden to remarry. Today, the law gives them better protection, but remarriage is still discouraged. Two-fifths of the widows were married before they were twelve years old and a third were widowed by the age of 24. Those widows interviewed said that they preferred to live in the ashram than go home where their treatment would be even worse. In some places, widows are permitted only one meal a day, sometimes no fish (because fish are a symbol of fertility) and must shave their heads.

In the past, women in India died in mass suicides by immolation and other means to escape capture, rape, abduction, and death at the hands of invaders. Baig (1988) mentioned such cases from the 10th to the 13th Centuries in India, and Lester (2010a) described mass suicides of Hindu women in India during the chaos

---

[10]   Supplemented by maternal mortality as a result of unhygienic lying-in and postpartum conditions.

after the partition of India (into Pakistan and modern India) in 1947. Baig (1988) suggested that these mass suicides by women may have contributed to the sati mentality in India.

Stein (1988) has written about the epidemic of the deaths of young married women in India by suicide or murdered by their husbands and in-laws, often pregnant at the time. Many of these wives are harassed by their in-laws over the dowry that they are expected to bring with them, and in-laws often demand additional dowry payments, creating additional stress.

Domestic violence is common in the Middle East and Asia, and women who are found to have behaved in ways unacceptable to their husbands, fathers, or other relatives are often murdered, a behavior known as *honor killing*. One form in Pakistan is called *karo-kari* (Patel, 2008), and Patel noted that, with emigration of Pakistanis to other countries, the practice seems to be spreading to other countries.

Nasrullah, Haqqi, and Cummings (2009) found 1,957 cases of honor killing in newspapers in Pakistan from 2004 to 2007. Alleged extramarital relations were the most common reason for the murder (92%), and 88% of the women were married. The murderer was most often the husband (43%), followed by brothers (24%), and other close relatives (12%). The most common methods for the murder were firearms (61%), sharp instruments (24%), and strangulation (9%). The annual rate was 1.5 per 100,000 per year.

Of course, enculturated women do not have to be murdered – they can kill themselves. Cakmak and Altuntas (2008) documented cases of *honor suicide* in a southeastern part of Turkey where women who have disgraced themselves by fleeing with a lover, by being raped, or by refusing to marry a local official kill themselves. Cakmak and Altuntas attributed this to the strong patriarchal society, poverty, the violations of human rights during the Kurdish-Turkish conflict in the region, the rapid urbanization of the region resulting in social disorganization, the low level of literacy in the women (many of whom do not speak Turkish), and the Islamic and Kurdish identity.

A related behavior is *dowry killing* in which, after a dowry is paid by the bride's parents to the groom's family, the marriage does not please the in-laws (for example, if a son is not conceived or if their dowry demands are not fully met). In this situation, the wife may commit suicide to escape the harassment or be set alight by her in-laws who can then claim that it was a kitchen accident. Narasimhan (1994) reported that 792 dowry deaths occurred in India in 1987 and 922 in 1988, despite the passage of a law specifically banning this in 1961, but she noted that many such deaths are classified simply as suicides.

An analogous phenomenon exists in modern society. Lester (1997) studied over a hundred suicides by famous individuals, famous enough to have biographies written about them. He found two instances of husbands who wanted to kill themselves and whose younger, subservient wives decided that they could not live without their husbands and joined them in a suicide pact. For example, Stephan Zweig fled the Nazis in Europe with Lottie, his second wife, to England but still feared for his life and moved to Brazil. When the Nazis swept across Europe, he decided to kill himself, and Lottie died with him. The second example was Arthur Koestler who was dying from Parkinson's disease and persuaded his wife, Cynthia, to die with him. Lester found no case of a wife deciding to kill herself and her husband deciding that he could not live without her! Lester noted that, earlier in Zweig's life, he tried to persuade his first wife, Friderike, to die with him. She refused and went on to become an academic and a scholarly expert on Zweig. Lester noted that "Lottie died with Stefan; Friderike built a career on him," a much better resolution.

Daly (1978) has documented the oppression and *gynocide* of women throughout the centuries and across cultures, including sati, Chinese foot-binding, genital mutilation, witch burnings, and even gynecological practices. She noted several components to what she called these *sado-rituals*: (1) an obsession with female purity, (2) a total erasure of responsibility on the part of the men for the atrocities performed in these rituals, (3) the tendency of the gynocidal rituals to catch on and spread, (4) the use of women as scapegoats and token torturers (such as blaming mothers-in-law for the widows' suffering), (5) a compulsive orderliness, obsessive repetitiveness, and fixation on minute details to divert attention from the horror, (6) behavior unacceptable in other contexts becoming acceptable and normative as a result of conditioning, and (7) legitimization of the ritual by "objective" scholarship, especially by stressing the role of cultural norms and customs in order to "understand" the ritual.

As a result of these observations, the role of the Hindu religion in sati is suspect. Women are oppressed by many religions, and they have long been oppressed in the West, where the right to vote was granted only in the early part of the 20th Century. Men have often sought to oppress women and have used religious and pseudo-scientific claims to justify this.[11] Female fetuses are aborted and female children killed in both India and China, two countries differing greatly in religious and political philosophies.

The role of Indian culture in the oppression of women in India may be relevant for a cultural explanation for the existence of sati rather than some other form of

---

[11]   Lester (1994) documented how, in 19th Century America, women who wanted to work and to gain
         independence from their roles as wives and mothers were "re-educated" to accept their traditional
         roles.

oppression. However, it is not relevant to the explanation of why some women in that culture commit sati whereas others do not.

The Research of Weinberger-Thomas

Weinberger-Thomas (1999) has written a book on sati that is of great importance. Weinberger-Thomas is not a psychologist, nor even a journalist. She is a Professor of Hindi and her concern, therefore, is with tying the practice of sati to the religion, myths, and culture of India and Hinduism. Despite this, she gives important clues to the understanding of sati. The first contribution is the brief documentation of modern cases of sati in India throughout her book, which I have listed in Table 1.

Can a wife avoid sati? Weinberger-Thomas noted that sprinkling the woman with water that has been colored with indigo is enough to make her too impure to become a sati. Being touched by an *untouchable* (a person of lower caste) also prevents a woman becoming a sati. In olden days, being touched by a foreigner would also suffice, and cases have been documented of widows throwing themselves on foreign spectators to avoid becoming satis. Weinberger-Thomas notes that a person can be tricked into impurity, for example, by sprinkling indigo dye on the coconuts placed on the funeral pyre. However, sometimes, widows simply refused to become satis. Weinberger-Thomas noted a case in the early 1800s when, after the death of the Rajah Bhanswarrah, not one of his wives committed sati despite urging from others to do so.

Roop Kanvar (known as Bala), who, at the age of 40, was prevented by the local police from becoming a sati after the death of her adopted son, has become a *jogini* (an emanation of divine energy) and has a temple in her honor.[12] Her case is interesting since her "husband" collapsed when he touched her at the wedding ceremony and died fifteen days later. Thus, she was seen as the "cause" of her husband's death. She was sixteen at the time. Bala was born in 1903 near Pipar (in Jodhpur District), was widowed in 1919 and adopted her nephew. This son died in 1943, and Bala announced her intention to die on his funeral pyre along with the son's daughter-in-law. The daughter-in-law was tricked into drinking indigo water and a blue veil was thrown over Bala. Both were considered impure and unfit to be satis. Bala lived until 1986, but maintained a total fast for those 43 years. This last point (about her 43 year-long fast) illustrates the myths that

---

[12] Weinberger-Thomas visited her at her temple.

develop about satis, making it very difficult to distinguish fact from fiction in their lives.

Weinberger-Thomas makes the same point about Hem Kanvar who committed sati in 1943, about whom many mythical stories have been told. For example, after the news of her husband's death and her decision to commit sati, she is said to have become white and radiant. Her house, which has become a temple in her honor, lived in and officiated by her in-laws, has become the site of pilgrimages and miracle cures.

> We must resign ourselves to the fact that we shall never know anything about the real life woman whose name was Hem Kanvar....[T]he "life stories" of the new satis....resemble one another to the point of confusion....The same vignettes, and occasionally the same cover illustration [of the publications], reinforce the sense of *déjà vu* that permeates the corpus. (Weinberger-Thomas, 1999, p. 139)

Weinberger-Thomas noted that the customs and rituals make it very difficult for a widow who states her intention (willingly or by force) to commit sati to later recant.[13] If she does try to recant, she may be forced onto the funeral pyre. The case of Javitri who committed sati on July 11, 1979, in Jari (in Uttar Pradesh) is relevant here. Her husband and brother-in-law were killed by hoodlums. Javitri's in-laws greeted her with curses when the news was delivered because, in that subculture, Javitri was seen as guilty for having cast a spell on her in-laws.

Unfortunately, Weinberger-Thomas reports nothing about the earlier lives of the satis she located. She mentions only one small detail about one sati. Dayal Kanvar showed a fascination with fire from an early age, always drawing close to fires and even placing parts of her body into fires. It is likely that much could have been learned about the earlier lives of the satis, some of which may have relevance for understanding their decision to become satis.

Discussion

There are two main issues in the discussion of sati. First, from a cultural, social, and anthropological perspective, the question is why sati became the method for oppressing women in India rather than some other form of abuse (such as genital

---

[13]   The same is true of female suicide bombers (Lester, 2010b, 2011).

mutilation or foot binding). This is an important question, but it is not the question addressed in this essay.

The second issue is psychological. Since not every widow dies on her husband's funeral pyre, why do some commit sati while others do not? The answer to this is that the choice was probably dependent on interpersonal and intrapsychic factors. For example, Stein (1988) reported the following:

> The first modern *sati* in the area occurred in 1954, in a family in which the family property had been equally settled among four sons. The death of the *sati* meant the consolidation of the property by the remaining three, since the wife of one of them, who was childless, was made the guardian of the dead woman's children. When this woman in turn became a widow shortly thereafter, rumors immediately started that she too would become a *sati*, the property going to the remaining two brothers. She escaped immolation, however, by sending an urgent message to her father, who obtained a police escort for the funeral. (p. 474).

One widow committed sati, the other refused. Why? What psychological characteristics distinguished these two women?

Postscript

What of Roop Kanwar, the 18-year-old widow whose sati on September 4, 1987, caused such a great debate in India? Only one journalist seems to have made an effort to find out some "facts" about the case. Mala Sen (2002), an Indian working in London, England, traveled on several occasions to India and, during her visits, became friends with Roop Kanwar's father-in-law, Sumer Singh. She also tracked down the first police officer to arrive at Deorala and who interviewed people in the village. What did she find out?[14]

The marriage had been arranged when Roop Kanwar was about five or six and Maal Singh was nine or ten. The contract was finalized in 1981, and they were married on January 17, 1987, in Jaipur. She was a city girl, and her father-in-law said that she was homesick in Deorala and so spent most of the marriage in Jaipur with her parents. Her husband was studying for his exams at this time. The low caste servants in the village who were, therefore, afraid to talk of the sati

---

[14] One element, modeling, seems to be ruled out. Roop Kanwar's father-in-law said that there were no previous satis in his or his daughter-in-law's family.

for fear of upsetting their employers, did tell Mala Sen's taxi driver that there was
crying and shouting in the house during the time Roop Kanwar returned to her in-
laws a few days prior to Maal Singh's death.

When the police officer, Ram Rathi, arrived on the scene, only the remains of
the pyre were left. He visited the village several times afterwards and spoke to
both the rich and the poor in the village. He found out that Roop Kanwar had
not loved her husband. In fact, she had a childhood sweetheart whom she was
not allowed to marry,[15] and she had been having an affair with him after her marriage in her home town of Jaipur, to which her lover had moved from Ranchi.
When her parents found out, they were horrified and ordered her to return to
her husband. She had become pregnant as a result of the affair, but hid this from
her parents. On returning to her husband, she tried to persuade her husband that
the child was his. However, their marriage had never been consummated because
her husband was impotent, and he had "mental problems," as did his mother.[16]
Although he had a BSc degree, Maal Singh was unemployed. Roop Kanwar
had lived with her husband for only three weeks of their seven months of marriage, a brief period after the marriage ceremony and for a few days before his
death. After Roop Kanwar came back to him, he tried to kill himself by swallow-
ing a large quantity of fertilizer. His family covered up his suicide attempt, and a
doctor took him to a distant hospital where he died on September 4, 1987.[17] His
body was rushed back to Deorala for a quick cremation in order to prevent an
autopsy.

The police officer was of the opinion that Roop Kanwar was "encouraged" to
kill herself. Although myths quickly grew surrounding her death (that her eyes
glowed red and her body generated an immense heat and she walked to her death),
the children in the village told Ram Rathi that she seemed unsteady on her feet, as
if drunk or drugged, and stumbled several times on the way to the funeral pyre.
She was surrounded by several youths armed with swords, and her eldest brother-
in-law (who was fourteen years old) lit the funeral pyre.[18] Reports that she waved
her arms as she burned and called out have been interpreted as agony and pain,
but supporters of sati argue that it was joy being expressed.

Remember that wives are thought in this region of India to be responsible for
illnesses and events that befall their husbands. If the husband dies or is killed, then
she is responsible. In this case, the wife had been unfaithful to her husband and

---

[15]   He was from a different caste.
[16]   Her husband told Mala Sen that his wife suffered from depression.
[17]   After the sati, the doctor, Magan Singh, fled and was not found for many months. After he was
       found and charged, he was no longer allowed to practice medicine.
[18]   Her father-in-law claimed to have been in a hospital many miles from Deorala after collapsing and
       becoming unconscious when his son, Maal Singh, was brought to Deorala.

conceived a child by another man. In many families, Roop Kanwar would have been simply murdered for these behaviors.

Whereas there are occasional modern cases where the parents of the bride saved her from committing sati, Roop Kanwar's parents disapproved of her true love and moved from Ranchi to Jaipur to put an end to the affair, to no avail. They, like her in-laws, celebrated her sati because now they were the parents of a new goddess and not simply business people who ran trucks between Ranchi and Jaipur.[19]

Roop Kanwar, therefore, like the female suicide bombers described by Lester (2010b, 2011), had few options. She could die on her husband's funeral pyre or face being murdered (or viciously persecuted for the rest of her life). Her suicide is best conceptualized as fatalistic in nature. By committing sati, she transformed her image from sinner to heroine.

References

Abraham, S. (1997). The Deorala judgement glorifying suicide. *The Lawyers Collective, 12*(2), 4–12.

Ali, S. (1987). A young widow burns in her bridal clothes. *Far Eastern Economic Review, 138*, 54–55.

Altekar, A. S. (1978). *The position of women in Hindu civilization*. Delhi, India: Motilal Banarsidass.

Anon. (2002). Stranglehold of obscurantism: Kuttu Bai didn't commit suicide; she was murdered. *People's Democracy, 26*(37). Available online at pd.cpim.org/2002/sept22/09152002_mp_sati.htm

Anon. (2007, August). India's widows singing for supper. *The Economist, 384*(8542), 35.

Baig, T. A. (1988). Sati, women's status and religious fundamentalism. *Social Action, 38*(1), 78–83.

Bhugra, D. (2005). Sati. *Crisis, 26*, 73–77.

Cakmak, H. C., & Altuntas, N. (2008). Reconsidering gender inequality and honour suicide with the frame of different liberal theories. *Muslim World Journal of Human Rights, 5*(1), article 4.

Cassels, N. G. (1965). The abolition of suttee. *Journal of British Studies, 5*(1), 77–87.

Counts, D. A. (1980). Fighting back is not the way: Suicide and the women on Kaliai. *American Ethnologist, 7*, 332–351.

Daly, M. (1978). *Gyn/ecology*. Boston, MA: Beacon Press.

Devereux, G. (1961). *Mohave ethnopsychiatry*. Washington, DC: Smithsonian Institution.

Durkheim, E. (1897). *Le suicide* [Suicide]. Paris: Felix Alcan.

Freed, R. S., & Freed, S. A. (1989). Beliefs and practices resulting in female deaths and fewer females than males in India. *Population & Environment, 10*(3), 144–161.

---

[19] Other reports say that Roop Kanwar's father was a school teacher.

Harlan, L. (1994). Perfection and devotion. In J. H. Hawley (Ed.), *Sati, the blessing and the curse*, pp. 79–99. New York: Oxford University Press.

Hawley, J. S. (Ed.). (1994). *Sati, the blessing and the curse*. New York: Oxford University Press.

Inamdar, S. C., Oberfield, R. A., & Darrell, E. R. (1983). A suicide by self-immolation. *International Journal of Social Psychiatry, 29*, 130–133.

Johnson, P. S., & Johnson, J. A. (2001). The oppression of women in India. *Violence Against Women, 7*, 1051–1068.

Kumar, R. (1995). From Chipko to sati. In A. Basu (Ed.), *The local feminisms*, pp. 58–86. Boulder, CO: Westview Press.

Lester, D. (1994). The rest cure of Silas Weir Mitchell in the 19th Century and Japanese Morita therapy. *Bulletin of Division 29 (American Psychological Association), 29*(4), 51–53.

Lester, D. (1997). The sexual politics of double suicide. *Feminism & Psychology, 7*, 148–154.

Lester, D. (2010a). Suicide and the partition of India. *Suicide-Online, 1*, 2–4.

Lester, D. (2010b). Female suicide bombers and burdensomeness. *Psychological Reports, 106*, 160–162.

Lester, D. (2011). Female suicide bombers. *Suicidology Online, 2*, 62–66.

MacLeod, W. C. (1931). The distribution and process of suttee in North America. *American Anthropologist, 33*, 209–215.

Mehta, M. J. (1966). The British rule and the practice of sati in Gujarat. *Journal of Indian History, 44*, 553–560.

Mukerji, M. (1979). *Ham in the sandwich*. New Delhi, India: Viking.

Narasimhan, S. (1990). *Sati*. New Delhi, India: Viking.

Narasimhan, S. (1994). India: From sati to sex-determination tests. In M. Davies (Ed.), *Women and violence*, pp. 43–52. London, UK: Zed Books.

Nasrullah, M., Haqqi, S., & Cummings, K. J. (2009). The epidemiological patterns of honour killing of women in Pakistan. *European Journal of Public Health, 19*, 193–197.

Parilla, V. (1999). Sati: Virtuous woman through self-sacrifice. Accessed June 11, 2012 from http://www.csuchico.edu/~cheinz/syllabi/asst001/spring99/parrilla/parr1.htm

Patel, S. (2008). Karo-kari: A form of honour killing in Pakistan. *Transcultural Psychiatry, 45*, 683–694.

Sen, M. (2002). *Death by fire*. New Brunswick, NJ: Rutgers University Press.

Sharma, A. (1978). Emile Durkheim on suttee as suicide. *International Journal of Contemporary Sociology, 15*, 283–291.

Sheth, S. D. (1994, July–August). Those who take their lives. *Manushi, 83*, 24–30.

Singh, R. N., & Unnithan, N. P. (1999). Wife burning. *Violence Against Women, 5*, 641–653.

Stein, D. K. (1978). Women to burn. *Signs, 4*, 253–268.

Stein, D. K. (1988). Burning widows, burning brides. *Pacific Affairs, 61*, 465–485.

Thakur, U. (1963). *The history of suicide in India*. Delhi, India: Munshi Ram Manohar Lal.

Vijayakumar, L. (2004). Altruistic suicide in India. *Archives of Suicide Research, 8*, 73–80.

Vijayakumar, L. (2009). Hindu religion and suicide in India. In D. Wasserman & C. Wasserman (Eds.), *Oxford textbook of suicidology and suicide prevention*, pp. 19–25. New York: Oxford University Press.

Weinberger-Thomas, C. (1999). *Ashes of immortality*. Chicago: University of Chicago Press.

Yang, A. A. (1989). Whose sati? *Journal of Women's History, 1*(2), 8–33.

Cultural Ambivalence and Suicide Rates in South Korea

B. C. Ben Park

In the last few decades South Korea has experienced a sharply rising rate of suicide. Since suicide is seen fundamentally as an individual act, the reasons for suicide are often sought in the life situations and personal problems of those who take their own lives. However, suicide in South Korea should also be viewed as possibly the result of broader social factors and as reflecting the shifts in and the forms of turmoil in the nation's culture.

Culture evolves over time, gradually forming traditions that shape the values and patterns of the behavior of a people. Yet, at the same time, culture is a dynamic force that undergoes change as it interplays with the socioeconomic structure and politico-historical location of a society. As people adopt ideas and tools from other cultures, cultural diffusion may occur, and changes in a culture may follow as people respond to changes in economic and political conditions. This process has been intensified in the modern world, with the expanding global economy, causing people to grapple with a new set of values and life-style issues that come with new economic and technological formulas.

As people are forced to adapt to new economic and technological milieus, they may collectively experience ambivalence about their traditional value system. This collective ambivalence is what Emile Durkheim (1897/1951) called *anomie*, which is a condition that creates serious psychological distress among a society's members. Cultural ambivalence stems, according to Durkheim, from a social condition in which an old set of values becomes blurred, while a new set of values is not recognized or accepted by its members. This pathological social condition, with its lessening of the normative regulation of the society, can lead many people to have an unclear concept of what is proper and acceptable behavior.

South Korean society is currently facing *collective cultural ambivalence*. Confucian values that have guided and meaningfully glued Korean people together over many centuries have been perceived as out of date. However, a new set of Western values that came along with the industrialization that began in the late 1960s and 1970s has been often in conflict with traditional norms, but gradually internalized by many individuals, albeit in different ways. Certainly, tension arises between interpersonal-directed Confucian values and individual-oriented Western values.

Such tension can be a source of distress, particularly when it is perceived by "una-ware" individuals as creating ambiguous social expectations regarding when to assert individual autonomy and when to display mutuality. In other words, contemporary Koreans are provided with no clear set of social expectations, only conflicting and confusing messages stemming both from mutual-help ethics, the legacy of Confucian tradition manifested in keeping up the interpersonal networking – what Cho (1995, p. 146) views as "a major means of accommodating one's needs" – and from self-advocacy, the Western value of individualism manifested in the neoliberalistic market's push for competition and specialization.

Clearly, this is not an either/or choice. Still, the conflicting demand is a stressful one for individuals given the context in which they are compelled to compete with one another but, at the same time, required to invest their time and energy to build mutual relationships with one another. As Michael Breen (2004, p. 31), a British reporter, observed, "Koreans are more gregarious than we are. They are so into other people that they don't read books much. ...They work hard at their relationships." But, "[t]hese gregarious people carry a tremendous amount of unresolved pain." Korean people seem to respond to this conflicting demand as if it were a part of modern life and do not pay close attention to the pain. Instead, it seems, many choose to let their lives be guided by the consumerist global culture, which provides only a weak psychological anchor.

South Korea's economic success brought the rise of consumerism. With it, Western values and life-styles became pervasive in contemporary Korean culture. In this context, it should be noted that, for some people, particularly the older generation, the acculturation stress produced in the process of adapting to new culture may be related to suicidal tendencies (Lester 1999). Furthermore, it is logical to assume that, if one person internalizes the meaning of a Confucian value, but another rejects it entirely, conflict may arise in the relationship, especially relationships within the family. Interpersonal familial conflict may be associated with suicide proneness. In fact, according to the data provided by the police department, nearly 10% of all suicides that occurred during the period of 2004–2006 in Korea resulted from family conflict (Lim et al., 2008, p. 41). Furthermore, the psychological distress and interpersonal conflict stemming from the incongruent value systems and unclear social expectations in contemporary Korean cultural context appear to have led to increased mental health problems (Rhi, 1998).

This essay will look at the changing patterns of suicide in terms of how these patterns have been affected by collective cultural ambivalence. The dramatic increase in suicide rates in Korea's recent history warrants intensive study. The rise in suicidal behavior is, without a doubt, caused by multiple factors. However, given the powerful role a culture plays in providing a map for human behavior, my aim is to describe how the changing nature of Korean culture creates strains which, in turn, are linked to suicidal tendencies among the population. Specifically, I will explore how traditional Confucian values still influence Korean people in the midst of globalization, consumerism, and technological advancement, which shape people's attitudes, beliefs, values, and behaviors differently from the ways in which they were shaped in the past. The resulting effect contributes to the rising number of suicidal acts. Using the official suicide data obtained from the Korea National Statistical Office, I will describe how the changing patterns of suicide fit into the changing cultural context.

Suicide Trends in South Korea

The number of suicides has sharply increased in recent history in South Korea (hereafter referred to as Korea). As shown in Figure 1, the suicide rate was 7.4

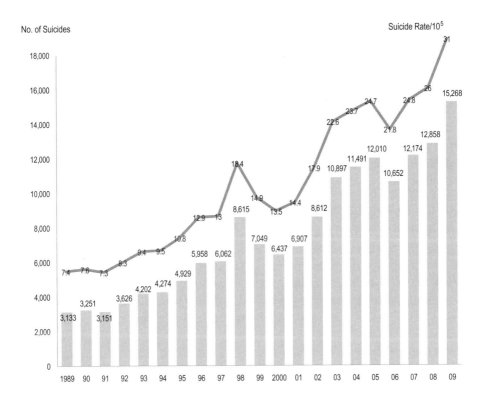

Figure 1. Trends in suicide in South Korea.

per 100,000 people in 1989, but in 2009, the rate climbed to 31.0. In just two decades the suicide rate in Korea has more than quadrupled. According to the Korean National Statistical Office Report (http://kostat.go.kr/), suicide was the seventh leading cause of death in 1998, but it has risen to the fourth leading cause for the total population since 2004. Such a drastic increase of completed acts of self-destruction in Korea leads us to ask what the cause of this is. What are the driving forces behind such a drastic increase of suicide in contemporary Korean society?

Some might argue that the lenient view of suicide in Confucian teaching could be a primary contributing factor to the rise in suicide. In fact, there is "no strict prohibition against [suicide], i.e., suicide is not intrinsically wrong" in Confucian philosophy (Lo, 1999, p. 74). In some situations, the act of purposefully killing oneself for noble causes, or to preserve one's honor or integrity, is viewed rather positively. However, if this were a valid argument, one has to explain why the suicide rate remained relatively low in the past. It should be noted that from 1983 (the first year of the compilation of suicide statistics) until 1996, the suicide rate remained within the range of 7 to 8 per 100,000 people per year. It is thus evident that an attempt to link a particular social phenomenon to a few traits in a culture does not satisfactorily explain the dramatic rise of suicide in Korean society. However, the question still remains: Why are there more suicidal acts today than in the past? We need to understand how the dynamic nature of a culture yields different mental health outcomes in different sociohistorical locations.

It is notable that Korean society has faced vast changes in its recent history. It has experienced a profound transformation in the past several decades as its economy has become integrated into the global financial system. As a result, there have been significant changes in many different areas, such as the social organization of work (which includes new forms of business and trade, with greater competition), fashion, new markets, and increasing social problems (drug use, crime, low marriage and fertility rates, divorce, unemployment, mental illness, etc.). More importantly, however, Korea's integration into the global economic structure has occurred with a shift of its cultural value system from interpersonally-directed moral values to individually-oriented materialistic values. This shift has created what I call a state of cultural ambivalence, which is then followed by an increased level of distress that increases the willingness of the population to consider and engage in suicidal behavior.

As suggested above, there is a link between cultural change and changing patterns of suicide. In what follows, I will discuss a few Confucian ideals that may be relevant to understanding suicidal behavior in the cultural context of Korea. The discussion of Confucianism is important to understand not only for its profound impact on the Korean psyche over many centuries, but also for its changing nature in modern Korean culture. I will then examine the changing patterns of suicide in reference to Durkheim's theoretical perspective. Durkheim's concepts are useful in understanding the connection between sociocultural determinants and changing patterns of suicide in modern Korean society. Finally, I will examine and discuss the suicide trends of how each age group – elderly (60+), older adults (40–59), younger adults (25–39), and youth (15–24) – is differentially affected by the contemporary trends of Korea culture.

Confucian Values and Their Relevance to Suicidal Behaviors

Confucianism was regarded as the principal sociocultural and political force that prescribed the basic rules of personal conduct and family life in Korea for many centuries. The philosophy was initially introduced in the fifth century AD and served as the political ruling ideology during the Yi dynasty (1392–1910). Confucian values have thus been profoundly ingrained into the psychological substructure of the individual to a much greater degree than any other "socioreligious values" (Slote, 1998). Although Confucian ideals emerged to guide people's way of life in agrarian society, they still remain alive in interpersonal relationships and are ritualistically practiced in modern Korea. However, Confucianism today has typically been portrayed as "hierarchical, authoritarian, and gender based" (Hahm, 2003, p. 358). This authoritarian, hierarchal structure is typically observed in the relationship between employer and employee (Breen, 2004). Because the Confucian legacy remains a strong cultural force in Korea that impacts contemporary attitudes and patterns of behavior, it is appropriate to discuss, albeit briefly, some of these Confucian values that are most relevant to the concept of self-destruction. With the belief that values are usually construed as the core elements of a culture, it is important to understand how the agrarian-based values, flourishing even in modern-era Korea, can create strain in the individual living in the competitive globalized society, and how such strain can contribute to the rising suicide rate in Korean society.

As stated earlier, Confucian teaching offers "no strict prohibition against [suicide]" (Lo, 1999, p. 74) in the way that the act is rather unambiguously denounced in the Western cultural context (Farberow, 1975). Implicitly, as Mencius, the best-known student of Confucius states, "Life is what I want; *yi* [justice] is also what I want. If I cannot have both, I would rather take *yi* [justice] than life" (Lau, 1984, p. 10). The purposeful act of killing oneself for noble causes is not condemned. This type of act is what Durkheim understood as altruistically motivated suicide. In history, numerous cases of altruistic suicide can be found in

Korea (Jang, 2004; Kim, 2008; Park, 1994; Park, 2004). In more recent history (i.e., during the period of 1970–2000) many students and laborers killed themselves to promote their respective movement's causes. Those who undertook this type of suicide were often labeled as martyrs (Park, 2004).

Although the purposeful act of suicide is viewed positively, it is important to note that the nonpurposeful, purely personally motivated suicide that Durkheim called *egoistic*, is regarded rather negatively. Under the philosophical premise that all humans have the capacity to be good, the focus of Confucian teaching was primarily on moral self-cultivation, which is the process of learning virtue or moral character. Confucius believed that the morally cultivated person would know how to live ethically and to fulfill the self, which ultimately would lead to building a peaceful and flourishing society. Thus, cultivation of the moral self is the way to build a good society. The family, Confucius believed, is the place in which one's moral self-cultivation originates. Children are taught to develop virtues, and they learn how to position themselves in the wider world by having exemplary relations within the family. Filial piety is, Confucius argues, "the root of virtue and the origin of instruction" (Goldin, 2011, p. 35). He further argues:

> You received your self, your body, your hair, and your skin from your mother and father: not daring to destroy or injure [these gifts] is the beginning of filial piety. Establishing oneself, practicing the Way, and displaying one's name onto later generations in order to manifest one's mother and father is the end of filial piety. The beginning of filial piety is serving one's parents; the middle is serving one's ruler; the end is establishing oneself. (as cited in Goldin [2011, p. 35])

The display of gratitude and respect for the parents who brought one into the world is the way to establish oneself. One's own renown later then brings glory on one's parents, which will be the ultimate end of filial piety. More importantly, from the concept of filial piety we are able to infer Confucius's attitude, even indirectly, toward self-harming behavior and suicide. Simply put, suicide is "understood as usurping the authority of parents" (Lo, 1999, p. 79). As discussed earlier, only the altruistic type of suicide that is committed for high moral significance may be accepted or praised. Unless the act of killing oneself involves "a protection of one's dignity, honor or integrity," it is generally condemned (Fei, 2009, p. 16). For this reason, the egoistic type of suicide is viewed rather negatively.

Confucius did not advocate blind obedience of children to authority in the family or in the larger world. The virtuous relationship between father and son, he argued, is based on mutual affection. There are detailed specifications about such a relationship (Tu, 1998). Listing them is beyond the scope of this paper, but it is important to note that Confucius called our attention to the importance of filial discipline at home to foster moral character. In the process of building moral character, Confucius stressed that love ought to be present in the father-son relationship. Nevertheless, as filial piety became institutionalized as a social norm, this ideal of Confucian teaching vanished. Instead, measures of dogmatic enforcement of filial piety have taken over. Later, I will discuss how this basic Confucian idea has created strain in the complex modern social structure, which, in turn, engenders stress for most Koreans.

In this Confucian cultural context, the death of a child by suicide brings to parents not only the feeling of loss but also a deep sense of shame. A man of virtue is not supposed to kill himself for personal reasons, but only for higher moral reasons. A death by suicide thus carries a stigma, not only for the individual who carried out the act, but also for the family, because it signifies parental failure in providing the discipline for cultivating a man of virtue. This negative cultural meaning attached to egotistic suicide leads many people to hide the fact from the public.[1] In other words, any suicide without moral significance is socially stigmatized in Korean society.

As mentioned earlier, Confucianism prescribed that the relationship between parents and child ought to be governed not by the filial duty of child to parents but by mutual affection. The same mutual affection and love is also emphasized in the husband-wife relationship. Essentially, human relationships are structured by mutual regard and voluntary cooperation, which involves reciprocity. Reciprocity can be characterized as the basis of Confucian ethics: "What you yourself do not desire, do not do to others" (Goldin, 2011, p. 15). This ethical principle in relation to one another extended to the community compact that "called for mutual encouragement in the performance of worthy deeds, mutual admonition in the correction of errors and failings, reciprocal engagement in rites and customs, and mutual aid in times of distress and misfortune" (de Bary, 1998, p. 59). The mutual help ethic is important for understanding the traditional social network system through which people were integrated into group life. More importantly, the residue of these ethics is still powerfully at work in modern Korean society, although with a personalized form.

---

[1]   This is one reason that professionals find it difficult to organize survivor's meetings or to study family members of a suicide. Understandably, an acknowledgement of a family member's suicide brings shame to the whole family. For example, the 26-year-old daughter of Mr. Lee Gun Hee, the head of the Samsung Group, a powerful South Korean corporation, died by suicide in 2005. It was initially announced that she was killed in a car accident, but later, due to foreign media coverage, the company's spokesperson admitted that her death was from suicide. What is critical is that initially an attempt was made to hide the fact. Even after the admission of suicide, the family has never mentioned or discussed it.

In the Korean context, Chang (2003) argued that the mutual help ethic (*hyangyak* in Korean) had already existed as a form of labor exchange in the Korean peasant community, even before the Confucian central government initiated the *hyangyak* movement (the community compact) in order to establish self-governing local communities and to teach the Confucian mutual help ethic to the local masses in 1506. Yet, the preexisting mutual help ethic that grew out of the need in a farming village became not only reinforced but also extended to various collective "efforts to protect themselves [those in the group] from unusual events, crises, or disasters, as well as to even more sophisticated informal organizations such as *key* (rotating interest association) which was designed to meet individual financial needs in a collective manner. The *key* (qi) was a traditional device for ensuring against special or crisis situations that the individual cultivator or household might encounter" (Chang, 2003, p. 93). The compact practiced in local communities thus became the central ground for solidarity among the community residents. The gentry class (elites) also formed their own separate mutual help system based on their kinship bonds, which later served as a semi-government organ assuming "the responsibility of establishing a new social order based on the Confucian moral precepts" (Chang, 2003, p. 95). The Confucian ideal of mutual help and cooperation was practiced separately in both groups. The peasant commoners and the elites had the goal of integrating members within each group, and this contributed to maintaining a strong social bond among members, which Durkheim (1897/1951) saw as a preventive force against suicide.

It is observed today that the Confucian tradition of mutual support continues to flourish in modern Korea, albeit in a personalized ritual. According to Chang (2003), Korean people in modern urbanized society are making great efforts to develop connections "through a shared lineage, or [because they have] attended the same school or short-term training program, come from the same town or province, or [have] served three years in the army in the same company" (p. 100). "[S]chool and university provide Koreans with the most important social network in their life.. . .If you are a graduate from a top university you can be confident that there are tens of thousands of 'seniors' out there who will do favors for you" (Breen, 2004, p. 65). The effort to create a personal network system through schools and universities is not only to take advantage of the reciprocal social relationships but also to enhance one's status. Cho (1995) sums up the phenomenon as follows:

> Koreans invested all their energy and "capital" for a more secure goal: to send their sons to schools of higher education. Once a son received higher education, the status and economic condition of the whole family improved. By sending him to a university, the family could secure not only a breadwinner,

but a new network through his school ties. Having an alumni network was extremely crucial for survival in a society where networking was a major means of accommodating one's needs. Korean society has depended heavily on individual networks rather than on building new institutions or forming voluntary groups. (p. 146)

However, this personalized network system in modern Korean society, especially for the elite society, is often perceived as leading to corruption and unfairness. It is, therefore, likely that one who fails to develop social connections with influential individuals may feel a sense of powerlessness or be perceived as a victim of favoritism.

Of central importance to this analysis is that the Confucian tradition is not the only cultural force that affects the attitudes, values, and patterns of people's behavior in modern Korea. It is also important to acknowledge that the Western ideal of meritocracy, which focuses on individual ability and effort, impacts many aspects of modern Korean society, particularly the educational and economic institutions. Young people generally grow up believing that Western values, such as the egalitarian ideals being taught in schools, are superior to the Confucian formula that is often portrayed as authoritarian. In the midst of the perception that Confucianism is an outdated philosophy, irrelevant to modern life, genuine Confucian ideals are rarely taught or discussed, a result that seems to lead the young to take little genuine pride in their own cultural heritage. In this social context, what I call *collective cultural ambivalence* naturally emerges. On the surface, the Western ideal appears to prevail, but, at a basic level, the traditional Confucian norm that once bonded Koran people together, although weakened, still exerts its power inadvertently in the domain of interpersonal relationships.

In order to understand the connection between cultural ambivalence and the increased rate of suicide, it is also relevant to take Durkheim's theoretical perspective into account. My analysis, therefore, attempts to understand, using Durkheim's concepts of social integration and regulation, the connections among the sociocultural determinants of suicide that are most relevant to Korean society.

Durkheim's Concepts in the Korean Context

Durkheim's (1951) theory of suicide is based on two dimensions: social integration and social regulation. Social integration is the extent to which people in a society are bound together in social networks. Low levels of social integration result in *egoistic* suicide, while high levels of social integration result in *altruistic*

suicide. Social regulation is the extent to which the desires and behaviors of the
members in a society are controlled by social values and norms. Low levels of
social regulation result in *anomic* suicide while high levels of social regulation
result in *fatalistic* suicide. These four types of suicide (egoistic, anomic, altruistic,
and fatalistic) all point to the strength or weakness of an individual's ties to society
and help us understand suicide (seemingly the ultimate individual act) in social
terms. What follows is a brief sketch of how each of Durkheim's three conceptual
frames (egoistic, altruistic, and anomic types of suicide) are relevant to sociohistorical trends in Korean society.

Durkheim argued that "excessive individualism," or egoism, increases the
suicide rate. When people have "excessive" freedom to pursue life as they see
fit and do not feel connected to a group or community that commands their loyalty
and participation, they are provided with an insufficient will to live and, therefore,
find it easier to consider suicide as a way to opt out. Durkheim's framing of egoistic suicide helps us understand the rising suicide rate in contemporary Korean
society which may be attributed, in part, to the increasingly weakened individual
ties to groups and to growing individualism. With the rapid integration of the global economic system, Korean culture has shifted sharply to the Western values of
individualism (Hyun, 2001; Yoo, Lee, & Yoo, 2007). This shift may have eroded
the ties of individuals to group life. More importantly, one's identity has become
more tied to an achievement orientation in the competitive labor market. The global market force then leads people to become less tied to a cohesive, tightly knit
traditional community and to kinship relations. Without a strong bond between the
individual and society, Durkheim believed that life would become perceived as
relatively meaningless, and the potential for suicide would increase.

It is plausible to assume that the increased individualism in modern Korean
culture has contributed to the rise of egoistic suicide. However, it is equally critical
to note, as suggested, that the Confucian norm of familism[2] may not have suc-
cumbed entirely, at least not yet, to Western individualism. The family in traditional Korean society was the social unit that had served the role of providing
its members a "sense of identity based on continuity through successive generations and a 'community' large enough to function as semi-independent economic,
academic, and sometimes even political units" (Hahm, 2003, p. 356). Furthermore, Kim (1990) noted that, "In external relations, a man acted not as an independent social being but as a member of the family." Under this normative
regulation of traditional familism, "[A]ll purposes, actions, gains and ideals of

---

[2]   Familism is defined as "a form of social organization in which all values are determined by
      reference to the maintenance, continuity, and functions of family group" (Kulp, 1925, p. 188).

individuals were referred to and evaluated by comparison with the fortune of family groups" (p. 411).

This normative cultural force still exerts pressure, to a certain extent, on individuals in modern Korea. However, Kim (1990) observed two profound changes that accompanied industrialization. First, the family structure changed from the extended family to the nuclear family. According to the Korea Statistical Office data, over 93% of Korean households in 2000 were categorized as nuclear families (http://kostat.go.kr/). Second, and more importantly, a transformation in the social norm of familism occurred, from community-oriented cooperative familism to modern competitive familism, which exclusively pursues individual interests. Yet, Kim observed that the change was not directed toward Western individualism. Instead, modern familism, diverging from the traditional one, puts the family interest as the top priority and utilizes the kinship network system largely for economic and instrumental reasons, not for emotional and expressive purposes. Moreover, the kinship (or a new) interaction network is much more narrowly perceived and exclusively formed with economic and instrumental objectives in mind. Individuals feel, therefore, pressured to compete in order to obtain wealth for their own family at the expense of others or for the public good. In this context, "people were eager to mobilize all the available resources within the [personal] network...to take a favorable social position in promoting their [nuclear] family interests" (Kim, 1990, p. 419). Because these features are distinctively different from the traditional familism that fosters cooperative behaviors of individuals, Kim labeled modern Korean familism as *amoral*.[3]

It is thus logical to infer that one could feel a greater sense of responsibility when one failed in the competitive market if one were a member of a nuclear family rather than of an extended family because the burden was less widely shared. As discussed above, a reciprocal relationship is a highly valued Confucian norm in Korea. People also have a psychological need to see themselves as an effective member of a social group, and not as a member that is burdensome (Joiner, 2005). Assuming that one is under the influence of Confucian norms of mutuality and reciprocity, one who perceives oneself as a burden to one's family could have difficulty maintaining meaningful relationships with other members. In fact, many notes left by elderly suicides in Korea seem to illustrate that they did not want to be a burden to their families; they therefore thought that ending their lives would benefit their surviving family members (Park 2010a). It is also possible to infer that a man's unemployment status may cause him to regard himself as

---

[3]   Amoral modern familism emerged, Kim argues, as a result of the policy for unbalanced economic growth that favors the elites. The choice was made by the Park Chung Hee regime in an attempt to quickly legitimize his power obtained through a military coup d'état.

a failure and imagine that his family would be better off without him. This may be the reason why the suicide rate is high during times of economic crisis, such as the one Korean society faced in 1997–1998. Similarly, young people who perceive themselves as not measuring up to parental demands may be likely to choose death instead of living as a ("perceived") burden to their family.

If these suicides could be categorized as altruistic (which generally occurs when there is an excessive social bond), a sizable proportion of suicides occurring in modern Korea would fit into this type. People who engage in altruistic suicide, according to Durkheim, do so as a result of the fact that they regard the life of the group as their own authentic essence because of their extensive, nearly total immersion into or integration with the society or collectivity in question. As people become so integrated into a group that individuality becomes weak, they place the group's interests above their own welfare, which may lead them to sacrifice themselves. It is evident that the traditional Confucian norm that stresses mutual support and harmony still regulates family relations, although the normative power has changed considerably to be more directed to the pursuit of individual "family" interests.

In the discussion above, it is argued that Koreans are exposed to cultural ambivalence and are forced to deal with the tension arising from ambiguous normative expectations, that is, the Korean traditional norm expecting cooperative behavior is coexisting with the modern Western expectation to be competitive and put self-interest before the interest of community. These conflicting cultural expectations can result in psychological distress for an individual who is experiencing the ambivalence. Such distress may lead to what Durkheim called *anomie* (from the Greek word for "lawlessness"). Individuals who are confronted with anomie, according to Durkheim, may commit a wide range of destructive acts, including suicide. Anomic suicide thus reflects a low degree of regulation over individual behavior due to the weakened common morality that bonds members together, a weakened morality that then leads many people to have a less clear concept of what is proper and acceptable behavior (Gelles & Levine, 1999). Disorientation about normative expectations of themselves and of society, I argue, stems primarily from collective cultural ambivalence.

Although the suicide rate has increased in all age groups in Korea, it is important to note that each age-cohort is affected differently by the historical and sociocultural trends. For example, because the youth of a country have comparatively low levels of commitment to a past they have not experienced, they bring openness to new ideas and social relationships. However, they are uncertain about the role of the enduring Confucian legacy on their thinking. By contrast, the changing culture can be seen by older adults and the elderly as cutting the common thread that connects their past, present, and future. In particular, those who hold on to the traditional value system may find their own norms and values less or no longer relevant and so feel a deep sense of cultural ambivalence, if not alienation and social isolation. Adults falling victim to cultural ambivalence may have an enormous amount of guilt because of conflicting messages they have to grapple with – the Confucian norms of filial piety and mutuality and the neoliberalistic market's push for self-advocacy. In what follows, I will describe how the conflicting cultural expectations existing in modern Korean society engender stress for four different age categories: elderly (60+), older adults (40–59), young adults (25–39), and youth (15–24).[4]

Elderly Suicide

Elderly individuals are survivors of the harsh Japanese colonial rule (1910–1945) and the painful Korean War (1950–1953). They served as the engine of Korea's industrialization (1960s–1970s) in their adult years. For the most part, they internalized Confucian values and sacrificed themselves for their children's education (the norm of filial piety) believing not only that their children's renown would bring glory to them, but also that their sacrificial investment would return as a form of insurance because they would be financially supported in their old age by their children. Furthermore, the parents' social status would be enhanced if their children achieved high positions in society.

However, as a result of the profound societal change that Korea has experienced in recent decades, the common thread that connects their past, present, and future has been severed. First, the economic change has made their children's position in the competitive labor market much more unstable than before, and this has required the children to have two incomes to support a family. In contrast, a family was supported with one income during the industrialization period. In the context of such change, many elderly members, instead of being cared for, must aid their struggling adult children. In fact, the norm of filial piety guided a large

---

[4] One reason to classify the age of 60 (instead of the conventional age of 65 in the West) to be a cut-off point to be elderly is as follows. One's 60th birthday in Korea (called, *hwan-gap)* has been considered a time of meaningful celebration because one has completed the zodiacal cycle. Yet, more importantly, only a few lived to be 60 years old in the pre-modern times, during which the life expectancy was estimated to be 35–40. Thus, the 60th birthday ritual meant traditionally a celebration of longevity. Typically, in the past, the *hwan-gap* party was lavishly prepared with lots of food and activities by one's sons and daughters, and guests were invited to celebrate the milestone of one's life. Today, the significance of the 60th birthday ritual has somewhat declined. However, the traditional notion that the 60th birthday is a symbolic mark of gaining extra years to live is still regarded meaningfully by many people. For this reason, it is culturally sensible to put the age of 60 and above into the category of old age.

segment of the elderly population to invest their resources in their children rather than to create their own retirement accounts, and so they have to depend on either their family members or relatives. Further compounding the problem, government assistance for the elderly in need, which was put into effect in 2007, is insufficient.

Second, and more importantly for the elderly, a profound transformation occurred in Korean culture that has made it even more difficult for their own values to be shared with younger generations. The so-called "digital revolution" prompted cultural values to become even more fragmented and personalized than they had been. In this digital culture, elderly individuals experience a greater level of cultural ambivalence than young people, and thereby feel a deeper alienation from social development, which also leads to weakened social bonding with others. In postmodern culture, the elderly's own norms and values are less relevant, or no longer relevant, and they "are forced to respond to conditions that they have little or no ability to control" (Clayer & Czechowicz, 1991, p. 685). Elderly individuals who hold on to traditional Confucian values face a greater disruption of their self-continuity and so feel a deeper sense of cultural ambivalence and social isolation.

The outcome of such a social trend is depicted in Figure 2, which indicates that the suicide rate of the elderly has sharply increased. The increase is much greater than that of any other age group. For example, while the rate of increase for the youth (ages 15–24) is about 1.5 times higher during the period of 1989–2009 (refer to Figure 5), the rate for the elderly is about 6.8 times (6.7 and 7.4 for males and females, respectively).

It seems very likely that the sharp increase in elderly suicide is due to collective cultural ambivalence created by the rapid transformation of Korean society. Durkheim posited that changes in socioeconomic structure, as well as higher levels of mobility due to urbanization and secularization, were the underlying forces that increased suicide rates. Such processes not only weaken common morality but also create social conditions conducive to egoism. It has been observed by the author that, as socioeconomic changes became more extensive due to Korea's integration into the global economy over the past few decades, the suicide rate climbed considerably. When Korea joined the Organization of Economic Cooperation and Development (OECD) in 1996, Korean society experienced negative changes in many different sectors. Moreover, it has been observed that economic development measured in Gross National Income (GNI) per capita is positively correlated with suicide (Park, 2010b, pp. 169–170).

Yip and Tan (1998) also reported increased suicide rates during the period of 1984–1994 in Hong Kong and Singapore, both of which are economically the most advanced in Southeast Asia. Additionally, the authors reported that suicide rates among the elderly increased rather sharply to about four to five times the

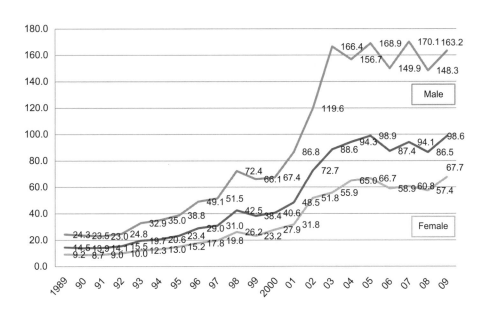

Figure 2. Suicide trends for the elderly (60+) in South Korea, 1989–2009.

average for the society in general. It seems that, as these societies became more deeply integrated into the global market system, the elderly became increasingly alienated from the larger social, cultural, and economic structures and, as a result, may have experienced greater ambivalence. Thus, these studies appear to indicate that changing suicide rates are tied to the disruptions that societies undergo due to the forces of globalization and modernization.

It is also Durkheim's argument that the elderly are more prone to suicide because the level of social integration decreases with age. However, this pattern of increased suicide with age is found mostly in developed nations. Girard (1993) argued that, as nations develop, people's identity becomes less tied to traditional kinship relations, and their ascribed social roles are more tied to an achievement orientation in the competitive labor market. One's job and wealth are set by the labor market, and security in old age is more a function of social security and pension plans than reliance on male children for support typically found in less developed nations. With increased age, one has more accumulated advantages (e.g., high salaries and high prestige) to lose from failure in the labor market. Hence, suicide rates tend to increase. In addition, older people, particularly those who have been widowed, diagnosed with terminal illness, or have experienced rapid physical deterioration, are much more likely than any other age group to see suicide as a release (Atchley & Barusch, 2004; Farberow & Shneidman, 1957; Glass, Jr. & Reed, 1993; Menninger, 1938). However, such an explanation is more applicable to Western societies.

One peculiarity that needs to be considered regarding the Korean elderly is that suicide is sometimes chosen for altruistic reasons. It is not uncommon to see, given the internalized Confucian norm to be a mutual and reciprocal member of the family, an old man, who perceives himself to be a burden to his family, end his life in an attempt to benefit his family. Some of these feelings of burdensomeness, of course, may result from a wish to avoid the negative view of others on the suicide's family.

To see this issue from a different angle, we may see that the social norm of filial piety prevailing powerfully in Korean culture prevents social policy makers from seeing the need for government intervention, leaving most of the burden to "amoral" modern familism. Despite the role that the traditional extended family served as a form of effective welfare and insurance for the elderly, the modern Korean nuclear family is placed in a financial muddle amid the unclear cultural expectations and the ever-increasing demand from the market-oriented neoliberal structure. The elderly, it seems, fall through the cracks more easily than those of any other age group because of their deeply internalized Confucian values.

The Suicide of Older Adults

Older adults spent their formative years largely during the industrialization era and under the military dictatorship, during which schools were expanding and college education was vigorously pursued by them *en masse* and supported, for the most part, by their parents, now the elderly. Because of their extensive schooling, they understand egalitarian ideals and long for participation in the democratic process of decision-making. At the same time, however, they internalized much of Confucian values to a greater degree than their younger counterparts. The internalization occurred partly because authoritarian political leaders deliberately reinforced the Confucian social norms, such as filial piety and loyalty to the ruler, as an easy way to legitimize their own power obtained through illegitimate means, such as military coups. For example, during the reign of Park Chung Hee regime (1961–1979), the Confucian ideas of filial piety and loyalty to the nation were heavily emphasized in its political propaganda slogan of "*indigenous democracy.*"

As discussed above, suicide notes left by some elderly people indicate that the choice to end their own lives was to make a final sacrifice as an attempt to lessen the burden for their children. The adult children are perhaps seen by their elderly parents as struggling in the neoliberalistic social condition, which has increased uncertainty given the competitive market-driven economy, while still striving to fulfill the cultural expectation of filial piety (the care of aged parents). It could be presumed that these older adults would be aware that their parents sacrificed themselves just to send their children to school. However, the older adult children of the elderly feel agony because they are unable to pay their parents back, that is, to support their aged parents. The end result is "a sense of guilt" when "they cannot live up to its demands" of the internalized norm of filial piety (Yim, 1998, p. 167). The feeling of guilt, if persistent, becomes a risk factor for suicide (Menninger, 1938).

As seen in Figure 3, the suicide rate for older adults (ages 40–59) has increased about 3.6-fold during the period of 1989–2009 (3.4-fold for males and 4.2-fold for females, respectively). Suicide is more common in men for this age group, as well as for the elderly, as the sex ratio was 2.7 in 2009. Still, the rate of female suicide is slightly high in Korea when compared to Western societies in which male suicide rates are usually 3–4 times higher than female suicide rates.

Given that the life expectancy is currently 78 years of age, the burden of caring for aged parents falls mostly on the older adults. Despite the significant sacrifice required, most adult children attempt to meet their parents' needs. However, in the current socioeconomic conditions, with an increasing specialized labor market, the added pressure to stay competitive so as to remain employed seems much greater today. Thus, older adults in modern day Korea have to deal with a greater degree of stress and guilt.

Furthermore, the cultural ideal of filial piety prevails so strongly that it prevents the government from moving proactively to help the struggling families, mostly leaving the burden of care to the family. The slow government response to the incongruence between the traditional norms and the modern economy contributes to the rising suicide rates for both adult children and elderly parents in contemporary Korean society.

The Suicide of Young Adults

The young adults (ages 25–39) grew up experiencing political democracy and being exposed to the global culture due to the extensive globalization policy of the Korean government in the 1990s. During their formative years, they enjoyed the fruits of Korea's industrialization and freely traveled to foreign countries, unlike previous generations. They internalized mostly Western values and were socialized to achieve their dream through competition in the labor market. In fact,

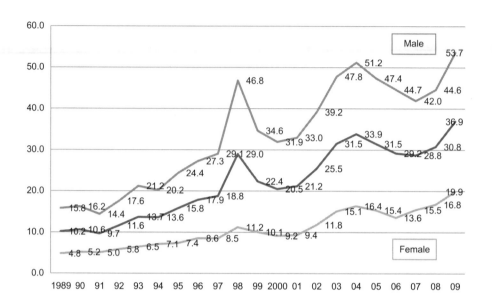

Figure 3. Suicide trends for the 40–59 age group, 1989–2009.

their interest in self-actualization is strong as a result of their global experience and education. However, they were indoctrinated by their parents in their early years to believe that their success in life depends on entering top-tier universities, where one could have a prestigious alumni network upon graduation. According to Cho (1995), "The rank of one's university determines one's worth as a social being." Upon entering the so-called top universities in Seoul, "one can look forward to a secure future – that is, a stable job, good marriage, and respectable social life" (p. 148). Thus, for the most part, this age group was compelled to compete in order to obtain material comfort and social prestige.

As seen in Figure 4, the suicide rate of young adults has increased about 3.0-fold during the period of 1989–2009. Of interest to note is that the rate of increase for females is greater than that for males (2.4-fold for males and 4.5-fold for females). The sex ratio for suicide in 1989 was 2.3, but dropped to 1.2 in 2009. Thus, it is important to understand the reason for the greater increase in suicide for young adult females.

One of the possible reasons for lower female (than male) suicide found in Western societies is that women possess better skills than men in making social ties with others and in adapting to changes in the life course (Stack, 2000). Girard (1993, pp. 556, 557) argues that, unlike men who "anchor their identities in competitive, [an] achievement oriented domain," women base their identities

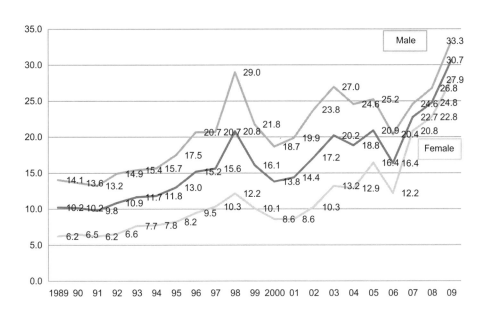

Figure 4. Suicide trends for the 25–39 age group, 1989–2009.

"on cooperation, social interdependence, and parenthood." Pescosolido and Wright (1990) similarly contend that, in general, women have better social support systems to draw on when they are in a state of crisis than do men. Such an explanation is somewhat challenged by the sharp increase of young female suicide in contemporary Korean society.

This trend in female suicide signifies a greater degree of cultural ambivalence among the younger generation of females in Korea. This pattern implies that young females discover themselves caught between the Western cultural ideal of gender equality and the Confucian values that support, essentially, the cultural tradition of gender inequality. In the Confucian tradition, women were segregated from the public domain, deprived of the opportunity to pursue an education, and forced to subordinate themselves to men. However, in modern Korea, women are expected to participate in the labor force. As a result, they outnumber men on university campuses, and they are also encouraged to compete with men for achievement of high status. Yet, they often experience the "glass ceiling," a limit to what positions that they can achieve. Moreover, due to the low value assigned to physical labor in Korean culture, many women avoid choosing a career that requires manual labor and thereby limit themselves to a narrow path. Thus, it is plausible to infer that women, who have internalized the Westernized ideals of autonomy, equal opportunity, fair competition for scarce resources and so forth, are more likely to experience stress as they face the invisible barriers that block their opportunities for achievement. What is worse is that they may have heard mixed cultural messages about their worth sociologically and biologically.

Young male adults also seemingly become victims of dualistic cultural messages. They are taught the value of competition to achieve their ultimate goals in life, but they have to face the barriers embedded in the informal personal networking system of the elite structure of most social organizations, the residue of Confucian values. Those who fail to enter a top university and gain stable employment may question their worth and perhaps perceive themselves to be burdens to their family members.

Youth Suicide

Korean youths (ages 15–24) today are heavily influenced by a consumerist culture and are much more individualistic than their predecessors. Thus, they find more common qualities with Western peers of their generation than with the older generation in Korea. They tend to be disconnected from cultural traditions, and they mistrust social, political, religious, and educational institutions. Yet they are struggling with the pressure from their parents to achieve academic success. During their childhood, they were sent by their parents to a *hakwon*, a private institute for extra schooling, just to get ahead. According to Cho (1995), "Those who did not go to *hakwon* comprised only 0.3 percent." The underperforming children were "afraid of going home" with poor grades, and so "had thoughts about running away from home" (p. 148). The majority, as a result, felt the pressure to study as a significant stressor.

The trend of youth suicide can be seen in Figure 5. The rate for both male and female suicide has increased about 1.5-fold during the period of 1989–2009. However, the increase seems to be led mostly by females (1.1-fold for males and 2.3-fold for females). Similar to the young adult group, the sex ratio in 1989 was 2.7, but dropped to 1.1 in 2009. The difference between male and female suicide rates, therefore, is small. In fact, the rate of female suicide surpassed that of males in 2005 for this age group.

The suicide rate of male youth, consistently high with a moderate fluctuation, suggests a high level of persistent stress, which can be attributed to high expectations from their parents for academic success. Being male, particularly being heir of the family lineage, he is expected to discipline himself to succeed in the world and bring glory to his parents. The first step to such a goal is to be admitted to a prestigious university. In other words, Korean youth experience a high level

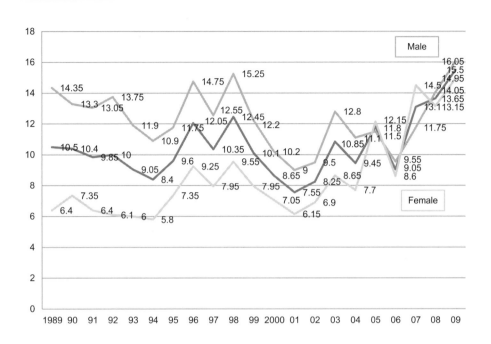

Figure 5. Suicide trends for the 15–24 age group, 1989–2009.

of stress stemming from the competitive academic pressure (Lee, Hong, & Espe-lage, 2010). Yet, it is interesting to note that students who are connected emotion-ally to their parents are less suicidal (Moon, 2006). Young people who are connected to their past via their parents, it seems, acquire better self-preservation skills than those who are not so attached. In times of social change, which can pose a threat to one's self-continuity, the study by Chandler and colleagues (2003) of Native Americans is illuminating. These researchers found that, given that cultural continuity is essential for one's selfhood, aboriginal communities that successfully preserve or recover their heritage and culture and that exercise some control over their future have significantly lower youth suicide rates than those communities that fail to recover and maintain their own cultural heritage.

As discussed earlier, the younger generation of females in contemporary Korea appears to be exposed to a greater risk of cultural ambivalence stemming from unclear gender role expectations as a result of societal change. Cultural ambiva-lence can lead to psychological distress, which, in turn, is a risk factor for suicide. In this era of globalization, along with the technological advancements in commu-nication, a young woman who has little interest in the ideas of the past but is open to new ways of behavior may face disapproval from those who have internalized

Confucian values. For example, a woman from a patriarchal family engaging in cohabitation or premarital sex may be shunned by her parents and relatives because those behaviors were considered, in Confucian culture, to bring shame to the family and clan. Shunning can increase her social isolation, which is a risk factor for suicide.

Conclusion

The original analysis of suicide by Durkheim focused on European societies as they emerged through the transformative modernizing processes of industrialization and urbanization in the late 19th Century. He argued that suicide should not be seen just as a sum of individual acts, but rather could be more fully understood as an indicator of how personal behavior can reflect the impact of macrosocietal changes. This analysis of Korea has looked at this Asian society in the late 20th and early 21st Centuries and has argued that it is useful to employ lenses that parallel those Durkheim employed. In Korea, as a century earlier in Europe, individual behavior needs to be seen in its societal context.

Culture should not be thought as either static or monolithic. Culture is evolving historically, often conflicting with new ideas, tools, technologies, or other cultures. I have argued that this dynamic nature of culture can become a different kind of social force in different historical locations. Contemporary Korean culture is in the midst of change, creating cultural ambivalence that, in turn, contributes to the rise in suicide rates. More specifically, the deeply rooted Confucian values are incongruent with the market-oriented neoliberalistic social structure. On the surface, the Westernized individualistic competitive culture appears to be predominant yet, underneath the surface, the traditional norms still govern many aspects of Korean attitudes and patterns of behavior. In other words, Korean people have neither abandoned the age-old traditional value of interdependency nor accepted fully the individualistic rational rules for competition in the market. The amalgam of incongruent cultural values is linked to various abnormalities in contemporary Korean society, one of which is what I call collective cultural ambivalence. This leads to unclear social expectations or the absence of clear rules of conduct, which, in turn, produce anxiety or stress for individuals. Culture provides its members with meaning (see earlier chapters). Yet, the ambivalent state of coexisting cultures makes the meaning blurred. The blurred meaning system makes it difficult to preserve one's selfhood.

All age groups seem to be affected by collective cultural ambivalence. The older people who are affected the most by cultural ambivalence are finding their own Confucian norms and values less relevant, or no longer relevant, to the individualistic, competitive modern social structure. Adult children appear to be stressed due to feelings of guilt stemming from the fact that they do not live up to the internalized norm of filial piety, while being forced to adapt to the specialized, competitive market-oriented economy. The younger generation is seemingly eager to break with the past and welcome today's postmodern culture, along with advanced technologies and new ways of behavior. However, the dualistic sets of rules seem to engender anxiety in them and clash with the enduring social institutions largely supported by Confucian norms.

Some attempts to resist the Western cultural influence and preserve the cultural traditions were sought for a purely political reason by the military government during Korea's industrialization and, later (in the 1980s), by some student movement groups. In recent decades, however, the sociopolitical trend seems to have moved in the opposite direction. Neoliberal policies that advocate small government and market-driven economies have been promoted by current Korean governments. While conservatives assert that traditional family values must be restored in order to resolve abnormal social conditions – the increased divorce rate, mental health problems, marital and generational conflict, elderly and child abuse, and the decreased marriage and fertility rates[5]– the global consumerist culture has flourished and become a significant cultural force in contemporary Korea.

If restoring traditional family values, as argued by conservatives, means strengthening the authoritarian hierarchical order of relationships or placing women and children in a subordinate position to the husband and father, then restoration would preserve or worsen the incongruence between the past cultural values and the current Western values, and this incongruence would worsen the problem. What needs to be done to reduce the suicide rate is to restore the continuity of the culture because cultural-continuity is essential for the preservation of one's selfhood. The continuity of the cultural tradition here does not mean prolonging the mechanical enforcement of the institutionalized Confucian norms. Rather, it means recovering the genuine meaning of cultural heritages that have been the core of Korean people's identity – the meaning of who they are and who they will become. The recovery involves the (re)interpretation of genuine Confucian ideals, the evaluation of successes and failures in the past, and the incorporation of new ideas into the traditional cultural legacy. This process would inevitably produce conflict but would lead to a new tradition and allow Korea to

---

5   Kim Dae-jung and Noh Moo-hyun were considered progressive presidents, but they supported
     neoliberal policies because they had to deal with the economic crisis. They also had to confront the
     strong conservative force resisting progressive policies. The current president, Lee Myung-bak, is
     conservative and an ardent supporter of neoliberalism.

build a moral community. Solidarity in such a community, according to Durkheim, would be the best preventive force for suicide. Abandoning the more than one thousand year-old tradition implies denying one's identity. On the other hand, accepting Western values does not make one become a member of Western society. It is clear that the Korean people have not abandoned Confucianism entirely, yet they do not abide by Western norms, either. The more that cultural ambivalence continues, the more it will produce victims. Is a wise balancing of the two competing forces possible?

References

Atchley, R. C., & Barusch, A. S. (2004). *Social Forces and Aging*. Belmont, CA: Wadsworth/ Thomson Learning.

Breen, M. (2004). *The Koreans: Who they are, what they want, where their future lies*. New York: St. Martin's Press.

Chandler, M. J., Lalonde, C. E., Sokol, B. W., & Hallett, D. (2003). *Personal persistence, identity development, and suicide: A study of native and non-native North American adolescents*. Boston, MA: Blackwell.

Chang, Y. S. (2003). Mutual help and democracy in Korea. In D. A. Bell & C. Hahm (Eds.), *Confucianism for the modern world*, pp. 90–123. New York: Cambridge University Press.

Cho, H. J. (1995). Children in the examination war in South Korea: A cultural analysis. In S. Stephens (Ed.), *Children and the politics of culture*, pp. 141–168. Princeton, NJ: Princeton University Press.

Clayer, J. R,.& Czechowicz, A. S. (1991). Suicide by aboriginal people in South Australia: Comparison with suicide deaths in the total urban and rural populations. *Medical Journal of Australia, 154*, 683–685.

de Bary, W. T. D. (1998). *Asian values and human rights: A Confucian communitarian perspective*. Cambridge, MA: Harvard University Press.

Durkheim, E. (1897/1951). *Suicide: A study in sociology*. New York: Free Press.

Farberow, N. L. (1975). *Suicide in different cultures*. Baltimore: University Park Press.

Farberow, N. L., & Shneidman, E. S. (1957). Suicide and age. In E. S. Shneidman & N. L. Farberow, *Clues to suicide*, pp. 41–49. New York, NY: McGraw Hill.

Fei, W. (2009). Cultural and religious traditions in China: The influence of Confucianism on suicide prevention. In D. Wasserman & C. Wasserman (Eds.), *Oxford textbook of suicidology and suicide prevention*, pp. 13–18. New York: Oxford University Press.

Gelles, R. J., & Levine, A. (1999). *Sociology: An introduction*. Boston, MA: McGraw-Hill.

Girard, C. (1993). Age, gender, and suicide: A cross-national analysis. *American Sociological Review, 58*, 553–574.

Glass, Jr., J. C., & Reed, S. E. (1993). To Live or Die: A Look at Elderly Suicide. *Educational Gerontology, 19*(8), 767–778.

Goldin, P. R. (2011). *Confucianism*. Berkeley, CA: University of California Press.

Hahm, C. (2003). Family versus the individual: The politics of marriage laws in Korea. In D. A. Bell & C. Hahm (Eds.), *Confucianism for the modern world*, pp. 334–359. Cambridge, UK: Cambridge University Press.

Hyun, K. J. (2001). Sociocultural change and traditional values: Confucian values among Koreans and Korean Americans. *International Journal of Intercultural Relations, 25*, 203–229.

Jang, S. H. (2004). Continuing suicide among laborers in Korea. *Labor History, 45*, 271–297.

Joiner, T. E. (2005). *Why people die by suicide*. Cambridge, MA: Harvard University Press.

Kim, D. (1990). The transformation of familism in modern Korean society: From cooperation to competition. *International Sociology, 5*, 409–425.

Kim, H. (2008). Micromobilization and suicide protest in South Korea, 1970–2004. *Social Research, 75*, 543–578.

Kulp, D. H. J. (1925). *Country life in South China: The sociology of familism*. Kwantung, China: Phenix Village.

Lau, D. C. (1984). *Mencius, VI, A*. Hong Kong: Hong Kong Chinese University Press.

Lee, S. Y., Hong, J. S., & Espelage, D. L. (2010). An ecological understanding of youth suicide in South Korea. *School Psychology International, 31*, 531–546.

Lester, D. (1999). Native American suicide rates, acculturation stress and traditional integration. *Psychological Reports, 82*, 398.

Lim, J. S., Kim, C. H., Kim, C. K., Seo, H. C., Hong, S. Y., Kim, C. W., & Park, M. C. (2008). *Study on investigating suicide causes and developing suicide prevention programs in Korea*. Seoul, South Korea: Gachon University of Medicine and Science.

Lo, P. C. (1999). Confucian views on suicide and their implications for euthanasia. In R. Fan (Ed.), *Confucian Bioethics*, pp. 69–101. Boston, MA: Kluwer Academic.

Menninger, K. A. (1938). *Man against himself*. New York: Harcourt, Brace & World.

Moon, K. S. (2006). The effect of academic stress on suicidal impulse in adolescence: Mediating roles of parent and peer attachment. *Korean Journal of Child Studies, 27*, 143–158.

Park, B. C. (1994). Political suicide among Korean youth. *Bulletin of Concerned Asian Scholars, 26*(1–2), 66–81.

Park, B. C. B. (2004). Sociopolitical contexts of self-immolations in Vietnam and South Korea. *Archives of Suicide Research, 8*, 81–97.

Park, H. M. (2010a). *Suicide, the second worst option: Understanding the actor's introspection and communication*. Seoul, Korea: Ehaksa.

Park, B. C. B. (2010b). Pathological conditions of Korean society: Rebuilding a community for suicide prevention. *Discourse, 13*(4), 159–186.

Pescosolido, B. A., & Wright, E. R. (1990). Suicide and the role of the family over the life course. *Family Perspective, 41*(1), 41–58.

Rhi, B. Y. (1998). Mental illness in its Confucian context. In W. H. Slote & G. A. DeVos (Eds.), *Confucianism for the modern world*, pp. 285–310. Albany, NY: State University of New York.

Slote, W. H. (1998). Psychocultural dynamics within the Confucian family. In W. H. Slote & G. A. DeVos (Eds.), *Confucianism and the family*, pp. 37–51. Albany, NY: State University of New York.

Stack, S. (2000). Suicide: A 15-year review of the sociological literature Part II: Modernization and social integration perspectives. *Suicide and Life-Threatening Behavior, 30*, 163–176.

Tu, W. M. (1998). Probing the "Three Bonds" and "Five Relationships" in Confucian humanism. In W. H. Slote & G. A. DeVos (Eds.), *Confucianism and the family*, pp. 121–136. Albany, NY: State University of New York.

Yim, D. (1998). Psychocultural features of ancestor worship in modern Korean society. In W. H. Slote & G. A. D. Vos (Eds.), *Confucianism and the family*, pp. 163–186. Albany, NY: State University of New York Press.

Yip, P. S. F., & Tan, R. C. E. (1998). Suicide in Hong Kong and Singapore: A tale of two cities. *International Journal of Social Psychiatry, 44*, 267–279.

Yoo, Y. J., Lee, I., & Yoo, G. (2007). How strong familiies encouter social challenges in the Republic of Korea. *Marriage & Family Review, 41*, 195–216.

Conclusion

Concluding Thoughts

Erminia Colucci and David Lester

This book began with Heidi Hjelmeland arguing that, even though the physiological model of psychiatric disorder has become the major basis for explaining human behavior, including suicidal behavior, there still remains a role for inputs such as culture for understanding suicide. Hjelmeland makes a strong case for this, and her argument is particularly cogent today in light of the strong attack presently being made against the physiological model of psychiatric disorders. Three recent books have made the case that, first, there is no sound research evidence that psychiatric disorders are caused by dysfunctional neurotransmitter systems in the brain, and, second, that psychiatric medications are no better than active placebos[1] in helping patients and, in fact, may cause long-term harm, thereby contravening the medical guideline of "Do no harm" (Carlat, 2010; Kirsh, 2010; Whitaker, 2010).[2]

In Chapter 2, Colucci also argues forcefully that culture plays a role in suicidal behavior and that, therefore, a cultural understanding of suicide is necessary for its prevention (in particular, an understanding of the cultural meanings, including gendered-meanings, of suicide). In Chapter 3, Lester discusses the need for researchers and commentators who value the study of culture to be more precise in their use of terms such as the *meaning of suicide*, both at the individual level of analysis and at the cultural level of analysis. Finally, in Chapter 4, Lester reviews the many ways in which the impact of culture on suicidal behavior can be studied.

It is in the second section of the book that the problems in studying the impact of culture on suicidal behavior are demonstrated. First, the report in Chapter 5 of a study by Colucci on suicidal behavior in students from three countries (Australia, India, and Italy) illustrates the incredible complexity of the phenomenon of suicide. The participants from the three countries differed in their own personal experience of suicidal behavior, their attitudes toward suicidal behavior, and their

---

[1] Active placebos are those that cause discernible side-effects, thereby leading patients to think that the medication is having a beneficial effect.

[2] For a review of these books, see Marcia Angell (2011a, 2011b), the former editor of the *New England Journal of Medicine*.

recommendations for preventing suicide. By combining both quantitative and qualitative research methods (including open-ended questions and activity-based focus groups), Colucci teased out the differing views between the participants from these three countries and, in addition, the variation *within* each country. We cannot assume that members of a culture are homogeneous and mere clones of one another.

However, Colucci's study also demonstrated that the impact of culture (assessed by nationality in her study, although she also inquired about participants' spiritual and religious beliefs and ethnic identity) was also affected by the sex of the participants, their social class, and their religion. Indeed, it is as if there are subcultures within these cultures based upon sex, class, and religion. Interestingly, these differences were apparent in both the quantitative and the qualitative parts of Colucci's study, but more so in the qualitative component, illustrating the benefits that can be obtained from incorporating qualitative methods into research on suicidal behavior (as observed also by Hjelmeland & Knizek, 2010 and, in this book, in the chapters by Hjelmeland and by Lester).

Chapter 6 by Lester indicated some of the problems that arise in cultural studies, the major problem being the choice of cultural groups. Lester's description of his collaborative research with Ahmed Abdel-Khalek indicates that the two researchers chose to study countries rather than cultures, a common method in cultural research, probably because it is easier to identify members of nations than it is members of cultural groups. The members of a nation can differ considerably and, in many nations, the subgroups are so different that it makes no sense to ignore this. Colucci's study illustrates this since many of her participants chose to label themselves by ethnicity or religion rather than nationality. For example, the Chinese are very sensitive to the differences between the different cultural groups under this umbrella of ethnicity, and Lester (1997) has explored the well-established differences between those living in the northern region of a country and those in the southern region.

Just as the subjects of research are often chosen out of convenience, Lester points out that cross-cultural research is often carried out by convenience (finding researchers who want to collaborate) and serendipity (chance encounters between researchers, especially at conferences). It is less common for the cultures that are compared to have been chosen purposefully to explore some particular aspect of behavior.

Lester's analysis of sati in Chapter 7, while clearly focusing on a type of suicidal behavior common in one culture, illustrates another problem. Those who have written about sati have often never been trained by mental health professionals, skilled in psychological autopsies (if the sati died)[3] or interviewing (if the sati was prevented from dying). Indeed, the best account of any sati that Lester located was by an investigative journalist, not a mental health professional.

Park's work (Chapter 8) concludes the series of contributions by showing the complexity of understanding the increase in suicide in a rapidly changing society such as that in South Korea.

From the studies reported in these chapters, it can be concluded that the task confronting the researcher who wants to focus on cultural aspects of suicidal behavior includes:

1) Defining clearly the term *culture* for the study (e.g., in Colucci's study this was operationalized as being born and living in the country under study, with both parents born in the same country).
2) Choosing the appropriate participants for the study (e.g., college students versus older adults in the community).
3) Choosing and training the appropriate people who will collect the data. Here issues such as sex, class, and ethnicity must be carefully considered, as well as the emic (insider) and etic (outsider) position of the researcher.
4) Choosing the appropriate techniques of data collection (questionnaires, structured interviews, focus groups, etc.).

Finally, it is important to be aware of the political issues involved in studying culture. Obviously, as we have noted above, all the residents of the nation do not consider themselves identical. They identify themselves by region (e.g., Welsh, Scots, or English), by language or dialect (e.g., Cantonese or Mandarin in China), by religion, by their parents' ethnic background (e.g., Italian American or Irish American), and so on.

In some nations, this diversity is celebrated. The US holds parades and other events on many days of the year in cities across the nation celebrating, for example, St. Patrick's Day (when everyone is Irish), Polish Americans, Black American History Month, and many other groups. However, in many countries, these cultural differences, especially if based on ethnicity or religion, threaten to divide the nation. For example, in some Muslim nations, the Sunni/Sh-ite distinction can be divisive. Not surprisingly, many nations seek to thwart divisive movements. Sometimes the government engages in a civil war to prevent division

---

[3] It is unlikely that a standardized psychological autopsy could be carried out in the social system present in the regions of India where sati is common. Not only would the caste system prevent many people from speaking openly about the events, but also those close to the sati would have many reasons for not speaking the truth.

as, for example, when Nigeria acted to stop a movement by the Ibo ethnic group to carve off Biafra as an independent nation.

In other cases, there is a long "liberation" movement until the region gets partial or total independence, as in the devolution of Wales and Scotland from the UK or the conflict between French-speaking Quebec from Canada as a whole. Nations such as Australia and the US have escaped much of this divisiveness, partly because the many ethnic groups are rarely concentrated in one region, but rather scattered across the country.

In countries facing divisiveness and liberation movements, recognition of ethnic minorities (and, even more so, the recognition of ethnic majorities in countries in which an ethnic minority is in command, as in some Middle Eastern nations such as Bahrain), there is a fear that studies of cultural subgroups might lead to further divisiveness, even to the point of civil war.

This fear can be found even in countries such as France where it is not possible to carry out research by culture, race, or ethnicity, or the UK where, as Lester noted earlier, his paper on suicide in Wales was rejected by the *British Journal of Psychiatry* as being "of no interest." An extreme example is Zimbabwe, where the Shona dominate the Ndebele. Reporting suicide rates by ethnic group is opposed by the government, which has in the past, and continues today, to suppress any liberation movement by the oppressed Ndebele. Lester and Wilson (1988) were able to report suicides rates in Zimbabwe only for Blacks, Coloreds, and Whites, not by ethnic group. Recently, Lester, Saito, and Park (2011) were able to calculate and report suicide rates for foreigners in Japan, even for Koreans living in Japan who form a large, but stigmatized, ethnic group, even if they have been born in Japan (rather than being immigrants to Japan). However, data on the suicide rates of aboriginal groups (such as the Ainu) were unavailable.

Cultural anthropologists have occasionally been able to report on suicidal behavior in ethnic groups, but epidemiologists and suicidologists rarely conduct studies on these groups. There is very little research on suicide in the Basque people in Spain (members of which have, in the past, waged war in Spain in order to gain independence) or on suicide in Gypsies in Europe (who are the target of prejudice and efforts to expel them, recently, for example, from France). There is perhaps no other area of research in suicidology that is subject to such political considerations, and this has hampered research into the impact of culture of suicide.

In spite of the conceptual, methodological, and political challenges that characterize research on culture and suicide, and the personal interests that might lead some scholars to look to mental health services and pharmaceutical therapies as the only "answers" to suicide prevention, people are not born isolated from their cultural contexts, and they do not die nor chose to die in a cultural vacuum.

Thus, as also argued in Colucci (2009), we need to understand as in-depth as possible the impact of culture and the cultural meanings of suicide, including the gendered-meanings of suicide, if we want to understand how we can help to save lives. It is our hope that this book will stimulate readers to explore the role of culture in their future suicide research and prevention activites.

References

Angell, M. (2011a). The epidemic of mental illness: Why? *New York Review of Books*. June 23.
Angell, M. (2011b). The illusions of psychiatry. *New York Review of Books*. July 14.
Carlat, D. (2010). *Unhinged: The trouble with psychiatry.* New York: Free Press.
Colucci, E. (2009). Cultural issues in suicide risk assessment. In U. Kumar & M. K. Mandal (Eds.), *Suicidal Behavior: Assessment of People-at-risk* (pp. 107–135). New Delhi: Sage.
Hjelmeland, H., & Knizek, B. L. (2010). Why we need qualitative research in suicidology. *Suicide and Life-Threatening Behavior, 40*(1), 74–80.
Kirsch, I. (2010). *The Emperor's new drugs: Exploding the antidepressant myth.* New York: Basic Books.
Lester, D. (1997). Suicide in Italy: The North versus the South. *Italian Journal of Suicidology, 7*, 19–21.
Lester, D., Saito, Y., & Park, B. C. B. (2011). Suicide among foreign residents of Japan. *Psychological Reports, 108*, 139–140.
Lester, D., & Wilson, C. (1988). Suicide in Zimbabwe. *Central African Journal of Medicine, 34*, 147–149.
Whitaker, R. (2010). *Anatomy of an epidemic.* New York: Crown.

The end...

"There is but one truly serious philosophical problem, and that is suicide. Judging whether life is or is not worth living amounts to answering the fundamental question of philosophy."

Albert Camus

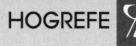

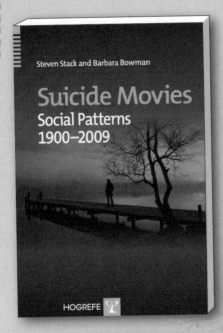
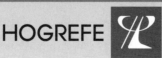

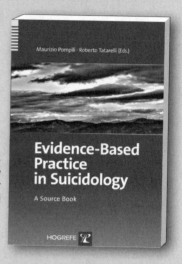
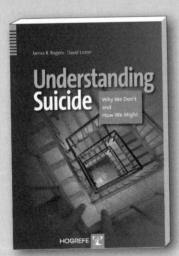
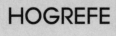